LES BA & ME

BRUCE JO

GREA

THANK YOU

I hope that anyone reading this book will appreciate its honesty and realise that to be true to yourself is what counts. I would like to dedicate this book to my late mum Irene, my wife Sandra and my children Jon, Steven, Lisa and Claudia.

I would also like to thank my good friend Ronnie Oliver for being there for me and my promoter Steven Lloyd and his brilliant team; including Malcolm Humphrey, Kevin Owens and our driver Stav for getting this book off the ground.

Also thanks to Barry Cox, Patricia Lennon, David Burrill, Chris Berry and everyone at Great Northern Books for believing in me.

I would like to thank everyone at ITV Granada, *Coronation Street* and to all my loyal fans and yourself for buying my book.

And to everyone I've forgotten please accept my huge apologies.

Bruce

Great Northern Books
PO Box 213, Ilkley, LS29 9WS
www.greatnorthernbooks.co.uk
© Chris Berry & Bruce Jones, 2011

ISBN: 978-1905080-83-0
Design and layout: David Burrill

Printed in Great Britain

CIP Data

A catalogue for this book is available from the British Library

CONTENTS

Foreword:	*Status Quo*	7
Foreword:	*Ken Loach*	9
Chapter One:	Les or Bruce?	11
Chapter Two:	Ian Roy Jones	13
Chapter Three:	Nearly Dead	21
Chapter Four:	Better Off Dead	26
Chapter Five:	The Misfit	29
Chapter Six:	Leader of the Gang	33
Chapter Seven:	The Weir	36
Chapter Eight:	Shakespeare Saved Me	38
Chapter Nine:	Pipes & Mods	43
Chapter Ten:	Married with Children	46
Chapter Eleven:	Freedom & Fatherhood	50
Chapter Twelve:	The Beast	53
Chapter Thirteen:	The Ripper	55
Chapter Fourteen:	Going Dutch	61
Chapter Fifteen:	Sandra & Me	64
Chapter Sixteen:	Go to Blazes	69
Chapter Seventeen:	On Stage	77
Chapter Eighteen:	Clarke & Jones	80
Chapter Nineteen:	Screen Time	87
Chapter Twenty:	Raining Stones	89
	Illustrations	97
Chapter Twenty One:	Roughnecks	114
Chapter Twenty Two:	Bob's Weekend	117
Chapter Twenty Three:	TwentyFour Seven	121
Chapter Twenty Four:	TV Times	123
Chapter Twenty Five:	Guilty of Being a Success	127

Chapter Twenty Six: The Full Monty   130

Chapter Twenty Seven: Coronation Street   132

Chapter Twenty Eight: Quo on the Street   158

Chapter Twenty Nine: Kirky & Me   167

Chapter Thirty: Lookalikes, Boots, Onions & Dying   169

Chapter Thirty One: George, Alex & Conwy United FC   172

Chapter Thirty Two: Deano, Diana Ross & Neil Diamond   174

Chapter Thirty Three: Kicked Out of Corrie!   176

                             Illustrations   *177*

Chapter Thirty Four: Oh Yes I Did!   202

Chapter Thirty Five: Sinitta   204

Chapter Thirty Six: Piers Morgan & Gay Byrne   213

Chapter Thirty Seven: On The Streets   217

Chapter Thirty Eight: Fish! Fish! Fish!   240

Chapter Thirty Nine: Road To Hell   243

Chapter Forty: Court   249

Chapter Forty One: Rehab   251

Chapter Forty Two: Rehab Worked   268

Chapter Forty Three: Charity   271

Chapter Forty Four: Agadoo's   276

Chapter Forty Five: Back On Screen & On Stage   278

Afterword: *Variety Club of Great Britain*   *283*

Appendix 1:   *Films on DVD*   *284*

Appendix 2:   *Major Films & TV Series Chronology*   *285*

FOREWORD

BY

Status Quo

We were delighted to be asked to introduce Bruce's book. His career, rather like our own we suppose, made him a fixture in the nation's living rooms. Everyone knew him, or thought they did. Like ours, his story is one of ups and downs; plenty of laughs, sure, but some seriously dark days too.

Our first meeting with Bruce came backstage at the Manchester Apollo on a particularly cold night in the Winter of 2004. He bounded in, much to the amazement of our manager Simon Porter who remains a huge fan of *Corrie*. He had with him a rather expensive, early model electric guitar that he asked us to sign. We did so rather reluctantly as, to be honest, it was a lovely instrument and our scrawls in marker pen didn't add to its beauty.

We had a good old natter and before long he'd been in contact again to see if we would make a guest appearance on *The Street*. He'd pulled some strings. Big time. Of course we were delighted [but not as excited as our manager who managed to make an appearance as an extra]. The storyline which resulted in Quo playing at Les and Cilla's wedding went out in 2005 and people always ask us about it. In fact it'll be in our obituaries.

The British public know Bruce for *Corrie* but it is easy to forget the charity work and also more serious roles he has taken on: the lead in Ken Loach's *Raining Stones,* a chunky role in *Band Of Gold*, a very small part [ahem] in *The Full Monty*! The public do tend to forget the appearance on *Celebrity Stars In Their Eyes* and the televised *Pantomime Cinderella* and that's just as well – but God knows we've had gigs we'd like to put behind us too!

The road that Bruce has travelled has not always been easy. We know too the trouble that the lifestyle that often accompanies the entertainment business can lead people into. We've been there and it's not a good place. What matters in life is responding to situations; making the best of them and moving on. In this book Bruce is honest, open and unafraid. These are great characters for any man – and the reason that we are proud to know him.

Rock on Bruce!
The Quo

FOREWORD
BY
Ken Loach

I first met Bruce Jones at an audition for a domestic cleaning product (well, it was the end of the eighties and it was a thin decade for most people). They were seeking someone who had a friendly face and looked as though he could do a day's work. He got the part.

A few years later I was working in Manchester directing a script written by Jim Allen. The film was called *'Raining Stones'*. It was the story of Bob, unemployed, married with a little girl, desperately seeking a job. Being a good Catholic, Bob wants to buy his daughter a dress for her communion. The film details his attempts to find the money.

Again, we had to find a cheerful optimist who keeps bouncing back from the knocks that life inflicts on him. Bruce came to mind. I think he was still working as a gas fitter. We tried out various imaginary scenes and he fitted the part exactly. As with all good casting, it became impossible to imagine Bob without seeing Bruce.

The film turned out quite well. It went to various festivals and played well, particularly in France. With fellow actors Julie Brown and Ricky Tomlinson, Bruce cut an impressive figure on the red carpet at Cannes and strolling on the Croisette.

It was not a great surprise when Bruce got more work in TV and then became a regular on *Coronation Street*. I always look out for his work and, of course, hope he does well. When we worked together I found his responses were true and he was a good pro. You can't ask for more.

All the best, Bruce!
Ken Loach

CHAPTER ONE

LES or BRUCE?

Who am I to you? Are you reading this book because you know me as Les Battersby? Are you really interested in me, Bruce Jones the actor? I only ask these questions because it is important to draw the distinction between me and Les right at the start. We are two very different people. One is a character in a fantastic TV series; and the other is me the real person, although I know many people see me as just the same as the on-screen role I played for over a decade.

If you're just interested in the *Coronation Street* part of my life that's fine. There are plenty of funny moments, great scenes and fantastic friends I made through being in the show to read about in here.

I'm delighted and honoured to have been involved in the nation's most enduring and best-loved TV show for so long and the most-asked question I get wherever I go is 'When are you going back in?' I won't deny it is something I would love to go back to if the chance ever arose.

The Street has played such a massive part in my life. It brought me national fame, as well as a degree of notoriety. Playing the part of Les was a joy, especially alongside the lovely Vicky Entwistle (Janice) and Wendi Peters (Cilla).

I'll talk about *Corrie* a lot, but this story isn't about Les. It's about a man who very nearly died as a child. It's about a man who has seen things no-one should ever see. It's about a man who has struggled to understand himself and why he does the things he does. And it's about a man who is facing up to his recent past and aiming to carry on what has been a great career. I'm now talking about me, Bruce Jones the actor.

Everyone in the entertainment world who has ever written their life story tells of using it to 'set the record straight' and I guess I'm no different. We all know how some of the media in this country, particularly certain newspapers, like nothing better than to kick a guy when he's down. I'm not saying they're all the same. I've had some great reviews over the years. But when the bad press comes along, and what they write has an element of truth, it's the way in which those newspapers portray the story that causes much heartache to people like me and my family. I have certainly been caused my fair share of pain through one or two of them.

You won't find me hiding anything away either. Every part of my life is in here. I'll talk about everything from the moments that have given me most pleasure to the times when I have been in the depths of despair. I know we all have ups and downs but mine would read a bit like one of those charts you see at the end of a hospital bed with the line going right to the top, then down to the very bottom, several times.

The highs include my two sons, my two daughters, my mum, my wife Sandra, my aunts and uncles, my cousins, the acting awards, the double act, films and TV series.

The lows include rheumatic fever, being in the presence of a serial killer, the horrific discovery of a mutilated corpse, coping with drink-related problems; and, if you read the newspapers at the time you will be aware of the story about grabbing the steering wheel of Sandra's car and vowing to end it all for the two of us in 2009.

My God, the lows sound just like they come from a TV soap don't they? But like I said, here I'm Bruce, not Les. I'm going to make a wild guess about what you may be thinking by now. Perhaps Les and myself really are the same and that I am protesting too much. In one newspaper report I am quoted as saying I had turned into the real-life Les Battersby. I never said that and whilst I liked playing the character I would never have wanted to be like him.

You'll make up your own mind I'm sure but what I can tell you here and now is that the real-life Bruce Jones is still the working class lad he was right at the start. I haven't changed. The celebrity status I took on board as a result of being in The Street never led me to forget my roots. I'm really not trying to be anything that I'm not.

I'm actually about to introduce a new character to you straight away. You see whilst I'm not Les Battersby I'm also not Bruce Jones!

CHAPTER TWO
IAN ROY JONES

'When I was young and lazy, as lazy as can be,
I said farewell to the mother-in-law and off I went to sea,
We sailed with Captain Skipper, aboard the Mary Anne,
And we all set sail down Collyhurst Road in a Black Maria van.'

CHORUS
'Oh, Collyhurst Road, I am forsaken,
And it's not that my poor heart is aching,
It's the whisky and the rum that I've been taking,
For that charming little girl down Collyhurst Road.

'Oh we got as far as The Vine and the rain turned into snow,
The snow got in the engine, and the engine wouldn't go,
So we wrapped ourselves in mainsails and stayed there for a year,
And all we had to bloody-well drink was a barrel of Boddie's beer.'

REPEAT CHORUS

'Well the law chased after me, and they put me in Number 3,
They said you are a Collyhurst boy, and you'll never get away from me,
They said the next time you go sailing, it won't be the Mary Anne,
Be down the Collyhurst Road to Collyhurst Nick in a Black Maria van.

REPEAT CHORUS TO FINISH

If you come from Manchester – and particularly my part of Manchester – this song needs no introduction. You also may have heard it sung at the City of Manchester Stadium, Manchester City's ground. They're my team.

It's called *Collyhurst Road"* and the reason for including the song here is because that's where I come from. It's the area I grew up in and where I have so many fond memories of family and friends before life started to get complicated. If you're an act booked to play a pub or club in the area and you play *Collyhurst Road* you'll have no trouble with the audience. I believe it was either written or sung by a guy called 'Bomber' who worked on market stalls in Manchester and was recorded by a local man called Billy Kite.

I was born Ian Roy Jones on 24 January 1953 but took my grandfather's Scottish nickname Bruce when I joined Equity, the actors' union, because there was already an Ian Jones registered.

Collyhurst was classed as one of the hard areas of Manchester at the time and I came into the world in a two-bedroomed flat in Davy Street, the eldest of six children. Collyhurst was a big council estate, the type of place that was just like you saw in old 60s films like *Billy Liar*. It was full of old women standing on street corners talking about their families and engaging in the latest gossip.

Mum and dad both worked really hard. My dad was a steel fixer and he worked all over the place. My mum Irene, who has probably been the greatest influence on my life, was a steam presser. We lost her in 2010 and I am still coming to terms with it. She did so much for me and my two sons. It breaks my heart just thinking about her not being here now.

My early childhood years were happy. We may not have had much but that didn't stop us from enjoying ourselves. Me and Bryn, my first brother to be born, would get sweets from my dad every Thursday. This was his pay-day and he'd bring the sweets home in a big bag.

When I was around three or four years old, we moved about a mile from Davy Street to a prefab just off the Rochdale Road, but still in Collyhurst. We stayed there a long time. The prefab house had 3 bedrooms. I remember it was always so cold and damp.

We had no central heating and the only time it warmed up at all was when the fire was put on. We were a typical, hard-working, poor Collyhurst family, of which there were thousands in the same boat, so you didn't think anything of it.

The people of Collyhurst were and still are fantastic. There's a

Facebook site now called *Collyhurst Forever* which shows just how much those who live there or have moved away still think about their area. Our community could never have been regarded as affluent but what we lacked in cash we made up for in spirit and togetherness. Collyhurst people really are the salt of the earth. When I lived there everyone would always rally round if anyone needed anything. There was no hatred or belief that one family was any better than the other.

My grandmother lived just up the road and all of my aunts and uncles on my mum's side of the family lived close by. That's the way it was for a lot of families in those days.

I went to a Church of England school called St Oswald's which has sadly been pulled down now. I started there at three years of age and I'd been there a year when my teacher gave me my first ever acting role as one of the three kings in the school nativity play.

My teacher was Miss Webb, one of only two teachers in my life who I've never forgotten and both of whom were partly responsible for my drama career.

I can't remember whether I was the king who brought gold, frankincense or myrrh but I do remember the opening of my line being 'I bring you a gift of…' I loved getting the costume on and getting ready to deliver my lines on stage, but what really sold me on the idea of being there was the applause at the end. To hear people clapping sounded as though I had done something right and that feeling has remained with me to this day.

Dad's job as a steel fixer and erector took him quite a distance from home at times and when I was little mum would often take me to work with her. I would sit by her legs. Life with mum and dad was great in those early days, but unfortunately it wasn't always to be that way. I don't know quite why, because I had a great time with my parents when I was a small child, but things just didn't work out between me and dad.

He was a great ballad singer and had a fabulous voice. He would often sing some of the wonderful songs from the 50s. He could have been Tom Jones could my dad – and he already had the right surname! He had been christened John William Jones but everyone called him Jack or Taffy, because he was Welsh. He came from Newtown in mid-

Wales. I would always go there for my six-week summer holiday each year, stopping with my grandmother. It was my favourite place to visit as a child.

Every Saturday afternoon my mum would get her hair done in a beehive fashion for going out ballroom dancing with my dad. Mum was ginger-haired, like me. I'm one of only two of my brothers and sisters to have her hair colour. The other is my brother John. My dad had jet black hair and was very good-looking.

Mum and dad were always immaculate when they went out together. Dad would wear a buttoned-up suit, shirt and tie. Mum just looked great in whatever she wore. They could dance every dance there was and I used to think they made a fantastic couple. They jived well and when the Teddy boy era came along they also got into rock 'n' roll.

During weekends I would go and stay with my aunts and uncles, in fact I spent a lot of time with them over the years. All of them have given me so much support, none more so than my Uncle John who is the leading authority on my acting career. There isn't anything he doesn't know about what I have done. In fact he probably knows more about me than I know myself.

Baking was one of mum's great specialities. I know most fellers will probably say their mum's baking was the best. I'd always stand by my mum's baking. It would definitely be up there. She baked everything from custard tarts to apple pies. Her stews were fantastic too. I can almost taste them even now.

My grandma made the best hotpot. She used to make this big meat and potato pie with a crust on. It was to die for. My granddad used to chase me out of the house because she would always give it to me before she gave him his. He was a 6ft 6 Glaswegian, a man you didn't argue with. His name was George Campbell and he was a bouncer at a local club, a hard man who taught me how to be tough.

In those days we didn't have a fridge, everything was just kept in the larder so everyone was popping in and out of their local corner shop. There were no supermarkets and in common with most areas we had a corner shop nearby. I was constantly running errands for mum and my grandma.

Rochdale Road was our main thoroughfare and it was full of shops. Bernard Manning was my grandmother's grocer. Yes, *the* Bernard Manning. It was actually his father's shop but Bernard worked in it before moving from semi-professional to professional in the entertainment world.

Friday night was fish and chips night. But for me and Bryn it was pudding and chips. Mum would get the pair of us a suet pudding. We'd call it a steak pudding. Bryn and I would get half a pudding each and share the chips. We always had bread and butter with them – in fact we had bread and butter with just about everything in those days.

Dad would normally be home around five or six o'clock for his tea, after going for a couple of pints at the local before coming home. Like father, like son in my case. Tea would be ready and we would all watch television afterwards. Dad was doing quite well at work at the time and we had a black and white television. I think we were one of the first to get a telly in our street.

Bonanza with Lorne Greene; *Ivanhoe* starring Robert Taylor; *The Lone Ranger* shouting 'Hi Ho Silver away!' with his mate Tonto; and *Flash Gordon* were some of my favourite TV programmes and films of the time. I also loved the *Old Mother Riley* films with Arthur Lucan. I never knew that it was a bloke who played that role until years later.

But life certainly wasn't all about staring at a television. I was an avid reader. I've always enjoyed reading and I used to read a lot of Enid Blyton books. I loved the *Famous Five* and *Secret Seven* stories. I would escape in a book and I still do. The *Just William* stories by Richmal Crompton were really fun too.

Other kids were more into *Dandy* or *Beano* and maybe *Roy of the Rovers* but I would always prefer to read a book rather than a comic. I remember one year someone bought me a *Dandy* annual for Christmas, but someone else bought me *Gulliver's Travels* by Jonathan Swift. I enjoyed the book so much that I must have read it at least three times. I loved this fictional land of little people and talking horses. In fact I've still got the very same book somewhere in my house today.

Collyhurst might well have been regarded as a rough place to some but I never thought of it as anything other than the place I lived. This was a time when parents didn't have to worry too much about where their children were when they were out playing, and as kids we had a great time.

As young kids my mates and I would play in the River Irk a lot. We would make our own home-made rafts and pretend we were pirates; and we'd use it for our own commercial gains too - to wash out the empty bottles we would find on the rubbish tip so that we could take them to the shops and get some money back for their return. We'd search for hours to get as many as we could.

Street games included my favourite called 'Rally-Vo!' The easiest way to explain the game is that it was a bit like cops and robbers, or escaped convicts and police. At the start everyone used to run off whilst the one whose turn it was to track everyone down turned around and counted to ten. That person then had to find everyone. If you were caught you had to stay in a corner of the street where you had to wait until everyone was caught, or until someone released you.

The game used to take a whole week to play. Me and my cousin Derek devised a great plan to make sure we wouldn't be found. We would go and hide in the loft, moving from one loft or attic to another, from house to house, to avoid being caught. We would sit there all night and never be found, then we'd come out at 10 o'clock when the game was over for the day. We would get asked where we had been and we'd say 'just roaming the streets'. We were the most elusive pair of any of them. I don't think we were ever caught.

You're probably not going to believe this next line, but I was also a choir boy and a cub scout. Cassocks and woggles aren't exactly what you would expect from a young Les Battersby are they?

St Oswald's was a Church of England school and that meant I always attended choir singing and church services. I started in the church choir when I was about five or six years old. We sang every Friday at school and on Sunday mornings and evenings in church services. I think it was the dressing up part of it that I liked most, all the robes and cassocks. My mates Kenny Coultas and Frank Cliff were in the choir as well.

My favourite hymn was *Onward Christian Soldiers*. We could all really belt that out and it's still one of my favourites to this day. My mum went and so did my grandmother (my mum's mum).

I'm sure that part of what made Collyhurst feel safe to me was that everything seemed to be in one place, all of the things I was involved with. I could walk through the school gate and there was the school door to the right and the church door next to it. It seemed as though my whole world was there in that playground and close by. Our prefab house was just down the road, only three minutes walk away, and we eventually moved even closer to the school.

Being in the choir became a useful money-earner at times too, because it meant that we knew not just some of the best hymns but also quite a few Christmas carols.

Me and my mates in the choir would go around carol singing. We used to make quite a bit out of it and I'd go back to my grandmother's and count the money - half crowns, florins (two shillings), sixpences and loads of other coinage. My grandma would say 'look at all this money'. I'd then go and use some of the money to buy presents for my mum and my gran.

How I became involved in the cubs was through talking with one of my friends. He said the troop were going camping. I'd never been camping so I joined up and really enjoyed it. We played all sorts of games. I remember one of the games was all about staying off the floor. If you touched the floor of the room and were tagged then you were out of the game. You could run across any item of furniture, going over cupboards, tops and desks, whatever was there really.

I thoroughly enjoyed being in the cubs and then joining the boy scouts. My outfit included a green jumper, brown woggle and a green and yellow neckerchief. I was involved in everything. I played football and basketball for our troop, started playing the drum in the band and took part in revues. I was awarded a Ralph Reader silver woggle and red neckerchief for taking part in the Scouts Gang Shows. I received mine at the Palace Theatre in Manchester.

Most scout troops had marching bands playing drums and bugles. I'd started playing the drum in my first year in scouts and became lead drummer in my second year. There was a very popular Whitsuntide Week March in Manchester that involved all scout troops in the area as well as lots of other bands. The march for us was about 3 miles from St Oswald's into Manchester. You would meet up with other bands along the way. You would have a brass band up at the front and a pipe band at the back. These marches were marvellous and I loved them. In fact I loved them so much I put my life in danger because of it.

CHAPTER THREE
NEARLY DEAD

I have had some highly emotional times in my life, but none more so than when I was just a mere 10 years of age. This part of my story remains the most difficult period of my life to talk about, let alone commit to print. Tears are already in my eyes as I start to tell you what I, and others who suffered like me, went through. I'm sure that psychoanalysts would have a field day in telling me that a lot of what has happened to me since that time harks back to what I went through at that time.

One thing is for certain. There were many times when I never thought I would survive – and when I wanted to give in.

I'd started getting pains in my legs. It had been happening for a while before my mum or dad took me to the doctor, our family GP, Doctor Sharpe. I took part in all kinds of sport and was pretty good at some of them, so at first the pains could easily be put down to either growing pains or tiredness.

But I knew it wasn't that. I was in real pain. It was horrendous.

Have you ever had cramp? What I was suffering from is a hundred times worse than that. My mum used to put this ointment on my legs three times a day and give me tablets. It seemed to ease the pain for a while but then it started to become unbearable again. My dad would help too. They were fine, my mum and dad, back then.

The pain started getting that bad that there were times I couldn't walk. The majority of the pain would come at night. It was in my arms and legs and eventually it started to affect all of my body. I know my brother Bryn was very worried too.

The doctors just thought it was a phase I was going through. If only they could have been inside my head I could have told them that this was no ****ing phase! As a kid I used to scream with the sheer agony of it all. I just couldn't stand it when it came on – and it kept coming on more and more. At this time I was still trying to be as much of a normal kid as I could. No-one had diagnosed what the real problem was.

The Whit Week March was coming up and it was the year when I was to be lead drummer in the band. I'd been practising hard and had been looking forward to it for ages. There was no way I was going to miss that march, it didn't matter how much I was hurting.

Mum knew what I was thinking. She knew how important the march was to me; but the night before the parade I'd had a really bad night and was screaming the house down. She told me I couldn't go on the march and that I'd have to stay at home. She was true to her word and kept me in on Whit Monday morning, even arranging for one of our neighbours, Pauline Thompson to look after me. Pauline had been my babysitter when I was younger. She and her family were lovely but nothing was going to stop me! I had been looking forward to this for a year and was going on that march no matter what anyone said.

Mum, dad, my brother Bryn and my aunties, uncles and grandparents had all gone off to watch the parade, as everybody did in those days, and whilst Pauline was downstairs I was upstairs putting on my uniform. It consisted of a grey shirt, blue and yellow neckerchief, woggle, green socks with yellow turnovers and green tassles. I put on my new black shoes.

Somehow, I can't remember quite how I did it, I snuck out of the house and joined the band. We all lined up and the march began. I was in excruciating agony, but I was determined to put up with all of the pain just for this one day. I wanted it that much and just wanted to get through it. As we marched we approached my family and I raised my head up high so mum and dad would see me. I wanted them to be proud of me.

There was a big crowd at the bottom of Rochdale Road, where we would turn left to go on to the Oldham Road and from there on to the Town Hall in Manchester. What happened in the next few minutes as we turned that corner was to be my last action for some considerable time.

There they all were - Auntie Joyce, Auntie Marjorie and Auntie Gladys and my mum and dad. I can still hear Auntie Joyce's voice to this day. 'There's our Ian, drumming.'

Then I heard my mum's voice. 'What's he doing here? I've left him in bed. His legs won't carry him...'

I remember collapsing there and then. My legs went and the pain tore right through the whole of my body. The march came to a standstill and I was rushed off to hospital. This was the moment when my mum and dad and all the doctors realised that this wasn't just some kind of growing pains or cramp.

I was sent to Booth Hall Hospital in Blakeley and put straight into an isolation ward.

When I woke up mum and dad were by my bed. They told me not to worry and that I had fainted. Their words didn't help much. I was now in so much pain and I didn't understand anything that was going on. I remember crying and asking mum what was happening to me. She couldn't tell me at the time because the doctors needed to conduct all their tests.

I was diagnosed as suffering from rheumatic fever and it was taking lives. The disease had no definite cure and there was a good chance I could have died.

I know I said the pain is a hundred times worse than cramp, but change that to a thousand times worse. There's no way you can understand what the pain is like if you haven't suffered it. I was in an isolation ward for two years with others who suffered from rheumatic fever and there were times when you could hear everyone screaming in absolute agony.

What it does to you individually is bad enough, but what it did to my family, particularly my parents, was even worse. I can't say for sure but I think the disease I had was one of the causes of mum and dad splitting up. It certainly can't have helped.

Parents would hear all of the screaming when they visited and all of the mums would be crying. My mum, grandmother and most of my family came to see me, but one of the things that hurt me most was that my dad only came to see me once – and I was in that isolation ward for two years. I think my dad thought I was dying and I don't think he could handle that. My sister, Glynis, went through pneumonia when she was very young, at roughly the same time as I was in hospital, and I'm told he didn't visit her very much either.

My grandmother came to see me when my mother was working. I

wasn't short of visitors, mostly my aunties. That's why I love my family so much. There's always someone there no matter what hard times you might be going through.

There was a girl next door to me in the ward and we used to tap on the window to each other. She was a bit older than me. That was the only communication we had.

Every visitor had to wear masks and gowns. There's no wonder everyone thought we were going to die. No-one knew how the disease spread and there was a very real feeling that once you visited someone you might be able to contract it yourself and then pass it on.

One of the main causes of rheumatic fever is living in damp conditions, and in my case it had been caused through living in that cold, damp prefab.

I honestly thought I was going to die. I remember telling my grandmother that at least if I died I would then not feel this horrible pain.

The nurses and doctors did everything possible. I don't think anyone really knew what rheumatic fever was and thankfully it's wiped out today.

I had enjoyed my sport before I went into Booth Hall but the doctors told me I would never play sport again. Imagine that! To say that to any boy in Manchester was like cutting their feet off. We all wanted to play for either City or United.

I ran away twice. I remember waking up one morning and I just couldn't stand it anymore, all of the screaming, the pain, the isolation. It does your head in. I ran away down Delaney Road to the Rochdale Road. I knew that if I turned left at the bottom that my house was just there on that road. I could just walk down Rochdale Road and get home. I was wearing my pyjamas.

But I didn't make it home. The police had been called and they picked me up. Actually that's not strictly true because when they found out I had rheumatic fever they wouldn't touch me. So far as they knew the disease was killing people and anyone who heard about it didn't want to stand a chance of picking it up themselves. They brought an ambulance out to pick me up and take me back to the hospital.

My second escape was thwarted by my granddad. Just my luck! I'd escaped on the day he was coming to see me. I ran into him on Delaney's Road. He just took one look at me and said: 'Come on, I'll carry you back.' And that's exactly what he did. I was crying, telling him I didn't want to go back and he just said: 'You've got to, you can't come home.' As my granddad carried me back I could see people getting out of our way. It was like being a leper.

As some of us gradually improved, the hospital staff would let us out on a Sunday morning, but not on our own. The hospital had a pony and trap, or they hired one, and the hospital staff would take us out for a ride around in the fresh air early in a morning. We wouldn't be allowed out at times when everybody was coming and going. We were pale and weak. We were the kids who had this terrible disease.

We'd had some schooling whilst we there. We had been taught two hours of maths and English and other subjects each day, but if the pain had kicked in and the wailing started, the teachers were out of there pretty quickly.

Seven of the nine of us on that ward died. I don't know why the two of us survived, presumably because they caught us with the penicillin in time. We got the injections and I guess that's why I am here today and the others are not. I wasn't left totally unscarred by the disease either. The illness has left me with a permanent reminder of what I went through as I have a murmur on my heart.

Many years later, I overheard a woman saying that, as a kid, she had suffered from rheumatic fever. I joined in the conversation and mentioned Booth Hall. She stared at me and then gasped: "You're that ginger kid! You couldn't stop screaming you were in such pain." I couldn't believe it. It was the girl I used to tap on the window to - she was the only other survivor from that ward.

What we both remembered was the ward getting quieter and quieter as the others who didn't survive left us. I know how difficult it was for me and for my family coming to visit and I know it put a strain on my parents' marriage, but I also feel for those parents who came to visit the ones who didn't make it. All of those young kids who never had a chance to grow up.

CHAPTER FOUR
BETTER OFF DEAD

When I was finally allowed home from hospital my mum and dad had brought my bed into the front room. We still had no central heating so they kept the fire going all night long. It wasn't really fair on Bryn because he stayed in the bedroom where I must have picked up rheumatic fever. We had shared the same bedroom in that damp house, but thankfully he never suffered from the disease.

I never thought about it at the time but I can now understand how Bryn might have felt he had his nose pushed out. All of our parents' attention was probably going my way, or it must have seemed that way. Mum had been spending a lot of time with me at the hospital and hadn't been at home with either my dad, Bryn and by now my younger brother Gary as much as they might have expected.

Maybe that's why dad didn't visit. Whilst mum was with me he was at home quite a bit with the others. I think Bryn became my dad's favourite, but thinking about it from his side, that was probably more down to me and my disease.

It was a strange time during those first months of coming home and it felt very different to when I had been at home before I had the disease. People were coming around but they'd be saying 'he's diseased, look how ill he looks'. It took a long time for some people to come anywhere near me, let alone touch me.

In the hospital there had been times when I didn't know whether I was going to live or die. Those are thoughts that no young boy or girl should have to feel. That's why whenever I see children in hospitals today my heart goes out to them and their parents. I understand what they are going through.

I told my mum, several times, that it would probably be better for everyone if I just died. She told me not to be stupid, but I really had thought it all through whilst I was lying there and it just felt like it would be the best way out for everyone. It might have held my mum and dad together more.

Dad was great when I first came home. He and mum seemed to be getting on like they had always done. He bought me a reel-to-reel tape recorder and a boxer dog. Dad just couldn't do enough for me, but it didn't last. Neither, unfortunately, did the boxer dog. It was stolen within weeks.

We moved to St Oswald Street shortly after I came out of hospital. Mum and dad didn't want any more of their children getting rheumatic fever, so we moved out of the prefab and its dampness. They bought a corner shop. We lived to one side of the shop and up above it. St Oswald Street was made up of terraced houses just like *Coronation Street*. The shop was mainly a grocery store and mum also made sandwiches for the local beer barrel makers.

This was a great place to live and immediately much better for my health. We were close to the school, the church and I had loads of family all around me.

My gran lived next door, my Auntie Gladys was next door but one and Auntie Jean was next door but two. I'd go from school to my gran's for lunch. I'd come out from the school gate, cross the road and there I was being fed.

Having your own family shop also had some tremendous advantages. One of those was that you had a never-ending supply of sweets! I loved wine gums, sportsman's mixture and black jacks.

But it wasn't long before it all started to go wrong between my mum and dad. They started arguing and to avoid the conflict, my mum would go out to bingo with my gran and aunties. Dad spent more and more time in the pub. When he eventually came home, he'd be drunk and they would start shouting again. The arguing escalated and vicious words were exchanged.

Dad would go out on a pay night and we would hardly see him all weekend. Then the shop started going downhill. I used to read a book by candlelight because the electric was turned off as my mum couldn't afford to pay the bills.

I couldn't stand hearing mum and dad argue so I spent a lot more time living with my Auntie Marjorie or Auntie Joyce or my grandparents. It wasn't a very nice time for any of us. My sister was ill as well. Everyone thought she was going to die. She was in an oxygen tent at one time.

Looking back, my mum and dad were thrown a really bad hand of cards with two out of their four children at the time having been pretty much on death row.

It was at this time that I started blaming myself for what was happening between my mum and dad. I would tell my aunties, when I stayed with them, that if I hadn't been ill my dad wouldn't have gone drinking and my mum wouldn't have gone to bingo as much. Like my mum, they all said I shouldn't feel guilty, that I was wrong, it wasn't down to me. But none of their kind words really helped. It was there, in my mind. I truly believed their break-up was all down to me, and by now I had the impression my dad hated me. I didn't know why, but it was there, I could tell. Then one day I felt I knew for sure.

In one of his tempers, he actually said one of the worst things you can ever say to anyone: "You should have died! If you'd have died everything would have been OK." Who says that to a child? Once you hear that, there is no way it is ever going to shift from your brain. I know you can put some things down to temper, but when you're a young boy to hear that from your father is absolutely devastating. I have never got over it - and I never will.

Now don't get me wrong, it wasn't always like that. Dad did buy me nice presents, train sets and the normal things you buy for your kids, when I was younger, but the whole affair with rheumatic fever and what it did to my mum and dad was just too much for him. I still loved my dad until the day he died, and I still love him now, but somewhere along the way I felt he blamed me for everything. You can't take away that kind of imprint on your memory. When he was dying he told me how proud of me he really was, but it couldn't make up for what he'd told me back then.

CHAPTER FIVE

THE MISFIT

I wasn't allowed straight back to school when I came out of hospital. I had to be clear of the illness and I really didn't look right at first. But when I did go back I was an outcast. I felt it right from the start.

You can't pass on rheumatic fever but just the mention of it is enough to make people back-off from you when they hear that you've had a 'disease'. It's the fear of the unknown I suppose.

So when I went back to school I was bullied. Because I was pale from having been in a hospital on medication for two years I didn't look the same as them. No colour in my cheeks. The parents were the ones who caused the problems for me. They were telling their kids that I had this disease and that I could pass it on. It was maybe just a warning but it made the others pick on me. And it wasn't just the parents either. Even the schoolteachers were iffy about me going back. My mum had fought like hell to get me back into school.

There was one family of kids who always bullied me and their antics went on for a few months after I went back to St Oswald's. It was affecting me quite badly because I'd been used to having lots of friends before I'd gone into hospital and now no-one seemed to want to know me. They just wanted me to go away.

I would come home and read a book. I'd be very quiet. Mum was starting to worry that I was getting my pains back again, but I wasn't. I was black and blue from the beatings I was getting every day in the playground. Kids can be really horrible at times and I was being put through the mill. I wouldn't show Mum or Dad my bruises. I just retreated into my safer world of reading books. That was it. I was a misfit. Lunchtime, playtime, whatever time it was I was getting beaten up. They slapped me, punched me, kicked me, spat on me, all the time telling me that I was ill and that I shouldn't be at school at all.

Then one day my granddad walked into the playground. When he used to visit me in hospital he was the one who used to kick me out of my bad thoughts. He would say 'Get out of bed you little shithouse.

You're not sitting in there all day.' That was his way of dealing with where I was. I liked it because at least he wasn't saying I was going to die. He was telling me that when I got out of there I would have to be tougher than I was at the time.

I don't know how he came to be in the playground. Maybe he was on his way home to my gran's and he saw me getting beaten up again. He was a hard man. When he walked in anywhere you knew who was going to win. He picked me up off the floor by the neck that day and said: 'Now you fight back!'

When you get a gang around you, bullying you, it doesn't matter how big you are. I was a reasonably tall lad for my age but there had been too many of them. Granddad was about to even up the odds. What they weren't ready for was that by now I was starting to put the weight back on that I'd lost through being ill and I was free from pain, apart from their beatings as a group.

Granddad said: 'One-to-one' to the bullies who had been picking on me. He also got rid of all the teachers who had seen him come in to the playground and told them they could call the police if they wanted, but that whatever they did his grandson was still going to fight.

I took each of the bullies on in turn and I beat all of those who fought. Quite a few backed off from one-to-one as you might expect from bullies. Most people backed off when my granddad was around! I had needed to stand up for myself and this was the start for me. No-one picked on me again at that school.

During my final year at St Oswald's I was back playing all kinds of sport. I was a centre forward at football, good with my head. I swam a lot. I used to swim for both the cubs and scouts teams. I was a racer, front crawl, and I won quite a few competitions. Basketball was another of my favourites, being a tall lad, and I played up front at that too.

Having gone through what I had in the hospital ward for two years, I had got it into my head that if I was going to die I'd rather die enjoying myself and doing what I wanted to do. Sport was back in my life. I was fit and healthy and I was doing everything that the doctors had told me I would never be able to do again. Now that I was living properly again I just wanted to be a normal kid.

But I was soon to return to Booth Hall Hospital; although this time it was for a far more different reason to being a diseased kid.

I'd gone to the pictures. The Essoldo was where we all used to go. I'd watch Disney films and cowboy movies. There were times when I thought I might act in a film one day. But I wasn't about to have stars in my eyes as much as having stars around my head.

There were some concrete steps you had to go down to get to the toilets after you had come through the curtains. They were those deep, heavy curtains to keep the light out of the cinema. I managed to get my foot caught in the bottom of one of them and fell down the concrete steps fracturing my skull. It was a bad fracture. Well it would have to be with me wouldn't it? I was in hospital for about a month.

You'd think a disease and a fracture would be bad enough wouldn't you, but there was more to come. A short while later, I was sitting by the kerb outside our house when a milk float ran over my foot. So I'm just out from having suffered rheumatic fever, I've had a fractured skull and now I've had one of my feet run over. Thankfully I was wearing what used to be called beetle boots (desert boots) and the heel of the boot stopped the milk float from crushing my foot so I was only in hospital for a couple of hours that time. They bandaged it up and I was on my way.

I remember the sister in the hospital, who was a lovely woman and very pretty, saying: 'He's never going to be out of here!' But that was the last time I ever needed to be in Booth Hall.

I was on the mend by now in all ways. The tablets they had given me for rheumatic fever they expected me to have to take until I was 21 but the doctor cleared me at 15. I'd had some wonderful support from everyone – family, friends and hospital staff – and at home I was getting fed up. No, I wasn't getting fed up in a disillusioned way. What I mean is that I was being well nourished and well looked after wherever I went.

This is the time when Grandma's hotpots became even more of a winner for me. She also gave me food like tripe and onions, and bacon ribs and cabbage which I still love now.

Going to Wales for my summer holidays had always been great when I was a little lad, but they started to take on an even greater meaning for me. I didn't just feel good because I was with my Welsh grandparents, it was also because this is where I met the first love of my life.

I was lucky enough to have two great sets of grandparents – one pair at home in Collyhurst and the others in Wales - and the happy times I shared with all four of them will always remain in my heart. I also developed a love of Wales and the people of Newtown, especially Elaine Jones.

Elaine was not a relative, although the way we were heading I think people thought we might one day be very closely entwined. She lived next door to my grandparents. We used to play together, going down the River Severn on rafts, and we started going out together. We were only about 12-13 years of age but we were developing a relationship and I think my grandparents even had the idea that one day we might get married. We got on so well together, but we were only kids.

My next relationship with a girl after that was in my early teens. Her name was Jacqueline Page. She was the daughter of my mum's best friend, Marjorie. We were all good friends as I knew Jacqueline's brothers as well. I started getting a thing for Jacqueline as we were getting a little older and I remember her mum catching us together in the bathroom one day. We were just exploring. I wasn't a misfit for very long you see!

CHAPTER SIX

LEADER OF THE GANG

We only lived in St Oswald Street for about three or four years. I wished it could have been longer but the shop wasn't working out and my mum and dad were now struggling with their marriage. Maybe it was money troubles along the way, but it can't have been bad news all the time because not long after we moved to our new home in Collyhurst Drive Southern Flats, the family had increased from four to six children.

There was me, Bryn, Gary and Glynis who had all lived in St Oswald Street – and then John and Carol who were born after we moved. Our next move was to a brand new house in Miles Platting on the Monsall estate. Wilsons Brewery was just around the corner. Our home was a brand new build, 4-bedroomed semi detached house with a front garden and back garden. We'd never had a garden before.

Like most other lads I would spend a lot of my time playing outside with a gang of friends no matter where we lived. We were all great mates and during the latter part of my schooldays at St Oswald Street School to the end of my time at Albert Memorial Secondary School we would always be together. Most of us had been inseparable from being little lads.

We were never really bad or unruly. We didn't get ourselves into serious trouble. It wasn't as though we were trying to be anything other than boys messing about, but as time went on we got more and more daring. In the end we were pulling all kind of stunts, things that maybe we really shouldn't have been doing. But it all started very innocently.

Derek Warren, my cousin, and I were always close friends. We used to build 'guiders' together, sometimes called bogies. They were the go-karts of our generation. We would make them out of wheels and other bits of wood and metal we would get from rubbish tips. We would go to a place called Redhills – a bit like the 'Red Rec' in *Coronation Street* - and dare each other to see who could stay on their guiders longest as we came down the hill. I'm sure we all picked up one or two knocks and bruises as we fell off. We ended up making our own bikes from reclaimed parts as well, so we were actually very productive. We would find frames and wheels and we would build the bikes with a crowbar handlebar.

We also had what we considered to be one of the biggest bonfires around and we used to protect ours before the big night because rival gangs would often raid each others' mountains of wood. We would build it on a croft on the street behind us. I don't think anything ever grew there again because of the fires we had.

My biggest mates at the time were Frank Cliff and Stephen Cliff, Philip Bailey and Kenny Coultas. We had all gone through infants school, cubs and scouts together, so we knew each other well. We would always look out for one another.

Postman's Knock was another of our childish games. We would knock on people's doors, run away and, from a vantage point where they couldn't see us, we would watch the adults come to the door and see there was no-one there. We'd love it. We were just kids, high-spirited kids.

Eventually we all had our own racing bikes. I got mine from Derek's dad, my Uncle Charlie, for a tenner. It was a proper racing bike and I used it on my paper round delivering the *Manchester Evening News*. Little did I know then that I'd be featuring in the newspaper so regularly.

We went everywhere on our bikes. We rode to Southport for a day at the seaside. It was red hot and I got sunburnt on my back. But that was nothing compared to what happened to Frank Cliff when we got back to Manchester that night. We had talked about the best way back. Most of us thought Rochdale Road but Frank decided to go up Collyhurst Road. Unfortunately for him it wasn't the right decision. He got hit by a truck and was in a bad way for a time.

Music has always played a part in my life. As well as being a drummer I also became a guitarist and with Kenny Coultas, his brother Terry and another Coultas brother we started a band playing stuff by The Beatles, The Byrds and The Yardbirds. Mum bought me my first guitar, which I think was a Hofner. We played anything that was easy to play. I played rhythm guitar. We used to play at The Essoldo and we did alright, we always seemed to go down well, and playing in a band was always a good way to attract the girls, which by now we were all interested in. I enjoyed playing in the band but the rest of them practiced far more than I ever did.

By now you're probably wondering when things started getting a bit tastier, when we started upping the stakes and daring ourselves to take things that much further. After all, there was nothing wrong with playing football, swimming, bonfires, cycling or playing in a band; but along the way we started getting a bit more adventurous.

We started out by taking cider from the dray wagons as they were making deliveries to local pubs. That all sounds a bit tame I know, but we graduated to the next level. We would go on to the railways and steal detonators from huts. They were fog detonators and we would put them on the road for cars to run over. The detonators would then blow the tires. Now that really was dangerous.

I enjoyed being seen as the leader and I have to confess that a lot of the ideas for what we would do were mine. Why did I do it? I think because I felt I had cheated death I reckoned that I didn't have that much to fear. But maybe again it was just being with a group of lads egging each other on.

One of the most emotional moments in our time together wasn't anything to do with robbing or causing others distress though.

CHAPTER SEVEN
THE WEIR

There were places we knew that we should never have played and one of those was the weir on the River Irk. It was near the Collyhurst Road, close to the rubbish tip, and it was to be somewhere that would remain in my mind forever. We loved playing there, spending hours messing around. It was somewhere you could go that didn't cost anything.

You always get one lad in a group who is a bit weaker than the rest. It's not their fault it's just how it is. We used to 'run the weir' near to the whirlpool that was the river basin. The basin itself was bad enough and was 20ft deep. We thought that the weir was easy in comparison, but it was never easy for our weaker guy.

The hardest part was always getting back across. The river flowed pretty quickly and it became a real tester at times. You had to be careful, because it was so easy to slip and typically, amongst our gang, if you didn't do it you were regarded as chicken. One of the gang always struggled in getting back and on this one day I had to be in for tea at 6 o'clock. All the rest of the lads had to be back soon as well, but our weak guy was even slower at coming back over with us than he normally was, so we left him. It was to be our worst decision in all the years we played together. We very rarely left anyone and we knew afterwards that we should have stayed to make sure he got back. We certainly never made the same mistake again, but hindsight always makes life easy doesn't it?

No-one knows exactly what happened after we'd left him to fend for himself, apart from three hours later the police came to our house asking whether I had seen him. I was shaking like a leaf when the copper came to our door. I said he had been with us down by the river. I didn't want to tell him we'd been playing on the weir because then I'd have got in trouble at home. The police just said he was missing, but of course I knew what must have happened. It was like a shot through my heart as I was being asked when I had seen him last. We all knew how dangerous it was down there and how putting a foot wrong could land you in serious trouble.

Later, we found out that our friend had drowned. We knew we should have stayed. He was always a bit unsure of himself and as mates we should have stayed with him. At least we might have been able to help if we had seen him fall. For a while, all I could think about was him slipping and calling out for help with no-one there. It was a really sad time for all of us and obviously even more so for his parents. I know we all felt guilty for letting him down. We were used to looking after each other but we had failed miserably and learned a severe lesson about friendship; and just how quickly it is to lose your life.

CHAPTER EIGHT
SHAKESPEARE SAVED ME

The times I had with my mates were generally great days. We all got on so well. My early years at secondary school were a different matter though. I had passed my 11+ exam and went to Clough Top Secondary in Blakeley but it wasn't a happy experience.

The first day I went to the school the bullies were waiting. You know the kind of thing that used to happen in schools. The older years would pick on the new ones. They knew that our uniforms were brand new so they threw us down this muddy hill. No doubt it was some kind of ritual, with every year group doing it to every new year's students coming in. But they chose the wrong target with me.

My mum had gone into debt again to buy me the uniform. She'd had to fund it herself because Dad wasn't around at the time. It cost a lot of money, more money than she could spare. It was a maroon blazer with a blue and yellow striped tie and a white shirt.

I went back home that day and explained why it was in such a mess. I told my mum that they wouldn't be doing it again. She said: 'You've worked hard to get into that school, don't blow it, don't start fighting.' She knew I was not going to take it from them again though.

I watched my mum take that uniform and clean it. It was immaculate by the time she had finished, just like new. She was brilliant with clothes and when she ironed a pair of trousers the creases stayed in all week.

Next morning everything looked brand new again. I got the bus, got to school and there they were again, ready for Round 2. They never threw me down that hill again! I threw the ****ers down that hill again and again. I didn't get in to school until 11 o'clock because I wouldn't stop throwing them back down the hill. They must have wondered what they had taken on that first day.

My future brother-in-law, Steven Bailey, went to the school and he was in the year above me. He told them that they shouldn't ***k with me.

But my actions didn't stop this other guy coming up to me in the school yard later that day. He came right up to me, in my face, trying to intimidate me. He almost spat out the words: 'You think you're really hard don't you!'

And I just hit him. 'Don't ever argue with anyone when they come on to you like that, just hit them.' That's what my grandfather said. And he said more: 'If someone's coming on to you, the more you talk the more chance they have of getting you.' So I just lashed out at him and broke his nose with one short, sharp jab. His nose splattered like a squashed strawberry.

Bashing up other schoolkids is one thing, but bashing a teacher? Well that's quite a different matter. I did both. The teacher bashing got me thrown out. How it came about was like this. Today it would probably be the teacher who would be banned.

Clough Top school had a park right next to it. We had been told in assembly that there was a prowler in the park. This prowler was molesting kids on their way to and from school but they hadn't caught him. We were all told that when we left school we were to get on our buses and go straight home whilst he was at large.

My English teacher was not the brightest spark. I argued with him over something he'd said and he kept us back as a class. It was winter and because he'd kept us back it looked like we were going to have to walk through the park whilst this molester was on the loose. Because I'd argued with him he slapped me across the head. I'd had a fractured skull. He'd hit me, so I battered him. I was kicked out of Clough Top.

I went to Albert Memorial School. I was now 13 and it wasn't long before I was in trouble there as well.

What was it with teachers that made them think they could slap you? I'm damned sure it doesn't happen today as they would all be done for GBH. At Albert Memorial another one slapped me around the head. My fracture was at the back of my head and that's where this science teacher hit me. Being hit anywhere just sends flashing blue lights to me; but being hit somewhere I'd suffered a fracture was like lighting the blue touchpaper. I went ballistic and attacked him. Then there was the RE teacher who threw a plant pot at me.

I was pretty much on my way out of the doors of my second

secondary school in so many months.

The headmaster, Mr Jordan, hauled me into his office. Mum was there. My dad even came along. It looked like I was more interested in fighting than being at school.

You'd think that would be the end of my school life wouldn't you? But it wasn't, thanks to one woman, a teacher who changed my life and who I shall be forever grateful to. If she's still alive I would love to see her to tell her the difference she made to me. Without her I would never have achieved the acting career I have had so far and will hopefully have for many more years to come.

Miss Brown was my English teacher. She came into Mr Jordan's office that day and said: 'Give him to me for six weeks and I'll change him. I will give you a different boy back.'

He didn't agree straight away. He told her and my mum there was no way anyone could change me, that I was violent and borstal was my next resting place.

I turned to Miss Brown and laughed at her not believing this woman would or could do anything for me. I asked her what she was going to do. This broadly-built woman was the saviour of my life. She took me out of that room and gave me a script.

'We're doing *Julius Caesar* as the school play – and you're going to play him. You're going to learn the script and I know you can do it. I've seen you in English lessons. The two lessons you really settle down to are English and History. You can do this.'

She taught me that if you portray Shakespeare you must do it in a certain way, that I must feel it, I shouldn't just say the words. I listened. This woman, this wonderful woman, was setting me on the path I wanted to be on. She put me through my exams and drama classes and it felt good.

Probably my favourite Shakespeare play of all is *Twelfth Night*. I love the characters and could play two or three of them in the play. I used to like playing one character for a minute and then go on to be someone else. I found it really easy to nip in and out of characters.

Whatever belief Miss Brown had in me she brought out. I went from a thug and being off the rails, with a reputation for hitting members of the teaching staff to being in every play she ever put on. I started to learn Shakespeare and there were even times when I didn't go out with the gang of lads I'd been going around with. I'd stay in at lunchtime to learn everything I could and I joined drama classes after school hours at a place called Queen's Park.

When I took the curtain call at the end of performing *Julius Caesar* and everyone applauded it sent my mind right back to the nativity play when I was just a little lad. It triggered all of those good feelings again and I never looked back. I started winning awards for my English compositions and I loved my acting world. Everything just seemed to fall into place – and it was all down to the belief that Miss Brown showed in me. She really was my guardian angel.

I didn't just have Miss Brown believing in me either. My Uncle John was right there too. He would come, with my Auntie Marjorie and my mum, and see me in all my plays. He took a real interest in me and what I was doing. He would talk with me and his encouragement was a great help. I never had that in the same way from dad. Uncle John would ask what I wanted to be. Where I came from you either wanted to be a footballer or nothing; but I told him I'd like to be an actor.

I became a reformed character at school, studied hard and went on school trips too, something I hadn't done before. I went to France and my mum and gran paid for it. I had settled down to schoolwork and the fisticuffs were in the past.

The only problem I had was that it wasn't exactly going to go down well with my mates if I told them I was going off to see a Shakespeare play instead of playing football. 'To the lads where I came from, the only response to that would be, 'Are you gay?'

I used to take my football boots with me to the drama classes I attended on a Saturday and when I came home I muddied my face up and hung my boots around my neck as though I'd played.

There were plenty of times I was still playing football though. I played centre forward for the school team and ripped the ligaments in my knee. No surprise there. Off I went to Crumpsall Hospital this time! At least it was a change from Booth Hall! I was on crutches for six months. My mum said I was the most accident prone kid ever born. I couldn't argue very much about that. Skull, foot, knee, I was running out of parts of the body left to injure. Now don't go making up your own stories about where my next injury would be!

I wanted to stay on at school. Quite a change from before Miss Brown had got hold of me.

My dad had gone again. He'd been gone for months at a time for the past few years and I thought he'd gone for good. One night I had found Mum crying. Dad had packed his bags and left. She had six of us to look after. It was a huge task. The least I could do was to contribute in some way. That's when I told her I was leaving school and going to get a job.

I went to the headmaster and told him I had to leave and why. Considering the bad place I'd been in years before when I was nearly chucked out it was a bit ironic that I'd have to leave just when I was enjoying school and doing well. I received a lovely gift – a book – as well as a toothbrush and toothpaste. They always gave you those when you left school. Maybe they had a sponsorship deal with Colgate. The book I received was of William Shakespeare's plays and sonnets.

As for my acting I just thought maybe that was it. I'd enjoyed it whilst it had lasted. Miss Brown once told me that she felt I would go far in the acting world, but what Mum needed at that time was someone bringing in some money. That was what I had to do.

What Miss Brown did for me in my time at Albert Memorial School is something no-one else has ever done. She gave me belief in my own ability and it is her and her alone that made sure I came out of school with a far better attitude than when I started. She gave me an aim in life. Acting, performing, writing - I didn't know how it was all going to influence me. But Miss Brown believed in me. I was no longer that kid who was diseased or the one who was off the tracks.

Without her influence, without her standing up for me and taking me under her wing at Albert Memorial I might never have ended up achieving what I have. Thank you Miss Brown wherever you are.

CHAPTER NINE
PIPES & MODS

My Auntie Joyce had a cousin who was an electrician and he got me my first job as an apprentice. I lasted 12 months. By then I had found it boring. Whilst I was on a job I watched some pipefitters. There was pipe everywhere and I enjoyed watching what they were doing. It looked a lot better than putting a wire in a wall and chasing the wires out. I managed to swap over to a company called Calvent Engineering of Stockport and began fitting everything from boilers to radiators. It was my kind of job - shifting, lifting and fixing.

I was working and bringing in money, but that wasn't enough for me. I needed some excitement. I was still interested in acting but I wasn't on stage and since school I hadn't joined an amateur dramatic society. I was now a teenager with a job who enjoyed going out with the lads, having a drink and pulling the girls. The excitement I needed at this time came from getting dressed up, but not for going on stage.

I was a Mod. I used to save up for smart suits, the Mods' usual sharp-looking outfit. I was a scooter boy for a short while and had a Lambretta SX200 but typical of me I kept falling off it. Friday nights we would all go out on our scooters and meet up in Middleton. We'd go to seaside resorts like Newquay, Brighton and Blackpool; and on a Sunday afternoon it would be time for Mods versus Rockers at Heaton Park in Manchester. The rockers would be on one hill with the Mods on the other. It went on for a while in Heaton Park. I've still got a scar on my wrist from a flick knife used in one of those fights.

Being a Mod was a way of life for a while. I liked the two-tone suits and the parkas. I had one of the proper fishtail parkas with 'Ban the Bomb' on the back. I also loved the music that Mods liked.

When I went out for a night in Manchester I would wear my white linen suit with matching shirt, tie and scarf. The shirt and tie were brown and I had a pair of black brogues. I gelled my hair the way the kids do today, so it was spiky and for a time I looked a bit like Sting in Quadrophenia. All very Mod. I always liked to dress smart to impress the girls and yes, I fancied myself as a ladies' man.

My best mate around this time was Steve Hadfield. We'd go everywhere together and he was best man at both my weddings! We were from different areas around Manchester, he was a Blakeley lad but we had a lot in common and enjoyed going to clubs together.

Steve and I went to a club in Cheetham Hill called Chilton's. It was a non-alcoholic nightclub and that's where we would meet up with the rest of the lads every Tuesday and Friday night. We ended up spending quite a lot of time there enjoying the music of the Beatles, The Who and soul music which was really popular with all the Mods.

Another of our favourites at the time was a place called Rowntree Sound. This was a big disco club in Manchester, near Victoria Station, and we could get a drink in there. That's where I first discovered what drugs can do to you. I've never taken drugs in my life but one of the lads from the regular crowd that went there died of a drugs overdose.

The closest Steve and I ever got to doing anything really bad was stealing some potatoes and carrots from Smithfield Market in Manchester. I'd take them home after a night out and put them on the table for mum, thinking I'd done a good thing, getting us some extra food. Next day I'd be in trouble from her, some real earache for a couple of hours, but she knew she needed help with food and money. By the time I was nearly 18 I was on £3 a week and I was giving my mum £2 of it. She would then give me a pound back to cover my bus fares and sandwiches.

Being with Steve and the rest of the lads was always more important than being with girls in those days. We would all look out for each other. It was a time when going to a club, meeting up and having a drink came first. Girls were a bit more of a game to us all back then. Sure, we were going out to pull the girls and it was a case of whoever pulled went off on their own.

I was a good looking lad, tall, and I met quite a few girls. I'm not saying I didn't have a few one night stands but I preferred going out with a girl and getting to know her a bit before we went any further. If a girl was willing on the first night you learned very quickly that she wasn't for you. You wondered where she would be tomorrow night!

I enjoyed being a Mod; the way we all dressed, going out with the lads, riding the Lambretta, going to clubs, meeting girls and dancing to some great music.

And it was music that brought me together with a girl called Sue Bailey.

CHAPTER TEN
MARRIED WITH CHILDREN

Sue was a beautiful girl. She was tall and dark haired; had a great figure with curves in all the right places and was about the same age as me. We had met at Chiltons Dance Hall in Seymour Road, Crumpsall and had started going out together everywhere. We couldn't get enough of each other. She loved Diana Ross and the Supremes, the Four Tops and all of the Tamla Motown sounds that were really popular in the early 70s.

Pretty soon we were inseparable and the lads I was knocking around with had to take a back seat. Blackpool was a favourite for us and we spent the kind of weekends you do when you're having a great time as a couple. We would laugh and joke all the time and do what comes naturally.

You don't really need me to tell you what's coming next do you?

That's right. Sue was pregnant and I'm fairly certain I know where Jon, our first son, was conceived, right down to the B&B. We were married on 12 June 1971 at St Oswald's Church in Collyhurst - Ian Roy Jones and Susan Margaret Bailey. Her mother and father and my gran paid a lot of money for the wedding. Tony Christie was high in the charts with *I Did What I Did For Maria* as well he might have done, but I did what I did for Sue. We had a lovely wedding with all of my family there, even my dad. He shocked me, not purely because he turned up as he was always doing that - but because of what he said to me on my wedding day just minutes before going into the church.

Dad offered me money to run away from it all, to do a bunk. He just told me quite simply and very seriously, in fact probably the most serious words he had ever said: 'Don't get married'. I don't know why he suddenly decided to tell me that, but maybe he had greater insight than I had.

I loved Sue, but it turned out that we were too young – or at least I was. The song that goes, 'You're much too much, much too young; you're married with a kid, when you should be having fun with me' by

The Specials was probably written about someone like me. I wasn't ready. I wasn't mature enough to handle all of the responsibilities that come with marriage and fatherhood. Of course I didn't realise this at the time. I was blissfully happy in our months just before the wedding and right up to the birth of our first child. I thought we would stay together forever.

When Jon was born everything was great. I had changed from being the flash lad-about-town in my white linen suit to the family man. I had dropped going out with my mates as regularly as I had been and I had sold the Lambretta.

I had also come out of my pipefitting work for a while because I wanted to be closer to home. I wanted to be a good husband and dad. A friend of mine called John got me a job with Dewhurst butchers. I just wanted a steady job to pay the rent and I'd been getting on really well with him. With all of the changes I'd made I felt as though I was trying very hard to get things right. I'd still go out for a quick drink after work on a Friday, but that was as far as things went without being with Sue. We would go out together on a Saturday night if I could get Glynis to babysit. But it wasn't enough. We weren't destined to play happy families for very long.

I know Sue's mum and mine thought we would have problems and I always felt that her mother didn't really like me for having made her daughter pregnant. I'm sure she thought I had taken away part of her youth and that I'd somehow trapped her daughter into motherhood. Sue's father Jim, God bless him, was a lovely man. I'd sometimes share a drink with him on a Sunday afternoon. We talked a good deal and had a much easier and friendlier relationship than I ever had with her mum.

I thought I was taking my responsibilities seriously, but maybe I was too immature to understand what Sue had gone through and how a baby changes a woman's life in so many ways. She had given up work and was now at home all the time. I don't think I realised what that does to someone's independence. I do understand that now, even though it's a good few years too late to have found out.

I was working hard to make sure we could pay the bills and afford a decent living. I thought that was my role, to be the bread winner. In my heart I felt that because I was working hard during the week this entitled me to go out and have a drink every now and again. I wasn't 'out with the lads' as such, I was just in a local pub. It wasn't as though I was out on the town, but it didn't go down at all well with Sue and the arguments started.

When we rowed it felt to me as though we were going the same way as my mum and dad, but a lot earlier in our marriage than they had. After a while I couldn't bear the arguments and started going out with my mates again, but that just made matters worse.

We were living in a place called Harperhay at the time and Sue was on her own with Jon. I'd go out drinking after we'd had a row and get back home when I wanted. Not very clever I know and not very understanding of me either. Things were at breaking point only months into our marriage and Sue walked out, leaving me with Jon. I can't blame her. I was the one who was making life very difficult and the rows were because I never understood what she needed from me.

Because I was working all the time there was no way I could look after Jon during the day. Jon was still only a baby and I know that Sue would never have wanted to leave him, it was just that our rows had affected her so much. So I moved back into my mum's house on the Monsall estate and mum looked after Jon while I worked.

It wasn't all bad news between the two of us though. Many young newly-weds find the first months of their marriage tricky, especially when there is a baby to consider, and a few months later Sue and I got back together. We'd met up, talked things over and decided to give it another go. We put our name down on the council list for a house. We became a family again. In fact things were so good that we soon went from being a family of three to a family of four. That's when our second beautiful son Steven was born.

We'd overcome our early marital problems and we were good together, this time for a couple of years rather than months. We lived in Darnhill in Heywood. I was working what seemed like every hour God sent and there was little time for anything but work and family. When I did go out for a drink it was with my Uncle Brian who lived in Heywood, near where we lived at the time. I was taking on as much overtime as I could, to earn as much as possible and because I was working so hard I felt I had earned the right to go out for a few drinks. That inevitably led to long nights out, and Sue was left at home with the boys. You can see the familiar pattern and what was going to happen next can't you? I was letting her down again, thinking of myself first. The rows returned and soon escalated. We were back on that rocky road.

It wasn't Sue's fault, it was mine. She could see I had my own freedom and I'm sure she wanted some freedom of her own. She left me for the second time and I went back to Monsall, to my mum's, this time with both boys. I told mum that this was it. We wouldn't be getting back together again, but we did several times. The boys were around one and three years old when Sue walked out on the second occasion. It must have been around 1974. From then on we had an intermittent relationship.

CHAPTER ELEVEN
FREEDOM & FATHERHOOD

Fortunately I always had mum close at hand and she was happy looking after Jon and Steven. When Sue left the second time it was mum who encouraged me to go out and enjoy myself. She knew I needed to be off with my mates. I started going out with the lads to discos again, mostly my two best mates at the time Steve Hadfield and Steve Broughton. Somewhat ironically I was also going out a lot more with my brother-in-law Steve Bailey. Mum gave me the chance to be a lad again whilst she made sure the boys were looked after. She took the boys wherever they needed to go and never once complained about doing it.

I had started thinking that nothing was ever going to work out for me, that maybe I wasn't cut out to be with someone. I decided that one night stands were the way. I hadn't had any before I was married because I wanted to get to know a girl first, but now it was different. I thought sod it I'll get what I can and get out.

I had my freedom back, especially with mum always there for the boys. She was with them far more than I was and that gave me a free rein to do what I wanted, so I took it. But I never felt I was taking my mum for granted, I knew just how much she was doing for me and the boys. I would ask her if it was okay for me to go out on a Saturday night. I think she liked it that I at least asked her permission.

Mum went one better than telling me it was okay. My brother Bryn had landed a job on the island of Jersey and mum suggested I should go over and join him. Bryn had enough work on to keep me busy and it was good money. I think mum thought it would also clear my head and give me chance to take a different look at my life. She said she would look after Jon and Steven. I had misgivings about being away from the boys, but I decided to go.

Bryn was working in St Helier. He was a painter and decorator and he'd won some good work on the island. It was the first time in our lives that I felt the two of us had gelled. We worked hard and I was earning more than I had been at home. There was another lad called Steve

Holland from Blakeley who was there too and we all got on together. The island was beautiful and the people were great.

Every Sunday afternoon it seemed like the whole island descended on this place called Belle Vue. Every nationality in the world seemed to be represented on those afternoons all singing their own songs. I even took up a bit of DJ work in one of the bars. I'd just felt that the guy who was already doing it in this bar was a bit of a pillock and I said I could do better. It went well and was a useful sideline.

I stayed a few months, until the work dried up. I phoned Jon and Steven every day. I will always be grateful to mum for looking after them and giving me the opportunity to go. It certainly helped me get over some of the sadness I was feeling in breaking up with Sue and I came back refreshed, with stories to tell and with money in my pockets. I gave mum all the money I had earned in St Helier. Without mum there is no way I would ever have been able to go to work in Jersey.

Girls, girls, girls - I couldn't get enough of them for a while when I came back – and I wasn't looking for relationships! Well not long lasting ones at any rate.

I remember not long after I had come back I took mum out for a drink. It was about one o'clock in the afternoon. We were in The Clarendon, our local on the Monsall estate when a blonde haired girl walked in and sat near to us having a drink. Mum and I had been talking about the boys but she saw how I was getting distracted by this blonde girl. I remember her saying: 'You've not been back two minutes, what is it with you and women?' I told mum I wasn't doing anything; but by four o'clock I was in bed with that girl.

I knew I was in trouble when I got home. I walked in the house about eight o'clock and the boys were sat there. Mum asked where I'd been although I'm sure she knew. 'You were supposed to be having tea with the boys. You had better put them to bed because I'm not.'

What could I say? 'I'm sorry boys but I've been with a woman all afternoon, that I don't really know, but I've had a great time?' I knew I hadn't put them first. I was being selfish again, so all I did was apologise to them for not being there.

They didn't even want me to put them to bed. But it wasn't simply because I was late that day. It had more to do with the previous months whilst I'd been away in Jersey.

'Nana puts us to bed.' That's what they told me. I said that I was going to put them to bed that night. I put them to bed, kissed them goodnight and then told them I'd take them to school in the morning. They said 'Nana takes us to school.'

Mum was both their mum and their dad. They would follow her everywhere. She knew their routine, she knew what food they liked, what they were like as individuals. I didn't.

It's then that I started to realise what I had done. It was like 'Woah! These are not my kids, they're mum's!' Again I'd put someone and something I was doing before them. I remember thinking I had dropped one of the biggest bollocks of my life. I had a job to do here to build the relationship I should have been building – as a parent and a good father. That's when I realised I had to spend some real time with my boys. I started taking them out, playing football with them, being a dad.

Sue and I got back together again. By now we had moved to Bagley in Wythenshawe. I was now in my mid-20s and working for UMIST (University of Manchester Institute of Science & Technology) on boiler maintenance. Hardly the career you might have thought after I'd enjoyed Shakespeare so much. The Bard wrote many plays involving tragedy, but he didn't generally write about serial killers. And yet my life seemed to revolve around them for a time in the mid 70s.

CHAPTER TWELVE

THE BEAST

Trevor Hardy was the 'Beast of Manchester'. He murdered three teenage girls in the mid-70s and was jailed in 1977. He used to go into one of my 'locals', The Friendship Inn in Newton Heath. I didn't know it at the time, none of us did, but he had probably already killed his first victim when he was coming in to the pub at the time I was there.

He was a horrible man. This one particular Saturday there were two young lads with their father in the pub. The two boys had learning difficulties, I think it was Down's Syndrome, and when Hardy came in, he stared at them and then said to their father in a menacing and nasty way: 'What have I told you about bringing those two spastics in the pub. They shouldn't be here.'

Every time the bloke came in with his sons, Hardy was the same, treating them really badly. I was getting bloody well sick of him.

One day I was in the pub earlier than normal. I'd had one of those Saturday mornings. We had been pipefitting and we couldn't fit a piece of pipe to save our lives. Every piece we had cut was too short and nothing worked out at all. We had given up on it as a bad job. By now we couldn't have cared less about the extra overtime we were going to get for working the whole Saturday morning. We'd had enough, so we left for home and I went for a pint.

There was only me and my mate in at the time. Then Hardy turned up. The bloke and his boys weren't there. I had started to think that maybe they weren't coming and they'd finally had enough of the stick they were getting from him. But then they arrived and before you knew it he was at them again.

I went over to Hardy and said: 'Look I'm not having it. Get out. Leave them alone.' I must have said it quite hard-hitting because my mate told me that my eyes had changed and I'd scared the living daylights out of him. He'd not seen me like that before. He told me I was banging my fist on the bar, not loudly but that my fists were getting redder and my knuckles were getting whiter.

I turned around when he wasn't going to go and hit him. It all kicked off from there. We had a real scrap and God knows what was broken in the process. The police arrived and he was arrested. I wasn't. The landlord and the bloke with the boys stuck up for me.

After Hardy had been carted off I didn't see him for a while. When he finally reappeared he looked nervous and stayed on his own. He didn't say much and didn't bully the bloke with the boys.

Years later we all read about Trevor Hardy – The Beast of Manchester and how he had killed those poor girls. The landlord said: 'My God, you should have killed him that day.' I wish to God that I had. There would have been three girls still alive if I'd finished him off that day.

CHAPTER THIRTEEN
THE RIPPER

The most dramatic event of my life, the most disturbing, horrifying and emotionally catastrophic was to take place on the morning of 10 October 1977. It was the day I discovered the mutilated body of the Yorkshire Ripper's sixth victim.

Nothing can prepare you for finding a dead body - and the memory of that horrific discovery will haunt me forever. We all know that whatever happens in your life has an impact on you and it's only when you hear or read someone's life story that you begin to understand why they are the way they are. I'm not trying to make excuses for myself here.

My day had started well.

I had been with UMIST for a couple of years and worked with a chap called Jimmy Morrisey. We shared an interest in gardening and joined the UMIST Gardening Society. Jimmy had found out that an allotment had come available next to Southern Cemetery in Manchester. Little did I know how close that would bring me to a dead body that was not in a coffin and hadn't been buried six feet in the ground.

We had spent a good deal of summer 1977 getting the allotment ready for the next growing season, preparing the land. We had planted cabbages, sprouts, potatoes and carrots. When autumn set in and with winter approaching we decided to put a base in for a shed. I had been picking some bricks out of the rubble of an old allotment. I'd been moving them for the past few weekends and we had got most of the base down and now half the shed was up. We were building the side where we would be putting up the cold frame. Jimmy was laying the bricks down whilst I did the fetching and carrying.

It was 10.30 in the morning and we were having a cup of tea before I started out to collect more bricks. I was pushing my wheelbarrow over what had been a flatter area of rubble. This particular morning I saw what at first looked like a tailor's dummy. My initial thought was that I wondered who had thrown it there and why. But as I got closer the stench was awful. I soon realised that it was what remained of a woman.

Her name was Jean Jordan. She was also known as Jean Royle and she had been killed on 1 October 1977. Her body was described by the police and media as the most grotesque find of any of the Ripper's murders and I can still see it today. He had tried to decapitate her, he had cut off her breasts and her body was rotting away. I won't tell you any more than that because I really don't want to give you any impression that I'm in some way getting any kicks out of recalling what I found. I was physically sick at the time and please believe me that when you have seen a sight like this it never goes away.

The body hadn't been there when I'd moved the last lot of bricks the previous day. What if the person who had dumped it was there now? I looked all around as quickly as I could, but as we now know Sutcliffe had been there during the night. He had come back to find the fresh £5 note that he'd been given in his pay packet and that he had given to Jean Jordan. He had realised that the £5 note was traceable back to him. When he couldn't find it he became angry with her even though she was already dead, and mutilated her body completely.

I thought I saw someone staring at me through a hedge with black, dark eyes. That's all I saw. We could have been that close to him, the man that caused so much harm, so much loss of life, so much distress to so many families.

What if we had caught him? How many lives could Jimmy and I have saved? How many families would not have had to live through the trauma, the distress. We really must have been that close to him, this monster Peter Sutcliffe.

I was in shock.

I saw a bloke coming up the footpath with his dog, a Jack Russell. I shouted for him to come over and I also shouted for Jimmy. The bloke with the dog came over and his dog started sniffing around the body as dogs do. The bloke told me that I should go and get the police.

I ran across the Princess Parkway. It's a very busy road but all I could think of was getting to the nearest phone box. This was a time way before mobile phones. I rang 999 telling them I had found a body on Southern Cemetery Allotments. I was panic-stricken. I went back to

Jimmy. The bloke with the dog was still there. Police cars arrived and the police walked over to us.

Whilst what I found was horrific and I was in a bit of a state myself, I wasn't ready for what happened next. All three of us were put into a police van – and the dog! I couldn't believe it! All we had done was to find a body, but we hadn't just found anybody. We had found Jean Jordan and this was massive. We were taken to Moss Side Police Station where we were questioned. All we could tell them was about finding the body, we knew nothing more.

The police officers took all my clothes and put me in a white suit. I asked why they were doing that but I understand now why they did so. At the time I just felt as though I was under suspicion. We were all under suspicion.

I was allowed to go to the canteen and as I was sat there this young copper casually came out with the comment, 'You know that the one that finds the body is usually the one that's done it'.

I just snapped. I was already stressed by the discovery of the body and I was frustrated about having to wear this white suit as though I was a suspect. I didn't have a police record and I had been at the station for hours. It was now about four o'clock in the afternoon. That young copper's comment gave me the impression they might be trying to fit me up. I wasn't about to take that. I went for him.

His colleagues had to pull me away from him. I remember vividly the canteen lady telling them 'it wasn't his fault'.

Anyone who finds a body is immediately under suspicion. You never realise this until it happens to you, but when it does it is harrowing. It is an ordeal.

The incident with the young copper didn't do me any favours either, as you might expect. It just added to my time in the police station as I was taken back and put in a cell. They did it to cool me down. I was eventually allowed home the same day after being in the police station for quite a few hours.

The questions they asked me were all the kind of question that it takes such a long time to think about. 'Where were you on such and such a day?' When you can't remember what you were doing you get the feeling that every answer is going to incriminate you, even though you know it shouldn't.

There's little wonder that some people just own up to crimes they have never committed just because they feel under pressure.

I never kept a diary. I don't know of many who do. When you're being questioned you get the feeling that the police are trying to twist you, or at least that's how it seemed to me. It's understandable when they are trying to find killers, but it is intimidating when you know that you're not one and yet you feel that they are trying to pin it on you.

I had absolutely nothing to hide and I told them everything I could. I wracked my brain to remember everything I had done on the days they were asking about.

It really gives you such a bad feeling that you start thinking 'was it me?' You know you haven't done anything but the environment and the questioning gets to you.

The police then went to my workplace to check the work cards or whatever else they wanted to in order to 'eliminate me from their inquiries'. They checked on Jimmy as well.

My head was all over the place for weeks and months afterwards. I couldn't concentrate. Nine times out of ten I would wake up thinking I'd heard a girl screaming for help. I couldn't go back to work at UMIST straight away. And it put more pressure on my marriage with Sue.

Years later I was asked whether I ever had counselling for what I saw that day and what I'd gone through but that kind of thing wasn't really heard of at the time. Apart from visiting my local GP I had to deal with it myself. You just had to get on with it. There was no-one who gave you anything like counselling.

I don't know whether people became scared of me at the time but I know that I was troubled. It had an effect on me. I would easily lose my cool. Every time I talk, or write as I am here, about this poor girl I can see her, her body, it's still too much even now...

I've left the dots at the end of the paragraph above so that we can all just pause a moment here and reflect on behalf of Jean and what happened to her.

I never went back to the allotment. That was it for me. How could I?

I couldn't sleep, couldn't get up in a morning and I was off sick from work for the best part of a year. I was neither use nor ornament. If I had been difficult to live with at times before I was even more difficult now. Sue tried to help, but there was no way anyone could help me during that time.

'Some years later, when I was working in *Coronation Street*, that whole day was brought back to me again when the landlord of the pub I was in said there was someone who was adamant they wanted to see me.

'He's got tears in his eyes, Bruce,' is what he said. 'I think he really needs to talk with you.'

I went over to see him thinking he was maybe just another fan who wanted a photograph or autograph. But his words hit me like an exocet missile, bringing it all back to me instantly.

'You were the last person to see my mum, Jean Jordan.'

It floored me. My legs wobbled, I clung to the bar. When I'd recovered a bit of composure he hit me with the next line.

'You were stood over her. I want to know what she looked like when you found her. Did she look alright?' The tears in his eyes showed just how much this meant to him. His pain would always be worse than mine, he'd lost his mother. But how could I help by telling him every last detail? What good would it have done? Even the small amount I have put in here could not possibly get anywhere near what I actually found. To go through it all with him wasn't going to do him any good.

I just asked what he had read? He'd read the newspaper reports. I said 'No, that was just the newspapers mate.' I told him that her body wasn't as they had made out and that for his own sake he needed to let her go. I knew that he couldn't. Who could? Christ, I couldn't let her go so God knows how it was affecting him. In the end I said, 'I really can't tell you any more, I really can't.' I had tears in my eyes too. This was too much for me. I was now trying to console the son of a girl who had been brutally murdered. Finding her body had been bad enough, being questioned by the police and taunted by the young copper had also been bad, but being face to face with a victim's child? You just cannot imagine that kind of situation and what you should say. All I can say is that I tried to handle it all the best way I could. He hugged me, we hugged each other, he was crying his eyes out and I wasn't far off the same. All the time we were doing that I could see her as I'd found her.

CHAPTER FOURTEEN
GOING DUTCH

Sue and I had several attempts at making our marriage work over the years from 1971 when we married until around 1977-78. She always tried to give it other chances during that time, but I kept letting her down. She would come back, things would be fine for a while; I'd go out for nights with the lads; we'd fall out again.

Finding Jean Jordan's body didn't help our relationship, as it warped my mind and I was finding it hard to concentrate on anything. Perhaps my inability to communicate my feelings properly during that time may have been the final straw for Sue, but I'm not putting that up in my defence at all.

We parted once again. This time it was over. Sue started a relationship with a man from Wales; and I began seeing a lovely lady who I cannot mention by name here as she has since married and has a family of her own.

Sue and I had one or two interesting moments over the months that followed. These primarily revolved around who was to take care of the boys and when, but we eventually worked it all out.

In coming to terms with everything that had been going on in my life around that time – finding Jean Jordan's body and finally splitting with Sue – I spent a lot more time with both Jon and Steven. I returned to work at UMIST after having been given an extended leave of absence. I was grateful to my employers for their consideration and it helped me get my life back on track again. I hadn't wanted to split with Sue but now that it had happened again I was ultimately resigned to us never being back together. It was what football teams now refer to as a time of consolidation.

Mum was my saviour once again, looking after the boys whilst I was at work and giving 'gran's treats' when I was out for the night. There were one or two occasions when I raised my eyebrows a little over where mum was taking them at times; although you'll see that there is a family trait here.

When I went out maybe around eight or nine o'clock, having put the boys to bed, she would get them back up again and take them to the pub until 10 o'clock. She could then have a drink herself and chat with her friends. That way she knew the boys were safe too. The boys would love it I guess, staying up late after their dad had put them to bed, then getting lemonade and a packet of crisps. Everyone in the pub knew my kids. They didn't come to any harm. They were safe and they had a good time. Funnily enough neither Jon nor Steven actually drink very much. Maybe they learned lessons about drinking very early on!

At this point I should also thank my sisters – Glynis and Carol – who took their own turns in looking after the boys for me. Without mum and them I would have had no option but to let Sue have them live with her. I owe all three of them. Here's to Irene, Glynis and Carol!

I was enjoying my freedom after having tried to become the dutiful husband for the umpteenth time with Sue and having failed. I went out regularly with Steve Hadfield and Steve Broughton and we would go to a club called Placemate 3, which was to become Placemate 7 and was once the famous Twisted Wheel northern soul venue on Whitworth Street. We had memberships there and it was a good place to meet girls! After all I was back in the market and was ready to spread my wings. It was time for me to fly.

The first time I ever went anywhere in a plane was when I flew from Manchester to Schiphol Airport in Holland with a group of friends. We'd gone for a lads' weekend in Amsterdam. Now before you start getting any ideas, it wasn't what you're thinking! We only went once into the Red Light District but that didn't appeal to me. If I've got to pay for it, I thought, there must be something wrong. I had always gone through life without having to pay for sex and I wasn't about to start there. No way Jose! Or maybe that should be 'No way Johannes!'

We went over for quite a few weekends. I'd met this Dutch lad Peter in Manchester and we stayed at his house. I think someone from his family was quite a big name at Ajax Amsterdam FC. There was quite an eclectic mix of us at the time – Americans, Dutch and British. It was a really good group of fellers and I loved the city, but I couldn't have lived there all the time. Their evening lifestyle is very different to ours. They don't go out until 11 o'clock at night and don't get in until seven or eight in the morning. I'd miss all my episodes of *Stargate* at that rate.

Our regular meeting place back in Manchester was the Portland Hotel in Piccadilly Gardens. We were deciding where to go next one night and one of the yanks was being a right pain in the arse. He wanted us all to go to Phillips Park Hall Country Club in Whitefield. It was a beautiful club but we'd had enough of him by then, so we were determined not to go where he was going. What happened next was to bring about one of those kind of nights that you look back on and think has fate leant a hand? As we were getting into cabs he got in one by himself, because we couldn't fit him in. The plan was coming together. His cab went in front of ours – again, another result. He was all set for Phillips Park and we were going anywhere but there.

We had simply decided, just in case he'd changed his mind, that when we came to a junction and his cab went right we'd go left; and if he went left... you don't need it spelling out do you? We were determined to lose him and we made damned sure we did just that.

That's the night we went to Alderley Edge in Cheshire, where quite a few Premiership footballers live; to The Sidings, which was next to the railway station. It's now called The Braz, before that Brasingamens and before that The Queensgate. This was the night when I met the woman who was to become my second wife – lovely blonde-haired Sandra. This was the year when Dr Hook had a hit with *When You're In Love With a Beautiful Woman*. Well I was, and I was hooked!

CHAPTER FOURTEEN

SANDRA & ME

Sandra and I got together in 1979. That night in Alderley Edge, which is about 12 miles south of Manchester, Sandra had gone with two of her friends. It was one of the girls' birthdays.

The Sidings was a disco-type venue that fitted in with the Saturday Night Fever era. Most clubs were like that at the time and it was noted as the type of place where singles met. Rod Stewart, my all-time favourite singer, had just had a hit with *Do Ya Think I'm Sexy*. It was that kind of a venue.

I asked Sandra if she wanted to dance but she turned me down, but I knew she fancied me. Nothing much else happened that night but she and one of her friends Diane came to the Portland Hotel in Manchester later that week. Diane had met one of my mates at The Sidings, Bill the Texan and things were looking good between the four of us. I hadn't thought about a long term relationship when we'd met at The Sidings, but that was quickly changing.

Neither Sandra nor I knew where we were going with this at first although it was getting pretty clear that we both cared for each other.

Quite soon after we had met up for the second time we went to Blackpool with Diane and Bill. Sandra and I both took our two children. She'd been married and had divorced, so she was one step ahead of me.

So when we went to Blackpool I had Jon and Steven; and Sandra had Lisa and Claudia. Diane had a daughter too, a little girl called Tina. It was quite a gathering walking along the promenade. Sandra's girls both had blonde hair like their mother; my boys had reddish hair and Tina had dark hair. Sandra said she could see people trying to work out who was whose child. We found it funny watching their faces.

We had a lovely day out and pretty soon Sandra was coming over to our house with the girls and I was visiting Derbyshire where Sandra lived. The first time I went down to Sandra's village of Calver, 5 miles north of Bakewell, was to go to her sister Maureen's wedding. I was going through my Rod Stewart phase at the time and I had bought a new white suit. I thought I looked pretty good in it. Well I would wouldn't I? We seemed to be heading in the right direction and I felt good. In fact I'd never felt as content.

Mum was happy with the way things were going between Sandra and me. She said she liked Sandra and that meant a lot to me. We were getting together more and more; and when we weren't together we would ring each other every night. In those days that meant I had to go down to a telephone box.

Sandra was by my side when we won custody of the boys around 1979-1980. I'm sure moments such as that, plus the love we were showing to each other, were the reasons behind mum telling me: 'You might just have a chance now.'

I could tell she was getting more confident about Sandra because she ever so gradually let us take the boys away from her. We went on holiday, without mum, and although I think it hurt her to lose the boys she knew it was the right thing to do. I know she missed them such a lot even though she never said.

Our first holiday as a family of six, plus my sister Carol, was to Abergele; which is a small seaside town between Colwyn Bay and Rhyl. I was back in Wales again. I'd done something to my leg and was on crutches after falling off a boiler at work. Accident prone, that's me. Anyway I couldn't drive so Sandra drove us there and we stayed in a caravan. It wasn't the best holiday we were ever to have. In fact it could easily have been the worst. We'd only been there a few days and Sandra became really ill – she was so poorly that she couldn't drive either!

The whole thing was turning into an unmitigated disaster. In the end, which came quicker than we had intended, we had to get some friends to come and drive our car back, as well as dividing the children up between our friend's car and ours. We found out that Sandra was suffering from glandular fever and that laid her low for a good few weeks. I was still hobbling about like Long John Silver. We were both a bit of a mess.

But we were getting on so well that it wasn't long, once I'd got over my injury and Sandra had got over her fever, before we moved in together. At first we were all at my mum's but then we moved to

Failsworth in the northern part of Greater Manchester. We had a house that had a nice big extension on the back and our neighbours were great. We managed to get all the four children into the same school and life was starting to look good. Sandra's girls were the same ages as my boys. We became a family of two sons and two daughters. In 1982 my divorce from Sue came through.

Sandra was a hairdresser and initially got a job in Manchester, but she didn't like going into Manchester every day so she worked more locally. She worked in Oakenshaw for a woman called Hazel and then a woman Sandra still calls Mad Enid. After that she started her own business.

This was the best time I'd had in my life. I had this beautiful, attractive, gorgeous woman who I loved dearly, more than I can ever say, and four kids who were all great. We were married at Oldham Registry Office in late July 1984. Sandra always looked fantastic but on that day, like every blushing bride, she looked absolutely radiant. I still look at the picture of her looking into the camera, wearing her pretty dress, with the marriage book in front of us and think how lucky I was. She was, and to my mind still is, a wonderful woman.

My sister Glynis once told me: 'Bruce, you've only ever had two relationships where I would say you loved the girls you were with – and you married them both.' She has a point.

Where did we go for our honeymoon? You've got it, we were back in Wales. We only had a few days there but we went to Newtown, where my aunts and uncles from my dad's side of the family were. We couldn't afford much else in those days.

We were both forever working to make sure we always had enough money, but these were happy times. I'd finish work on a Friday night, get Saturday off, then I'd be in for 6 o'clock Sunday morning until 6 o'clock Sunday night. Sandra was bringing money in from her business too. We were both doing our level best for our four children.

Whilst it was the best time in my life it still wasn't all rosy. We had a few problems over Jon and Steven seeing their mother. They were difficult times for all of us and led to things being a little uneasy. When you are trying to deal with estranged partners and young children who don't understand why their natural mum and dad are not together it can be tricky. When you're also trying to make things work with a new partner at the same time there is such a lot of mental effort needed to keep a lid on feelings and emotions can run high.

This is where Sandra was great and it's where she has always been great, trying to sort things out. I'm not the best at this kind of stuff because it needs diplomacy. I'm not very diplomatic to put it mildly. I think it has been said that I could start an argument in an empty house.

Jon and Steven saw their mother every other Christmas or New Year, Easter and 3 weeks in the Summer.

Like most blokes, proper family blokes which I now felt I was for the first time, I would go out with Sandra either on a Friday or Saturday night and I played darts during the week, but only once or twice a week. I got on to the darts teams at The Willow Tavern and The Brown Cow in Failsworth. My best mate in Failsworth at the time was a bloke called Brian Taylor. We got on well and he also taught me how to fish as he was a keen angler.

Life was good and we decided to move to Marple, a lovely village near Stockport. This put us about halfway between Mum's house and Sandra's family. Not a lot of people know this but Agatha Christie's character Miss Marple came about because she was sat waiting for a train at the station and liked the name. Now there's a bit of trivia for you.

The house we bought was a 3 bedroomed semi-detached and it had a massive garden. For the first time since finding Jean Jordan's body I felt able to go back to digging and planting. That's what I'd wanted to do at Southern Cemetery Allotments but never had the chance to because of what happened. I put in my own vegetable garden. I really was turning into a proper suburban dad, working hard, still enjoying a drink, family man and most importantly with Sandra.

Once we'd got settled in at Marple I started playing darts for my new local pub team. The pub was The Bowling Green and the people who had it at the time were Ricky Hatton's mum and dad Ray and Carol. Sandra had been friends with Carol for a while and I knew Ray from being a kid. We made some good friends in Marple and the lads in the darts team were great to be with. There was this guy who bred budgies, called Phil. Then there was John and his wife Jean. Sandra and I became good mates with them.

It was about now that I started getting involved with some charity stuff, things that were going on in the pub, and we had some fantastic nights. This was my first step into the entertainment world since I had been at school. Admittedly it wasn't much of a step, but it started a flicker of an idea in my brain.

Ray and Carol put on a 24 hour charity day-and-night entertainment. They booked this rap singer called Sammy and all the darts lads were together having a bit of a laugh at his expense. He took it in good part and said that if any of us could do any better we could give it a try.

Off the top of my head I came up with this song called The Bowling Green Rap. It was a scream. I hadn't a clue what I was going to say next but everyone had a laugh over it and I ended up doing it on a local radio station. A star was born! I don't think so, but it was great fun.

CHAPTER SIXTEEN
GO TO BLAZES

I'd been with UMIST for eleven years and whilst we were at Marple I felt it was time for a change. I'd been stuck inside for most of that time and was feeling a bit institutionalised. I fancied being back out on the road again and got together with a mate called Dave. He ran a boiler engineering business fitting and maintaining alarm systems on boilers and boiler repairs. I became quite good at all that. We were also asbestos movers and tank movers too. Since I learned of the dangers of asbestos I have tried my best to raise awareness as well as funds for the people who suffer from asbestosis.

Whilst I was working with Dave I also took up another job. It had come about through Phil and John from the darts team. Phil was a fireman and in the course of conversation they were talking about retained firemen. I'd never heard the term before but they explained it meant you were a part-time fireman.

I asked whether it was a job you got paid for and Phil said it was and that if you liked it you could go on and train for full-time. It appealed to me straight away and I told him I wouldn't mind having a crack at it. I remember John saying: 'Are you daft? You could get killed.' I just said: 'I could get killed crossing the road!' Or actually in my case have my feet run over by a milk float. I know it wasn't the same thing but you get the idea.

We needed the money. We always needed money, who doesn't? In fact I could do with a bit now, so thanks for buying this book. Hope you're enjoying reading it. Anyway, back to the fire service.

I told Sandra I was going to see what it was like, so I went up to a training night, as Phil had said I should do. I met John Clark, Pete Clark, Ken Rowbottom, who was to become my leading fireman, and Paul Dolan. Paul had just come along for the first time that night too. We were the new boys. I met all the other retained firemen and really enjoyed it. Paul and I both signed up that night.

I remember Sandra saying to me that it was alright when you're in the station but what about when I would actually be on scene at a fire or whatever else we would be called out for? She was right. It was different, but it didn't alter what I thought of being in the fire service. Everyone involved saves lives and that is such a good feeling. These guys who risk their lives every day are proper heroes.

Me and Paul went through all our training together, along with a bloke called Bill who was Paul's leading fireman. We were on separate watches. One of the qualifications in becoming a retained fireman was that you had to be able to get to the station quickly, either by car or running. I think we had to be there in two minutes when we were on call.

When we were ready to go out on jobs we were told not to be too hasty to ride on the appliance (fire engine to you and me). It was a warning that the thrill of attending our first fire or road traffic accident might be just that when we were on the appliance heading towards a disaster, but that the reality of what we were about to see would soon kick in. The thing was we'd all done our training and all we wanted was for the lights to be flashing and to be in the cab on the way to rescue someone. Probationists are marked out by a red spot in the middle of their yellow helmets. We had ours. We'd had our training and we were ready to go. Don't get me wrong, we didn't want bad news but when you've gone through your training it is only natural that you would want to be able to do the job.

For the first few days after we were officially ready nothing happened. We were all sat in our respective houses just waiting for our bleepers to go off. We were still in our first week out of training when our bleepers went for the first time. My heart raced, adrenalin kicking in. We were off! I got to Marple Fire Station in record time, got all my gear on. The engine started up. You're only told what it is you're going to once you're in the appliance.

We were going to an RTA (road traffic accident) on Disley Road, near Lime Park. We were told 'persons reported' which means that when you get there the incident has already claimed a life or lives or that a person or people are badly injured. It was one serious RTA. What remained of the car looked to me like a Ford Sierra Cosworth. It was a bendy road and the car had hit a bus head on. The bus had ended up on the other side of the road and the car was a mess. There were three bodies in the car. This was our first incident.

I took one look and thought there was no-one getting out of there alive. We were told to cut them out, wait for the coroner to pronounce them dead and then we were to bag them. We used what's called a jaw clamp which widens the doors so that you can get the victims out more easily.

I'd be lying if I said I didn't have mixed emotions about joining up when we were making our way back to the station. On the one hand this job is heroic, on the other you see some truly awful sights. You'd think I'd be getting used to death by now wouldn't you? I'd stared it in the face a number of times either being in hospital with rheumatic fever or finding Jean Jordan. I did have doubts in my mind, but I carried on.

My first really happy moment, when I felt we had made a difference, was when we attended another RTA. Everyone thinks the fire service is all about fires and rescuing kittens from trees, but there are far more incidents you have to get to than that. This particular RTA involved a collision between two cars. One of the car drivers was a woman who was badly injured. We were trying to get this woman out when we all stopped for a second. We'd heard another sound. It was a baby crying, but we couldn't find out where the baby's noise was coming from. It turned out the woman had put the baby in the back seat and when the seat had caved in on impact the baby had slipped into the boot and had been covered by its child's seat. The seat had saved its life. All hell broke loose trying to find where the noise was coming from and we saved the child.

The first fire I attended also involved a fatality. It was in Marple on a new housing estate. It was the first time I had ever put on what they call BA (breathing apparatus) and seeing the flames we were walking towards definitely got to me. Sandra's words were brought home to me, what would I be like when tackling a fire for real? I now knew. God was I scared. Well yes I was, but I'd had the training, and this was what it was all about.

We went inside the house. We were feeling our way in, checking for other potential dangers, such as debris falling on you. We started dousing the flames. Then I saw a guy in a chair. I shouted back to the rest of the team that he looked alright and I started to make my way towards him.

'Woah!' That was all I heard from my leading fireman. I was pulled back quickly. I had all sorts of stuff to learn, such as 'flash over' which can cause whatever may be unsteady above you to fall in your way.

When we did get to the guy he looked perfectly normal. But when I went around to the other side of him I knew why he hadn't moved and why he was still there. I'd hoped he had just been overcome from the smoke and that there was a chance of rescuing him, but that was way out of the question. Everything had burnt off his other side. He'd fallen asleep with a cigarette in his hand.

What the firemen do on their way back to the station is to tell jokes. It doesn't matter how bad the joke is. When I first heard them I was annoyed. Why were they doing this? Didn't they have respect for those who had died? Then it came to me and I understood. They would tell jokes to get the fire, or whatever the incident had been, right out of their mind; or at least as best they could.

The biggest fire I ever attended was at the Swizzels factory, where they made Love Hearts, Parma Violets, Refresher chews and Drumstick lollies. The fire swept through the factory in New Mills, Derbyshire about 15 miles from Manchester. This was a big sweet factory and it went up one night somewhere between 8-10pm. The place was so much ablaze that I believe they evacuated some residents from the town of New Mills. We had about 40 appliances there with engines drafted in from neighbouring counties such as Yorkshire, Lancashire and Cheshire. That night I received a quite different assignment to anything else I had in my three and a half years as a retained fireman, although definitely not what I would have expected. It wasn't something I'd been trained for at all.

Someone came down the line and said the Chief wanted to see me. Hell, what had I done? I didn't think I'd done anything wrong.

'Your name's been put down for a job, a big job.' That's what I was told. Apparently Paul (Dolan) had been put up for it but he'd run down the wrong side of a towpath where we were going to pump water from the canal and had slipped in! Poor Paul!

When I got to the Chief he told me what my really important role was: 'I want you to go into New Mills (it was now 7 in the morning by the way) knock up (that means get them up by the way, nothing more) the chip shop owners, get them to start frying 200 lots of fish and chips.'

I think I said something like: 'Where are they going to get the fish from at that time in the morning?' But he just said to let them worry about that and that they could send the bill to the fire service.

Two hundred lots of fish and chips! This was my big job. So off I went into New Mills. There were two chip shops. I went down to the English chip shop but the guy told me to bugger off. I think he thought I wasn't for real. I mean, who orders 200 lots of fish and chips! But the Chinese chip shop opened up. They sent a couple of guys off to the market whilst they started frying the fish they already had. That chip run was for all the firemen and the Chief knew what he was doing. It's a bit like you can't run an army if they're not fed.

Of course with the best will in the world there are times when things go slightly wrong. Fortunately those were in some lighter moments where no-one got hurt. One instance was when we were called to a house where a lady's kitten had gone missing. She said it was up her chimney. We heard it meowing and it was definitely coming from the chimney. We reckoned the only way we could get to it was by taking her fireplace out. Then when we heard the kitten again we thought it could just be in the vent, which wouldn't have needed us to take out the fireplace. It was a beautiful stone fireplace when we'd arrived, but now we'd chiselled it and pulled it apart. It was such a mess. The kitten wasn't in the chimney, it had been in the vent. I turned around to Ken Rowbottom and said 'the cat's here'. He swiftly picked it up, dropped it into where the fireplace had been, covered it in soot, picked it back up again and proudly strode into the kitchen to present it back to its owner with a big broad beaming smile on his face! We were all a bit like the fireplace was in the end – cracking up!

But it wasn't all like that. We learned lessons all the time and Big Stevie Dyer taught me a very good lesson one day. We had gone to a chip shop fire in Hazel Grove in Cheshire. I was going to put a fire blanket over it, but Big Stevie just said: 'This is the best way.' And he picked up a big tub of spuds and put them into the fat. The potatoes cooled and calmed it down immediately.

Whilst most fires and incidents are accidents there are people who don't really help themselves and are a damned nuisance to firefighters. I only had a short time of involvement in comparison to some but I don't know whether I could cope with the abuse firefighters, ambulance drivers and paramedics now get from some sections of the public.

I went to houses where we had to break in because they were houses of drug addicts who had locked their girlfriends and babies in the house. One drug addict had gone to sleep with a cigarette in his mouth. I had my breathing apparatus on and was having to fight another addict off me. It was crazy. They now throw bricks at the fire service in some areas. Fortunately that never happened to us.

There were plenty of times when I never thought I was going to get out of the fires we attended and for people like me that's where your reliance on the rest of the team, each other, and your leading fireman gets you through.

I would follow Big Ken (Rowbottom) anywhere. We went into a fire at a school. We were heading down a corridor walkway when the fire flashed over and trapped us. I felt my feet burning and suddenly thought that we weren't going to get out of this one. Everything goes through your head in those moments – you think of your wife, your family, the kids, everything you hold dear just appears in front of you flickering from one face to the next. It's all over in split seconds, but it happens. Then Ken noticed something and took us over to a wall. Someone was breaking in to get us out. That's why you work as a team and that's one of the many lessons I learned from these great men and women who put their lives on the line daily.

I loved Ken. He was the bravest man I have ever met and died of a heart attack on a motorway, but even then he was a hero in doing so. He was a truck driver as well as a fireman and as he was having his attack he manoeuvred his truck off the motorway so that no-one was killed.

I had been down to Thompson Street in Manchester to put in an application to join the fire service full-time but yet another accident in my pretty well accident-strewn life meant I had to leave the service behind.

During the time I had been a retained fireman I had also changed my full-time job. The work out on the road with David's business had come to an end and I had got a job in a factory where they made sheet metal cowlings for boilers. I used to fit them, now I was making them.

But I wasn't making them for too long. One of them sprung from where I was working and sliced through my left wrist. What have I hurt so far? The list goes on.

Sheet metal goes easily through flesh, did you know that? It severed my veins and I had an operation. Yes, I was back in hospital to have my wrist put back together. I was off work again for over a year and this was a really difficult time. Sandra knew I couldn't go back to work at the time and as usual she was there to help.

I couldn't even fasten my buttons. But doing up buttons was the least of my worries as it turned out. This is when I started drinking more than I had for a long time. I was lonely and felt useless. I'd been used to earning a wage, going out every day to work, putting in the hours and this injury had stopped all of that. The accident and the fact that my wrist was in plaster for nearly a year led to problems at home.

The first few weeks didn't bother me but after a while I was not just bored but in a bit of a mess financially. Sick pay only lasts so long and is only a proportion of your actual wage. We used what savings we had and we received an insurance claim. That helped to pay the mortgage. This was the high interest rate mortgage time of the 1980s. I felt so inadequate. I wasn't doing what I had been used to doing ever since school – providing the family with an income.

Boredom set in and because I couldn't do anything else I started going to the pub about mid-day. I'd just go down there thinking I'd stop for an hour but one hour led to two, then three and four. I'd only gone down there for something to do. Sometimes I stayed, drank more and just talked. Other times I would stay, drink more and get involved in some kind of argument over the most trivial matter.

Sandra would be home from work and I would still be in the pub. She was right to get angry. She was the one bringing in the money not me. I started getting really awkward with everyone at home. Sandra would make the tea and then I wouldn't want what she had made. I'd just explode over the slightest thing. I think I just felt things weren't fair on me.

Eventually I was able to get back to work. I tried my hand at being a postman, but that really wasn't my kind of job; I became a bus driver, which I stuck at for a year. Then I took a job back on boiler maintenance at Waterford Dairies in Dukinfield. It was shift work starting at 4 in the morning and working through until 2 in the afternoon, but I took it. We had to get ourselves back on our feet.

But by now my new career, that was to make my face known to millions on every street in the UK, not a good thing quite a lot of the time by the way, was in its early stages. I wasn't exactly what you call an overnight success was I?

CHAPTER SEVENTEEN

ON STAGE

I love being on stage. I loved it that first time when I received the applause as a three year old. I loved it when I was in the Ralph Reader Gang Shows. I loved it when I was playing *Julius Caesar* for Miss Brown at school. I loved my drama classes. But I hadn't done any acting for quite a few years.

Whilst I'd had a number of jobs through my 20s and 30s acting was never far away from my thoughts. It was just that when I was married at 18 and then had the boys I had responsibilities, even though at times, early on in my boys' lives, it might not have looked as though I had.

Providing for my family has always been a priority for me though. So the desire to act, that I'd had at school and that I had studied on weekends, was still there but it was just a dream, something that wouldn't happen in real life.

I had taken a course in method acting and I've always been fascinated by it. You hear of actors who have immersed themselves in the character they are playing so much that they find difficulty coming out of it. I've experienced some of that, where you go to a certain place in your head and it becomes your real life.

Somewhere along the way I told Sandra that I loved acting and that's what I wanted to do. We sat for hours in a car park one night and she said if that's what you want to do you should do it. We were in Failsworth at the time and Sandra came with me when we went along to Sale to see about joining an amateur dramatic group there. I was going to join them but at the time we were just in the process of moving to Marple.

Once we'd settled in at Marple I went up to The Carver Theatre. It's a lovely theatre and the people are so committed to their art. They are what you would call a highly professional amateur dramatic company and they put on five productions every season.

I learned a lot about stage technique and timing at The Carver. It was like going back to school for me, a school where I wanted to learn and

I listened. I had two great teachers who became very close friends – June and Tony Broughton. They have both appeared in *Coronation Street* and Tony is the real life son of the actor Arthur Leslie who played Jack Warner, the Rovers Return's first landlord. Tony has played four roles in *Corrie* over the years, his last appearance being in 2008. June was a cleaner at Mike Baldwin's place for a while.

Tony directed me in a number of productions and I always talked with him about acting. I was with them about 3 or 4 years in the mid-80s, by now I was in my mid-30s. I used to get nervous as hell before I went on and then Tony told me that if I wasn't nervous it wasn't worth being there. It's still like that for me today. Once I'm on stage I'm fine but just before I'm going on I'm a wreck.

I regularly went to their house which was in another neighbouring village called Marple Bridge. The first time I visited I saw they had a big pub bar. Tony told me where it had come from: 'It's the original bar out of the Rovers' Return'.

Before long I was getting some really good reviews and it made me think that I might be able to make it as a professional actor if the opportunity arose. I was up for an award for one of the first productions I appeared in – *Bonny Brid* - which was set in Victorian England. Lancashire poet Samuel Laycock wrote the poem of the same name. The production was part of the Carver Theatre 1985/86 season.

The following year I landed a lead role as Spadge Hopkins in *Cider with Rosie* in the 1986/87 season. He was the trouble causer. Once again the reviews were pretty good and I felt great. I didn't take a part in all the productions because some didn't have a part the producers felt suited me or because of work commitments. I also appeared in pantomime and found myself usually cast as a comic character. 'Oh, yes I was!'

In between *Bonny Brid*'and *Cider with Rosie* I also joined Stockport Operatic Society. They concentrated on musical productions as you might have guessed. They had a fantastic theatre on Stockport Road. This was very different from amateur dramatics. This was music and dance. The first musical I took part in was *Love from Judy* and I got a speaking part. I was in *Oklahoma* and a number of others, as well as continuing with my acting roles at Carver Theatre. The last musical productions I'd done were over 20 years previously in the Ralph Reader Gang Shows and I had a few problems with the dancing side of things. I was alright on my own but dancing in chorus lines I found hard. Sandra says that she could see me counting the steps whilst I was on stage! Maybe that's why *Strictly (Come Dancing)* have not approached me yet!

Just as they had supported me by coming to the school plays my mum, Uncle John and Auntie Marjorie, and Uncle George would come to every production. They have always been so supportive.

Like many others who join dramatic or operatic societies, or both, there are sometimes difficulties in fitting everything in. There were plenty of times when a production was due for curtain-up at 7.30pm and I would only be getting home from work at 7pm. I know a lot of people who take part in amateur productions – and some professional ones - will be nodding their heads at this point, but that's how it is. Your adrenalin gets you there.

The more I was on stage the more I dreamed about getting a break to go professional. The reviews helped with the way I felt. Uncle John used to just tell me to carry on the way I was going and I'd be alright.

CHAPTER EIGHTEEN
CLARKE & JONES

Laurel & Hardy; Morecambe & Wise; Cannon & Ball; Little & Large –
do you remember them? Of course you do, but what about Clarke &
Jones? You do surprise me.

During my time with Stockport Operatic Society I met up with a great
guy called Eddie Clarke. We hit it off with each other right from the start
and we would talk endlessly about all sorts of things. Eddie then joined
me over at the Carver Theatre with Marple Amateur Dramatic Society.
We appeared in a few productions together and there was a chemistry.

I saw something in Eddie and me that I thought would work as a
double act. I hadn't a clue how to go about getting booked; and I'd never
been a comic before, but I knew how to write and come up with sketches
that would make good visual gags.

We were really fortunate to have a third member of our double-act if
that makes sense. His name was Brian Hargreaves and he became our
manager. He worked in the oil business for Shell and travelled a lot.
He'd heard what we were up to, mainly because we were talking about
it all the time, and Brian took a real interest in us. He would take notes
as we devised the sketches and routines in our kitchen. We asked Brian
whether he would manage us. He was a hard task master. If we didn't
do things right he'd be on at us all the time.

He was after perfection and it was good to have him push us, although
there were times when we thought he was too fussy and would wish he'd
just let some things go! His other fault was that everywhere we went
he'd drive too bloody fast. We'd have a right go at him about it, but he
was excellent for us. We'd never have got as far as we did without him.
He did a great job with us and it's probably Brian I should be thanking
more than anyone for setting me on my way into the professional world
of entertainment. He got us started and booked all the gigs.

Six months after coming up with the idea of the double-act we were
ready to perform our first show – or at least we thought we were!
Everyone must look back at their debut set and think 'how did we get

away with that?' That was definitely the case for us. Our first effort was at an agents' revue, a showcase for new talent, new acts that are looking for bookings. It also gives the hotels and clubs a chance to see a lot of acts all at once.

We hadn't performed anywhere! And our first show was to be in front of a group of people who must have been expecting at least some form of experience before coming in front of them. It was held in Cheadle Hulme and Brian had got us in. The club was quite full and I remember being really nervous as I waited in the wings.

The opening to our act had Eddie on stage and he'd be singing the song that Russ Abbot had a hit with, *I love a party with a happy atmosphere.* Then I'd burst on wearing just a towel. And I mean a towel and nothing else! We thought of ourselves as a Morecambe and Wise-type of act. They were our heroes, the ones we wanted to aspire to.

He'd stop singing and I'd tell him, and of course the audience, that I'd been mugged. We would use the name of the roughest area near to where we were playing so that we got the right reaction and tell a few gags about the place in with the routine. Then we would crack on with the rest of the show. Visually a man coming on without a stitch of clothing apart from a towel was always a winner. We both played guitar and sang, as well as doing the comedy routine.

We got our first six bookings out of that night and we were on our way as Clarke & Jones. It was to be a hard-working yet very satisfying four years of my life working with Eddie and Brian. We became the top comedy double act on the North West circuit at the time, not bad when you consider some of the other names who were around.

Coming up on the scene just behind Clarke & Jones were Spikey & Mikey. Dave Spikey was playing the circuit for years before he became famous with Peter Kay and *Phoenix Nights* and then quite rightly with his own solo act. Dave was always funny and we both liked him a lot.

We really weren't that good in our first year. We were learning our trade, but from 1986-1989 we went everywhere. We played up and down the country in clubs, holiday camps, hotels, marquees, gents toilets, the lot. Okay, maybe scrub the gents toilets. But that was another job.

We were never off the road – apart from maybe once or twice when it seemed as though we would be with Brian's driving!

We built up the act and ended up having a wealth of material. Bobby Ball came up to me one night and said,. 'We nicked one of your routines. We'd come along to your show and thought we'll have that.' I probably thought you cheeky b***ard at the time, but looking back now that was quite an accolade. When other acts start pinching stuff off you that's when you know you're getting it right.

Like every other act on the circuit we also had our share of good times and bad times, nights when things really were perfect and nights when things went wrong - or the places you were going weren't where you would have liked to have been sent. Let's do the worst of the worst first.

One bad night was in a catholic club the other side of Preston. We had our own sound system but for some reason we weren't allowed to use it, we had to use theirs. We didn't swear in our act, we never swore. Ours was good family entertainment. Typically, because they had told us we had to use it, their sound system broke down and I'm stood there in my towel. There's someone trying to fix it and I'm stood next to this concert secretary. Sometimes I think Adolf Hitler must have modelled himself on our concert secretaries!

I asked him why he wouldn't let us put our gear on. He told me 'everyone uses our gear' and I said 'Well it doesn't f***ing work does it!' I was raging at him by now. 'You f***ing jumped up little sh**.' And with that, as I was opening my mouth to say the words, but before I'd had chance to realise, the sound system came back on, and my words – not a part of our act – are bouncing around the room. Eddie and Brian were stood there thinking 'Oh F***, we've had it here'. But we still got paid. We didn't add swearing to the act though.

We'd had a great time touring up in Scotland and had been offered the North East. We were booked for a number of dates. We didn't know the area well and had no idea of the reputation of some of the clubs. I'd just like to say that the North East is now my favourite part of the UK and I have some great friends I love to visit, but back then I just wanted to get out of the area as soon as we could.

Our first problem was The Downhill Club in Sunderland, a renowned graveyard for clubland acts. Of course we weren't told that before we got there. We arrived at the Downhill around 11.30am because we were playing a lunchtime and early afternoon Sunday gig. It was a wet, windy day. We had to be set up by 12 noon because they had strippers and bingo on as well. The place was packed with 400 men, no women. There were some tell-tale signs that should have told us how bad it was going to be.

A crowd of kids had already greeted us outside with their insurance scam of asking for 50p to look after our van. Apparently it was a very worthwhile insurance premium to pay because otherwise they would slash the tyres and burn the van. It was certainly the cheapest insurance Brian ever paid!

Suitably impressed by the standard of care that was now to be offered to our vehicle, we set up and went to our dressing room. We opened the door and two half-naked women were getting ready for their act. When they asked if we'd appeared there before and we told them it was our first time they laughed and said not to expect much. A big guy then walked in and said to one of the girls: 'Right, which one's first for the slaughter?'

The first stripper went on to loud booing and jeering. We were told this meant the audience was in a good mood! When she finished she came off effing and blinding calling the men every name under the sun. I had never heard a woman swear like that before. She said some idiot had grabbed her and felt her boobs. The big guy came back and told us to get on. We didn't argue.

We went on to complete silence which lasted for every second of the 35 minutes that was our first spot. All we could see was 400 newspapers held up to their faces. Apparently this was their Sunday ritual regardless of how good or bad you were. We were told that not all North East clubs were like Downhill, some were far worse. What we experienced in Middlesbrough was to bear witness to what we had been told.

Middlesbrough was the last club on the tour. It was a big working men's club and as we sat in the dressing room the singer/guitarist who was also on that night walked in. He said: 'Comedy double act?' We nodded. 'Not up here son, not up here! They hate comics up here.'

We started the act. Eddie opened up as usual and then I came on. I was just about to open my mouth when a bell was rung. The f***ing concert secretary's bell!

It was like Robot City. Everybody in the club, and I mean everybody, stood up from their seats and started forming a queue. I couldn't believe what I was seeing. They'd seen the start of the act and they knew we were just getting under way and now this. It was the most ignorant, rudest thing I ever witnessed at any club. They simply didn't care about who was on stage and they clearly weren't at all bothered about being entertained. The singer who'd warned us about this hadn't told us that it would be like this. We just thought he meant that the audience took a lot of winning over, but this was something else.

The concert secretary said: 'Don't worry lads, you can carry on in a bit, they're just getting their bingo tickets.'

'Bingo tickets!' I said: 'What are you talking about mate? We're a comedy double act here. Once we start we don't stop and start. It doesn't work like that.'

He puffed out his chest a bit and in a deep voice he said: 'Middlesbrough son'. It was as though that explained everything, that we'd entered a different country, a different world, a universe as yet unexplored – the planet Middlesbrough.

They collected their bingo tickets and then, once they'd all sat down, he said: 'Right lads, you can carry on now!' I said: 'You can piss off!' And with that I walked off. We got paid, but we never went back there. What a way to treat the people you are paying to entertain you! I still can't get my head around why they would want to do that but I know there are plenty of other entertainers who have received similar treatment.

Our best moments had to be when we were voted Best Comedy Act in the North West. We won the award twice and received gold medals for both. The first year we won we received our award at The Viking in Blackpool. It's one of Blackpool's biggest hotels and also the top cabaret venue to play. We just thought 'we're playing The Viking!' We knew then that we had arrived.

Everyone was there at Blackpool, all the family, my mum, Uncle John, of course, and all of our friends. It was an amazing feeling getting the award and we performed what was one of our favourite routines where we put together our own tribute to the great double acts including Laurel & Hardy, Flanagan & Allen, Morecambe & Wise and Cannon & Ball. We'd finish as ourselves. By now we had incorporated several dressing up routines, making our show visually very entertaining. Eddie was great at holding the stage whilst I went through so many quick changes. We received our second Gold Medal at a big club in Eccles.

Believe it or not my accident-prone life still hadn't come to rest either. Brian's driving finally claimed me as a victim when he managed to run over my foot, the left one, and I ended up in Jimmy's (St James' Hospital) in Leeds. We had been doing a gig for the officers at Armley Prison in Leeds. We'd been quite wary of doing it, but I should have been even warier of our manager. Brian asked me for the keys to the car as we were about to load up after the gig. He reversed the car up to the door and that's when he ran over my foot.

At Jimmy's I met up with some mad woman who was a clairvoyant or something like that. She said I had a lovely aura and that I'd be back there soon. She wasn't wrong. I don't know how far she could see into the future though because Brian let go of the wheelchair whilst I was outside, I banged my head, knocked myself out and was carted back inside until I recovered.

We'd had our Equity cards for quite a time. I was no longer Ian Roy Jones to the outside world. I was now, for the first time in my life, Bruce Jones. We were now a very popular act and there was talk of us making the next step up to television. I remember when we quit it was £7 a night to see us in some places. Back in 1989 that was quite a bit of money for an act that had never been on the little box in the corner of your front room, but we were playing to sell-out audiences.

Clarke & Jones never made it to television, though we did have one slight chance. The BBC was trying out double acts and we had talked about going down to London where the auditions would be held. I wanted to go but Eddie had a really good job at British Aerospace. He couldn't risk quitting and then finding a television contract wasn't there. I could understand, but I didn't think we would lose anything by going down to London to give it a try. We had a row on the way to another sell-out show in Stoke-on-Trent. I stormed out of the car and walked away. We hadn't gone too far from home by then so I didn't have far to walk, but I didn't see Eddie for a while after that. Four years on from when we had started Clarke & Jones was over.

I ended up going down to London on my own. I sat alongside David Baddiel and Frank Skinner. The BBC people put me with other comedians but it wasn't the same for me. I needed Eddie – a bit like Eric Morecambe needed Ernie Wise. I saw Eddie for the first time in years in 2011. We both appeared in a new film called *Down Our Way*.

Having acted in straight drama on stage in the theatre and now made a success of being on the road as a comedian I now started to consider whether I could combine serious acting and comedy.

CHAPTER NINETEEN
SCREEN TIME

By now I was working for Waterford Dairies and I was still taking part in productions either at Marple or Stockport. I had my Equity card but felt I needed an agent if I was to get anywhere professionally. My first agent was a lady who specialised more in looking after child actors. With the best will in the world you couldn't call me that. She was a really sweet lady and she did at least land me my very first TV roles. I appeared three times in *Brookside* – as an irate dog owner; a garden centre man and Bobby Grant's bagman. You'll find that Ricky Tomlinson, who of course played Bobby brilliantly for years, crops up more than once or twice in my career.

I switched agents after asking around the dramatic and operatic societies and chatting with friends. I made an appointment to see Patrick Nyland, an agent based in Manchester. I remember he was quite keen on me straight away but his partner in the business wasn't. Patrick said he thought there was something about me that would work. Patrick, and subsequently his brother Tony, have now been my agents for 22 years. They are two of my closest friends and I hope they always will be.

Patrick took me on despite his partner's reservations and started finding work for me, although it wasn't quite what I'd expected. I appeared in one episode of *Waterfront Beat* as a detective in the Phil Redmond cop show produced by Mersey TV for BBC1, but I was getting used far more in TV commercials. I did one for British Beef, another for a cleaning bleach and toilet cleaner producer called Viakal, and another for British Rail.

By the way, if you look on some websites there is a Bruce Jones credited with appearing as a character called Jack in a film called *Party Plane*. This isn't me. It was an American film released in 1991 and judging by the DVD cover it's probably a bit raunchy.

Anyway back to the ads. The British Beef commercial saw me on television for quite a while. I had to ride a bike, go home, fall off the bike and then have beef for tea. No surprise there, I wonder whether they knew I was being typecast. I don't think I had serial accident-prone on my CV.

It was the Viakal commercial that led to my big breakthrough and brought about the role that was to launch a career that has given me so much. Never knock actors who get parts in TV commercials because you just never know where they can lead.

When I turned up for the commercial I couldn't believe who was directing it. Ken Loach had directed *Kes* and *Cathy Come Home* as well as plenty more. I could never have dreamed I would be working with him, or that I would end up appearing in one of his films, but that's exactly what happened. At the time of the commercial all I thought was that it would look good to put on my credits that I'd worked with this great man.

But once Ken had finished and we had all said our goodbyes I decided I needed to contact him. It wasn't because I was going to plead to him to put me in one of his films either.

I had been called back to remake some of the commercial but when I got there Ken wasn't to be seen. I asked where he was, but the answer was just a case of 'forget about that, let's just get on with it'. Maybe they couldn't afford him for another day? Anyway I thought it was a little bit odd so I got hold of Ken's number and called him. All I said was that there was something wrong. 'They're making the commercial without you Ken, and they've called us back to reshoot some of it.'

Ken thanked me for the call and I went back to the reshoot.

Now I'm not saying that phone call made any difference to what happened to my career, but three or four months later Patrick called me to tell me that Ken wanted to see me. 'He's doing a movie set in Manchester and he wants you to try out for it.'

That movie was *Raining Stones*.

CHAPTER TWENTY
RAINING STONES

Ken Loach's trademark has been in making typically British gritty, real-life films. They are scripted, but they also use improvisation. Ken used both in *Raining Stones*. He likes using unknown actors, people whose life experiences can be drawn upon for the roles and by now I had plenty of life experience, for better or worse.

If I was to name my favourite professional role I would have to go for the character Bob that I played in *Raining Stones*. That might surprise one or two who read this book, in fact it might well surprise most of you, but it's definitely my favourite. It brought me a European Actor of the Year award, the film received an award at the Cannes Film Festival. It was also nominated for the (London) *Evening Standard* awards for Best Film and Best Screenplay. Basically it put me on the acting map. But it was the role itself and where I had to go with it that were the reasons for me putting it above Les Battersby and everyone else I have played over the years.

The film title is meant to convey how tough life is for Bob who has had to cope with no job, a succession of failed attempts to try and find work, and getting behind on his bills, plus the pressure of trying to make sure his family feel good about themselves. For Bob life isn't just raining on him, it's raining stones and no matter what he tries to do he ends up feeling like a lot of people in the same boat, that he can't get out of the mess he's in. He feels hard done by, but he never gives in. If you've never watched the film you can get it on DVD. It's also shown on Film 4 and I think it is my finest work so far. I will remain proud of it until the day I die. Hopefully one day I will get another part as good as this.

But getting the part of Bob took quite a bit of time.

Ken's audition process is very long, or at least it was for me and the rest of the cast in *Raining Stones*. That's because he was looking for 'real' performances, the kind of performances he believes are best coming from people who have experienced the kind of life and emotion that is called for in the characters.

He will try you out on subjects that he feels you should know instantly rather than letting you go away and research, or even have five minutes' thinking time. I can understand why he does it that way. Everything is then much more real, especially when you're improvising. There is a belief that you can't really improvise playing a role where you haven't experienced the subject matter.

When I went along to audition for Ken I hadn't seen any outline for the film before I was introduced to others, and I didn't see one at the audition either. The cast, or at least who he felt were going to be the cast, were all sat in a room. Ken would tap you on the shoulder, say a word and you would have to talk about it. He wants to see what you've got and what you can do.

'Ballcock!'

That's the word I got. It was like manna from heaven for me, or a Guinness from the Gods. I'd been fitting things like boilers and pipes and cowlings for much of my adult life. I had a ball with 'ballcock' and it seemed to work well all around the room, everyone was cracking up. Ken films these auditions and I'm told he has used my 'ballcock' to show student directors what he's after from other actors in his films.

I landed the part probably on the strength of that. The rest of the cast were all told they had landed their roles, but no-one knew who was going to take the lead role. I felt I was going to be in the film but because we never saw a script there was no way of knowing whether you were just going to get a small part or a bigger one. Then I was called into Ken's office and he told me that I'd best phone my agent as I was wanted for the lead role!

I didn't just land the best role I've ever had in my life I also landed £1000 a week. We're now in the early 90s. Casting took place in 1992. The film was released in 1993.

I'd never earned that amount of money in my life. I remember buying Sandra a new kitchen out of what I earned. During the big years when I was earning lots of money Sandra had more new kitchens than Gary Rhodes, Jamie Oliver, Nigella Lawson and Ainsley Harriott put together. There's been at least one new one for every house we've ever lived in since I took the part of Bob in *Raining Stones*.

The first scene I ever filmed for Ken wasn't the most demanding scene in the film. I'm seen knocking on doors in Middleton in Manchester, asking whether people need their drains cleaning. We got all of that done in one afternoon, so far so good. As a new boy I was, not to put too fine a point on it, sh***ing myself.

That's because in the cast were Ricky Tomlinson, who was a big name already as Bobby Grant in *Brookside*, and Tom Hickey who was a big soap star as Benjy Riordan in *The Riordans* in Ireland. Ricky played my mate Tommy and we got into some scrapes together. Tom played Father Barry. He's played fathers, priests, bishops and even a monsignor! By the time he got to me he'd played a father so many times it was like his second trade.

The story revolves around Bob's daughter Coleen needing the traditional white dress, shoes, veil and gloves for her first Holy Communion. Raising the money for this whilst also being in debt causes Bob and his wife Ann – played by the brilliant Julie Brown - huge problems. But he's a survivor and he will try his hand at anything to keep his family afloat. He's not a weakling. He might not have much of a life but he does try.

I spent six weeks learning how to be a Catholic, being with a priest and going to a Catholic church then we filmed for six weeks. By the time we came to start filming I understood about Holy Communion, how it works and what it means, and also how a child's first Holy Communion can prove a challenging time for parents who haven't much money. You really can go into a lot of debt. Bob and Ann were both out of work. They lived in a council flat and getting the money for the dress was to lead them into the hands of a loan shark.

Ricky and I are seen sheep rustling in the opening scenes and then trying to sell the meat in a local pub. We didn't do very well at selling it, but it showed how desperate we were. It set the tone for the rest of the film. For those scenes, the one in the pub, there was no real script. Ken would tell you what he wanted and then it was up to you to put in a performance. We would get something like half a sheet of A4 paper in a morning with some kind of dialogue and what Ken was after, Ricky and I would talk about it together and with the other cast members in the scene. When we were selling the meat to the women having a drink in the pub we were ad-libbing most of the time. You also didn't do a lot of takes with Ken directing.

I would only be given a page of script every night. It was the same for all of us. You had to go through that page of script and interpret it through improvisation. You had to think on your feet. I find improvising is like living on the edge; it's one of my favourite parts of acting because when you're into your character you know what they will say and how they will react. Improvisation is the natural way forward with characterisation.

Whilst the film deals with my character Bob going through some really tough times, some of the scenes were very funny, but maybe not for me. One of the funniest scenes in the film for the camera crew was when I cleaned the priest's drains. This was a prime example of Ken's work and why he always tries to use actors who have a feel for a job they are doing. Ken said: 'If you had to go down there and rod out the drain for real what would you do? How would you go about it? Go down and show me.' As far as I knew I wasn't supposed to go down there in the script, such as it was, but I followed his direction.

Remember I was the new boy! I didn't even know they had rigged it up what was to happen next. They had everything set and they just needed me to get down there. They were waiting for me. I was being set up, but for all the right reasons.

Ken just wanted everything to look so natural, so when what was down there exploded into my face and covered me from head to toe my surprise was natural, rather than acted. I go down there and then I'm saying this is how you do it. Next thing I know I'm covered in shit. Actually it was digestive biscuits mixed in gravy browning, always a winning combination for that kind of effect apparently, but all very new to me. It's a comic moment in the film and one that works a bit like a Laurel and Hardy scene when Olly gets himself into 'another fine mess'.

That scene might well have been a memorable moment for comic reasons but there were two scenes that took everything I had out of me. And I mean everything, both physically and mentally. I used what I had learned about method acting for both of these scenes.

Acting is not a simple job and method acting can be dangerous. I wouldn't go as far as to say that famous method actors such as Montgomery Clift and James Dean lost their lives because of it, but getting into your part through experiencing the life your character leads and not being able to return to your own life straight away is definitely unbalancing.

When you play a role using method acting practice it changes you inside. It takes you to places that you wouldn't be going in your own life. Whether it's method acting you are practicing or not, the important thing with each part is that you are not you. You're playing someone else and the emotions that you deliver, either on stage or screen, are not your emotions but your character's.

I have employed method acting a number of times in my career and whenever I have done so my performance has always been labelled a critical success. The crazy thing is that when I have finished my day's work in that zone I really don't know what I have done. I am usually so physically and mentally drained by it all that I just need to be on my own for a while, collecting my thoughts and returning to being Bruce Jones. Sometimes the process can take hours to get back to being who you are. For me it's as though I need to shed not just the skin of who I am but also replace my heart and soul.

The first, of the two scenes in which I employed my method acting assimilation, was the fight scene in the club where Bob had finally landed a job. You will have to watch the film to find out why, but I get battered by the people I'm supposed to be working with.

None of it is stunted, everything you see actually happens to me. I was battered absolutely black and blue. I fall down the steel stairs. I break down because I take a big kicking. They kick the f*** out of me until I can take no more. I kept letting them beat me and knock me down these steel stairs. I kept doing it because I believed in what I was doing. Eventually, after I had been thrown about once too often, one of the women on the set threw in the towel for me and the producer said: 'He can't take any more tonight'. Yet I kept doing it because I believed in what I was doing and I was following the method acting school of thought. I wanted it to be as realistic as it could be because I felt I now was that character, there were no blurred edges of me being Bruce Jones as I fell down those stairs.

That night I could hardly walk. They took me back to the hotel where I took a look at my body that night and it was not a good sight. I thought 'oh shit'. I couldn't believe just how bad I looked. I think the production team must have been a bit worried about me because they brought two women in to give me aromatherapy treatment. They were putting all sorts of stuff on my body. I was in agony but I knew that the pain had been worth it, so long as the scene didn't end up on the cutting room floor! They used it and I'm proud of it. Realism was what the film was meant to be about and you don't get much more realistic than that scene.

The greatest scene I have ever played and one of the scenes I will never forget was between me and Tom Hickey. It's near the end of the film and has a great twist to the story, something you're not expecting. Once again I'll not tell you everything about it because I would really like you to watch the film if you haven't.

At this moment in the film I believe I have caused the death of a man, the loan shark. I've just beaten him up. He is in his car. It crashes. I go back to the priest. I've gone there to tell him, to admit it. The scene is between the two of us. It finally looks as though I'm not going to survive this latest problem in my life. What follows in the script is a remarkable storyline, something that no-one expects.

Once again Ken didn't give me the script until the night before I played the scene. There had been a number of scenes that were only sketchily scripted and where improvisation was used but this was the only scene in the film that was scripted completely. Ken also only gave Tom and myself our own dialogue, so we didn't know exactly what was coming from each other. This was a real experience and it is a great way of filming. I was told that the script for this scene was the crux of the whole story, the most important part of the job. The film had already been a massive learning curve for me but this one scene was something special.

When I got my half of the script for the scene I looked and thought just how am I going to do this? I spoke to Ken who told me that he wanted me locked away that night and tomorrow. They put me up in a hotel even though I just lived down the road because they didn't want me doing anything or to be with anyone. Ken wanted me to feel isolated, on my own. I felt that way.

Now I was Bob and he was me for that night and the following day. The next 24 hours was one of the most incredible acting experiences of my life. I think it is this scene above any other in the film that led to the European Actor award.

We started the scene in the morning. It's quite a long scene and there were a lot of camera angle changes. I remember talking with Tom and him saying that this scene was going to be hard. Every time they finished with me I was locked back in a room away from everyone. I had a cup of coffee and a biscuit but that was all, I couldn't have a meal because I was told it would make me lethargic. They didn't want me coming out of that mood of isolation and I wasn't allowed to break that concentration. In the story I was in fear of losing my wife, my kid and I was going to go to prison for life in my mind.

I got to the point in the script where Bob broke down and cried, during the afternoon's filming. Ken disappeared. I thought what the f*** have I done now? One of the cameramen came to me and said: 'You've got to him mate, he's crying. You've done this scene and we can't shoot it anymore.'

I know this might sound odd, but I didn't think anything about what I'd just done. I was playing my role and just did what I had to do. Like I said, I was Bob and he was me for that 24 hours. I knew I had to break down. I knew I had to admit that I'd killed this guy. I knew I was fighting for my wife and daughter. I knew what I'd done was wrong and that I was going to lose everything. Bruce Jones didn't have a life at that moment. I'd invested everything into Bob.

Ken Loach took the whole cast out that night. He took us to a pub where a friend of mine, Dave, who used to work on boilers, saw me and asked how I was. But I couldn't talk to him, in fact I couldn't talk properly with anyone. I remember saying to Ken: 'Did we get it?' What I meant was had we got the scene right. He said: 'Did you what? You had us all there.' I just came back with: 'What did I do? Tell me, because I just don't know.' I can still vividly remember the day and that we filmed but I still don't know how I did it, how I went as far as I did with Bob.

The next day I wasn't called in because I think Ken could see what the day had done to me, what it had taken out of me. He knew I needed time to get my head back together. He understands actors and he understood me. I had to come out of that state I was in and it took time.

When I came back home Sandra knew there was something wrong. She asked me how I was. She could see something was different but I wasn't very gracious. I could have reacted a lot better but I was still not back from where I'd been to and that's what I said: 'You haven't got a clue where I've been. You don't know. You really don't.' How could she? I didn't even know myself!

In the hours that followed I had no passion for anything. My head was all over the place. I was still that part, the character of Bob, and I was still trying to get back. That's why I know method acting can be dangerous. It can bring about magnificent performances, but it can take its toll on you. If you go into a role as deep as some have done, myself included, you must come out of it. But there is no telling the damage that you can cause.

Cannes Film Festival – that's one hell of a way of bringing an actor back to the realisation he is just that, an actor. And for a lad from a tough end of Manchester it was like a dream when I was told that's where we were going. We were up for an award. My first film, and with me in the lead role, was not just up for any old award, but one of the top awards in Cannes. I couldn't believe it. My Uncle John was so proud when I told him. *Granada Reports*, our local news programme on ITV, ran a story about it. Three of us from the cast were going – me, Ricky and Julie.

Raining Stones took the Grand Jury Prize. We were award winners. *The Piano* starring Holly Hunter got the Palme D'Or and David Thewlis took the Best Actor Award for *Naked*. I talked with David and we found we had quite a bit in common. He's another Lancashire lad, coming from Blackpool. Famous Hollywood actors like Michael Douglas were there too. I couldn't believe I was in their company. It was a great four and a half days.

But those lonely moments, when I felt so isolated, were still there. One night I just disappeared. I didn't want to be with anyone. The Festival had shown the scene with Tom and me and everyone in the theatre was

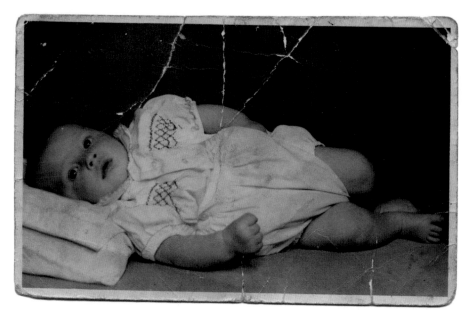

You see, even as a baby I was acting. Here I'm playing Long John Silver as it looks like half my left leg is missing!

My mum and dad – Irene and John William Jones.

Me with my brother Bryn.

Mum and Dad with me and my brother Bryn.

Collyhurst's finest at St Oswald's School – can you tell which one is me? My teacher Miss Webb is on the far left.

Lovely looking lad that I was! This was me at a Gang Show in the Palace Theatre, Manchester.

Me and Steve Hadfield
at my first wedding –
Steve was Best Man at
both my weddings.

My Rod Stewart days!
This was taken on holiday
in Newquay.

Fire Service time! Here I am with my good mate Paul Dolan.

No – I wasn't advertising for Strand cigarettes at this time.

Wedding Day – Sandra, looking absolutely gorgeous as we sign on the dotted line.

My two
fantastic sons –
Steven and Jon.

My two
lovely
daughters –
Lisa and
Claudia.

One of my earliest acting roles was as Spadge Hopkins in Cider with Rosie at The Carver Theatre in Marple. Here I am all set for going on stage.

My two main screen awards. The Screen Actors award for The Full Monty and my European Actor of the Year award for *Raining Stones*. They're heavy these things!

My character of Robert Askew in *Bob's Weekend*.

Ricky Tomlinson and me on holiday in France.

The cast of my BBC TV series *Roughnecks* which ran for two series.

With the wonderful Liz Dawn and the brilliant Bob Hoskins.

Bob Hoskins, the greatest screen actor I've worked with, beating me up in the film *TwentyFour Seven*

The make-up for the fight scene where Bob and I fought for real in *TwentyFour Seven*. This was filmed in Nottingham.

Bob Hoskins and me - getting it on in *TwentyFour Seven*.

Me and the great Kev Kennedy. We're the best of friends.

No doubt about it in my book – Vicky Entwistle is the best actress I've worked with and a great laugh too!

The lovely Jane Danson. I'm so proud of how both Georgia Taylor and Jane have gone on to achieve so much.

Myself and John Savident (Fred Elliot) in action during an episode of *Coronation Street* at Aintree Races.

Me and Sir Norman Wisdom when he played Ernie Crab in *Coronation Street*. One of the all-time greats.

Bill Waddington (Percy Sugden) was a real character. He owned a string of racehorses and yet would ask our local landlord for a lettuce leaf or tomato to take back home for his sandwich.

Dougie Almond, restaurant owner, who taught me how to cook in his hotel.

Me and Ricky Hatton on The Street, with Max my dog.

on their feet applauding. When they showed the scene it scared me, I thought I was going to get lynched. I don't know why, but it sent me back there, back to that day when we were filming. Ken had told me they were cheering me but it had made little difference to the way I felt.

There was a couple who turned to me and said they'd come all the way from Collyhurst to see us pick up the award. They told me I'd done Collyhurst proud. None of it made any sense to me at the time.

I remember being sat in a café at one o'clock that night. I was thinking about whether I should be an actor, whether I could hack it. I was starting to think that maybe I had made a mistake and that I should have gone full-time as a fireman. I tried ringing Sandra but it must have been too late to get hold of her as I couldn't get through. At that moment I needed someone, a friend. I was in a foreign country and everything was foreign to me. My world has just turned upside down again by watching that scene. I'd not seen it since we'd filmed it because I hadn't been able to make it to the premiere. I was just sat in the café bar on my own, along with the barman.

Suddenly I wasn't on my own. A guy came in and tried to mug me. He must have thought I was an easy target, a man on his own. He probably thought I was drunk. Unfortunately for him he was to find out just how much I wasn't at all drunk. He chose the wrong man at the wrong time.

I was back from being deep in my thoughts. That night I took all my pent up feelings and emotions and battered him. The café man was going to ring the police to report the mugging attempt but when he saw how I handled this guy he changed his mind. The guy ran off, probably to lick his wounds and try his luck elsewhere. I now had blood on my clothes and looked bedraggled from the smart state I had been in. When I got back to the hotel David (Thewlis) saw me and asked what had happened.

That night saw what can happen to you as an actor if you go in too far. You can win awards for it, but it can also send you close to the edge.

But the awards ceremonies didn't end there. Later on I received a European Actor's Award and I had to go to Pescara in Italy to pick it up. That was my first of two major international awards.

CHAPTER TWENTY ONE

ROUGHNECKS

It wasn't long after *Raining Stones*, just a few months, when I received a call to go to London. Patrick (Nyland) rang to tell me I was up for an audition for a new TV series called *Roughnecks*.

The series ran on BBC in 1994 and 1995 and was all about the lives of a group of people who worked on an oil rig in the North Sea. It was created and written by Kieran Prendiville who was a presenter on *Tomorrow's World* and *That's Life*. He also created *Ballykissangel* and wrote *Boon*. The theme tune was written by Mike Post the American who also wrote the theme tunes to *The Rockford Files* with James Garner; and *Hill Street Blues*. The cast included some great actors, once again I was with Ricky (Tomlinson); and the wonderful Jimmy Cosmo; John McGlynn; George Rossi; Colum Convey; Anne Raitt; Hywel Simons; Liam Cunningham; Teresa Banham; Clive Russell; Paul Copley; Alec Westwood; Ashley Jensen; and John Kazek. I played Terry, the boss on the rig.

We had two great seasons and filmed 13 episodes. We were contracted for two years and we would film for 6-7 months of the year. Filming was on location in Aberdeen and on an oil rig itself. It was a fantastic series to work on, very different from my role as Bob, so at least I wasn't getting typecast. The location was so different too.

Aberdeen is a great place. I loved it up there. They call it the jewel in the crown, not because of the money generated by the oil production but because when the sun hits the granite it glistens. It's a fantastic sight. They are also very Scottish. I know that sounds obvious but by that I mean they are fervently patriotic. We weren't allowed into Aberdeen city centre on a Saturday morning because they used to do these 'English Out' marches. Me and Ricky were stuck in our hotel one morning and watched it. It was frightening listening to them and looking at their faces as they marched past. You were okay to go shopping in an afternoon. They just wanted to make their point I guess. It put the fear of God up Ricky and me anyway.

Each time we were due for our stint on the rig we would fly into Aberdeen, check in at our hotel and next morning take a helicopter flight to the rig. We would spend four to six weeks on the rig at a time dependent on the weather then we would film around Aberdeen itself. We would film quite a bit of the interior stuff at Bray Studios in London. We'd be in studio for about 3-4 months of the year.

Filming on an oil rig in late summer was lovely but when we got to the winter period some of the helicopter flights were more than iffy. We had to go on a number of safety tests before we were allowed on to a rig at all. One of them involved a situation where the helicopter had turned over in the water. It's at times like these when you find out things about people that you didn't know. This is when I found out something that Ricky couldn't do!

'I can't swim', said this certain person from Liverpool. 'Get me out!' With Ricky you sometimes don't know whether he's having you on or not but here he was deathly serious. He really couldn't swim. 'But when we were auditioning you told them you could swim', I said. It was another lesson for me. If you want a part badly enough or simply want to keep in work you will say you can do anything to get the job.

We went through all the tests that they could put us through and off we went from Aberdeen to the rig. What we all found out, as actors, is that the people who earn their living working on oil rigs in the middle of the North Sea all deserve a medal for doing so. In the winter we had one night when it got so bad that the rig snapped an anchor and the whole rig turned. You just never know what weather is going to come your way in the middle of the sea. We were all worried, the whole cast was meant to be lifted off the rig, but the people who actually worked on the rigs were going to stay, so we stayed. We rode out the storm. Next morning the storm had died down and a boat came out and re-anchored us.

The scariest thing on the rig was the gymnasium. It was down one of the legs of the rig that was sunk into the bottom of the sea. It had a platform and that was your lift down into the bowels of the rig.

We also had a bit of fun with each other. We used to make up ghost stories about the rig being haunted and Alec Westwood who played Davey became our target. We worked on him and he got so worried that we decided to take things a bit further.

When I talk of 'we' I'm talking about my accomplice and me. If you haven't guessed it already by now it was that Liverpudlian feller again, the one who couldn't swim.

We wired Alec's room up with fishing wire. It was tied to a chair and a light. When he went to bed we waited until he'd got settled and started reading then we started pulling the wires so that the chair and light moved. Next thing we know he is screaming like a banshee as he runs out of his room and down the corridor.

I got done as well! I tried my hand at fishing off the rig. I thought I was doing okay, and then I thought I was doing even better when I actually caught a fish. I was over the moon. I started shouting to the others: 'I've caught a fish. I've only gone and caught a bloody fish!' You can imagine the big smile on my face. I was ecstatic.

The others, who had set it all up, and you don't need any prizes for guessing one of them do you, said: 'That's great Bruce. Well done mate. What fish have you caught?'

'Mackerel', I said more proud than ever that I had not even caught a fish but that I could name what fish it was. We ate mackerel on the rig so that's probably the reason I thought it was that.

They fell apart! 'Mackerel! He's caught a bloody mackerel!' That's when I knew that like the fish I'd been done hook, line and sinker. They'd managed to get my line out without me noticing. They'd got a mackerel out of the kitchen and stuck it on the hook. By now they're all howling, with ring leader Ricky louder than ever. They knew they'd done me! It was a fair cop.

Practical jokes were played quite a bit but when it came down to the serious acting work we really were a great team. The riggers were great people too and I have been back to Aberdeen a good few times to play in charity golf events there.

CHAPTER TWENTY TWO
BOB'S WEEKEND

During the time I had between filming the two series of *Roughnecks* I appeared in a Christmas episode of the ITV series *Heartbeat*. I also picked up guest appearances in a few other TV series once *Roughnecks* had finished. My next movie saw my second lead role.

Bob's Weekend was the toughest movie I have ever made. That might sound daft when you watch *Raining Stones*; or *TwentyFour Seven* that I did after *Bob's Weekend*, and see some of the scenes I do in those, but it was also such a funny film to do. I don't think I earned much if anything out of it but it was one of those scripts that probably don't come along too much in an actor's lifetime. For me acting really is about the parts you get, not the money. The director was Jevon O'Neill who I'd worked with on a TV commercial about Blackpool. He hadn't put together a movie before but he'd built a great reputation producing TV commercials. When we had been working on the one for Blackpool I had told him about the movie I'd just been in (*Raining Stones*) and that I'd just come back from Cannes. He went to see the film expecting me to be in it for about 5 minutes and was impressed by what he saw.

Jevon phoned me. He also called Patrick (Ryland) and he came up to see me in Marple. I read the script and told Jevon I'd love to do it. It was a great script, a great story and a really different kind of film. Bob Askew is a security guard in an office block. He's married but his wife is having an affair. His step daughter doesn't like him. He's ridiculed at work. He loses his job. Everything seems to be going wrong in his life. He has no purpose. But there's a lot more to it all than that, and the reasons why Bob feels the way he does about life. He decides to end it all in Blackpool, but the beauty of Jevon's film is that's where it all starts coming together for him.

The director of the Edinburgh Film Festival, Mark Cousins, headlined it as Britain's answer to *It's a Wonderful Life*. Jevon had never watched the film but he did later and saw the similarities. This feller, Bob, is a nice guy who hasn't done anyone any harm in the world and yet his world is caving in. He reaches the point of no return when his wife, played by Anna Jaskolka, who was also with me in *Raining Stones*, comes home with another man.

Ricky (Tomlinson) was in this movie too playing a cameo role as one of my colleagues at work; and I also played alongside the brilliant Brian Glover. It was Brian's last film as he passed away before it was released. He stayed in Stockport whilst filming was taking place for his scenes. He'd told me how ill he was but just listening to his stories about his wrestling career and his acting career in movies like *Kes* had me spellbound.

There are some magical moments in this film and whilst it was the most challenging movie I have done it was also the most fun to make. How many movies do you know that have a character dressed as a Bolivian Admiral walking down Blackpool Promenade wearing a Samurai sword, pulling a shopping trolley full of encyclopaedias and a rope.

Jevon had decided that he wanted me to walk along the promenade like this. All very well you might think, but he wanted me to do it without a camera and sound crew in sight and without telling anyone what was going on. That meant I was being set up like some kind of nutter, walking on Blackpool's busiest stretch, during the period when the Blackpool Illuminations bring tens of thousands of visitors every day. I knew the crew were all laughing at me from where I couldn't see them. I was wearing all this regalia, and had to keep a straight face whilst I could see the expressions on the faces of those I was walking past.

It was like Moses parting the sea as I walked along. Holiday makers fled to either side of me. Everyone was looking and I could see people were on their mobile phones to the police because obviously they had seen the Samurai sword. 'There's a lunatic down here, with a sword', I heard one of them say as I went past. I just kept walking. Next thing I know there are blue lights flashing and the boys in blue have arrived. Fortunately I didn't get arrested. Jevon hadn't wanted to let people know that we were going to do it that way (even the police) because he wanted to record their reactions of this oddly-dressed man with a lethal weapon. I wouldn't mind but Bolivia hasn't even got a navy. It's a landlocked country. And I was supposed to be Admiral of its fleet. It was that kind of film.

There were some really weird but wonderful scenes. In one of them I go down to the public conveniences in my normal clothes and get shaved by a lady who is preparing me for life, death and the after-life; my journey. In another I go into this antiques warehouse and come out a bit like that children's TV series *Mr Benn* in a different outfit – the Bolivian Admiral.

Two things save Bob in the movie, which has a lovely happy ending. One of those is the character of Angela, played by a great young actress called Charlotte Jones (no relation) who becomes my guardian angel. It was Charlotte's first film and she played her part superbly. I don't quite know why she didn't go on to get some other really big roles because she was wonderful to play alongside. The other thing is Blackpool itself. Jevon loves Blackpool and so do I and in a way the movie is also about showing people what the seaside town is all about. It shows the tower, the promenade, the Pleasure Beach and North Pier which are all icons.

We had to go to the top of the tower where there is just a railing between me, Angela and down below. I'm scared of heights, not as Bob but as me. And we had quite a bit of dialogue to get through up there.

For me part of the magical quality of the film was when Charlotte and I had to dance together in the Blackpool Tower ballroom. Bob and Angela dance the waltz to the Tower Ballroom Wurlitzer organ.

Blackpool is known for its plethora of wonderful hotels and bed and breakfast establishments. I'm mentioning that here and now because although it's known for them we didn't find the right one.

Whilst we were filming in Blackpool we all stayed in this B&B with the landlady from hell! Her husband had left her for a younger model, or so we heard. She was always in such a mood and even threw a bottle at us one night. She would sit at her bar in the B&B and was always spouting on about her husband. In the end we had to have a word with her and told her we were going to all pull out because of her moods. That seemed to bring her round.

Apparently the problem was that one of us looked like her husband. I hoped to God it wasn't me!

The movie was a real challenge for me because I'm in nearly every scene. It was completely different from anything I'd done before because of the brilliant script written by Jevon and Jayson Rothwell. I truly believed in the film and I'm immensely proud of what we all achieved in making it.

There was only one problem that I found tricky to get my head around. My role of Bob saw me as a Manchester United fan. I'm a big Manchester City fan and I had to reel off this monologue about all the great Manchester United players. The things we do for our art.

CHAPTER TWENTY THREE
TWENTYFOUR SEVEN

I make no excuses for jumping from film to film and a major TV series here, even though there were TV appearances in between and there was the matter of how things were going at home, but really everything did happen for me in a short space of time. *Raining Stones* was in 1993; *Roughnecks* took care of much of 1994 and 1995; *Bob's Weekend* was filmed in 1995 and released in 1996; *TwentyFour Seven* was filmed in 1996 and released in 1997.

TwentyFour Seven was a different movie again. In this one I play Geoff, Tim's dad. I'm in a handful of scenes in the film and every one sees me angry, hot-headed and in the most dramatic of all getting well and truly beaten up by the main character in the film Darcy, played by the absolutely brilliant Bob Hoskins.

I've acted alongside some of the best talent in Britain but I'd have to go for Bob as my absolute favourite I've worked with. I got on great with him right from the start and got to know him well. His background and mine are similar in a way, we both come from working class backgrounds and worked hard at home.

Working with Bob was like the icing on the cake for me. I'd played lead roles in two great films; I'd been in a cracking TV series for two years, playing alongside some brilliant talent. But this marvellous actor has played in so many big movies such as *Mona Lisa* and *The Long Good Friday*.

One of the main things I learned from Bob was that if you can get away with it you should never use stuntmen in action scenes. I'd already done that in *Raining Stones* but to hear it from a legend like Bob was reassuring. He told me that it was always better to do them all yourself because that way you get a better deal in the end. The big fight scene we have between the two of us is the biggest scene in the film. Darcy, Bob's character, runs a boxing club for boys in Nottingham, and my lad Tim has just gone into the ring for his first ever bout when Geoff, my character, pulls him out.

I'm a noisy, foul-mouthed, horrible man in the movie intent on destroying any hope my son has of succeeding at something. You never find out why I am that way because my role is not explored, but I bait Darcy so much that you're left to think that he's beaten me up so much that he's killed me. For me that whole fight scene works well because we both did it for real. Again, like I was in *Raining Stones*, I was black and blue in the end, and so was Bob, but it created the right effect. It was for real.

This was Shane Meadows' first big film as a director and he wrote it as well, with Paul Fraser. It's filmed totally in black and white and is a great British film.

Bob paid me a great compliment when we talked. He said I would go on to do great work and he asked me to go across to America and do some stuff with him over there. Of course I said I would love to, who wouldn't? But the week before we finished filming I got a call to go to Granada where I was wined and dined for a new role in a TV programme called *Coronation Street* – not that I knew it was for that at the time.

Who knows how life could have worked out differently if I'd gone to the States with Bob?

CHAPTER TWENTY FOUR
TV TIMES

Before we get to *Coronation Street* there's a bit to tell about those other TV programmes I was appearing in during the down times in *Roughnecks* and in between the movies. Basically I wasn't out of work as an actor for very long at all from starting out in 1993 with Ken Loach until I finished in *Coronation Street* in 2007. I guess I've been very lucky that way as most in my profession have long breaks between jobs.

Heartbeat was the first TV series where I appeared in a guest role. I played the part of Fred Parkin, a single parent, in *The Winter's Tale* and one of my three children was dying of breathing problems. It was another challenging role and I played alongside Twiggy. It was the *Heartbeat* Christmas Special of 1994 and the children's mother had died. My son and daughter were pinching Christmas trees from Lady Janet Whitly's (Twiggy) land, to sell so that they could raise money for my other son to go to Switzerland. It was the only place it looked like there might be a cure. Lady Whitly eventually found out about why the children were acting the way they were and there was a typical Christmas happy ending.

We filmed up in Goathland on the North York Moors and by God was it cold. I don't think I've ever been so cold in my entire life! The episode was directed by Tim Dowd, who I was later to meet up with again on *Coronation Street*. This was the first time I'd ever had to film whilst a snow machine was being used.

I stayed in The Mallyan Spout Hotel in this lovely village where the sheep graze freely across the village green. The cast also drank at The Goathland Hotel (which doubled as The Aidensfield Arms) so I frequented both establishments during my four week stay. Some of the regulars in the cast at the time were Nick Berry (PC Rowan), Niamh Cusack (PC Rowan's wife) and Bill Maynard (Greengrass). They were a lovely team to be involved with and the series was still relatively new at the time. I think it was into its third series. It's a shame that it's gone now.

The cast and crew would play a few games of pool on an evening and one night I was chatting to Bill Simons who played PC Ventress and who lived in the village. He happened to say that he was painting his cottage and since I had a day off from filming I offered to help him. I painted the guttering as I remember.

Band of Gold was my next guest appearance in 1995. I was Brian in an episode called 'Caught'. It was a fun part to play as I was a knicker salesman, lingerie to the more refined amongst you, and I was bribing all the prostitutes into bed with the offer of free sexy underwear! The series was set in Bradford and featured some great actresses: Geraldine James; Cathy Tyson; Barbara Dickson and Samantha Morton. Julie Brown from *Raining Stones* also appeared in this episode, as did Mark Addy who went on to appear in *The Full Monty* and Sue Cleaver who went on to play Eileen Grimshaw in *Coronation Street*.

During 1995 and 1996 I also appeared in *Hillsborough*; *A Touch of Frost*; *Crewe Stories*; and *Johnny Watkins Walks on Water*. I was hardly off the television in this time, which was great for me money-wise but it was starting to take its toll on my home life, my family life.

Hillsborough was shown at the end of 1996. It was all about what happened at Sheffield Wednesday's ground when 96 Liverpool fans were crushed to death in front of the cameras, before and just 6 minutes into the FA Cup Semi-Final against Nottingham Forest in April 1989. I'm in it throughout as the video technician who lived through it all on the day. He tried to get the message through that there were serious problems but it seemed no notice was taken.

The movie follows three families through their trials and tribulations as events unfolded before the game, during the six minutes that were played, the aftermath and the months that followed, including the court case. It was the kind of TV film that you couldn't help but to get caught up in. Just what those families have had to live through since then God only knows. Crushed to death at a football match, who would have thought of it happening? I think we were all touched by what we were reliving for others. I hope those whose families lost loved ones felt that the dramatisation was appropriate.

A Touch of Frost was another of those moments for me when I knew

I was working with a master. It was aired in 1997 but filmed in 1996. The episode was called 'Penny For The Guy'. You can always learn something from anyone but in David Jason's case there was so much you could learn from. I played a security guard in a supermarket (Tommy Dunstan) who had been caught stealing. I was on the take and whilst I was in the nick Frost (David) leant on my character to find out the information he needed to solve the case.

What I really learned from David was discipline. He was a true professional in every way whilst he was on the set. I found out that when he wasn't working he enjoyed the horses, checking form.

Crewe Stories was a series of four plays all set in the town of Crewe. Each week I played a different main character. The one I remember most was when I played the part of the school inspector and one of the delinquents pees in my briefcase. It's not something you forget very easily. I played the part of a local councillor another week.

During the shooting of *Crewe Stories* I remember reflecting on when I was laid on my hospital bed not knowing whether I would survive. At that time I was the same age as some of the kids now acting alongside me. I remember thinking that I had wanted to die, but then thinking that if I had died I would never have played all of these wonderful roles. Okay some of what you play might be a bit weird, in fact sometimes the roles can be downright strange and sometimes a bit warped, but they are still great to play.

I had stopped believing in God and the church at one time, especially when my head was filled with Jean Jordan and the Ripper. Then you think there is a God because 'I've got all this, I've got my dream'.

When I played the role of the school inspector it made me realise how many kids have stopped dreaming. That's when I really started thinking about charity work. I guess I felt guilty about all I now had in life. I felt guilty in some way. Can you understand that?

Johnny Watkins Walks on Water saw me play the part of a priest for the first time in 1997. Me, the guy who played Les Battersby, as a priest! This was a short film (10 minutes) that was part of a BBC 10 x 10 season. It was all about a girl called Mary whose father is a Beatles fan and runs a second hand record shop. If you like far-fetched storylines try this one out. Johnny is meant to be the 'Second Coming' and in the final scene he walks on water! And guess who was also in it with me? You've got it, Ricky T, this time as Mary's dad. Ricky had also appeared in *Hillsborough*.

And that was my lot for TV! Well, all apart from a little old thing called *Coronation Street*!

CHAPTER TWENTY FIVE
GUILTY OF BEING A SUCCESS

'You're in my heart, you're in my soul
You'll be my breath should I grow old
You are my lover, you're my best friend
You're in my soul
My love for you is immeasurable
My respect for you, immense
You're ageless, timeless, lace and fineness
You're beauty and elegance
You're a rhapsody, a comedy
You're a symphony and a play
You're every love song ever written
But honey what do you see in me.'
Rod Stewart *You're in my Heart*

I love Rod Stewart. I always have. And I have always loved Sandra even though as I write this we are apart. She really is in my heart and soul, maybe the line in Rod's song about my respect for Sandra being immense can be called into question and maybe the last line of the song 'honey what do you see in me' is the reason we're not together, but she's still there regardless. I don't want anyone else.

The reason why I've started with one of Rod's songs is because I've been going on about all the film and TV work I was involved with from 1993-1997 but not really mentioned our home life too much. Sandra would probably say that's because I wasn't home much at all.

The money was good. I wasn't out of work for any length of time during these years and when I was I had earned enough from the contracts to tide us over. *Roughnecks* was a guaranteed income for two years of that time; and thanks to Patrick all of the roles I was offered, apart from *Bob's Weekend*, carried decent money too. But that film was different. I really did want to do it and I am pleased I did.

Money isn't everything, although we all need it. After *TwentyFour*

Seven had finished Sandra and I had a massive fallout. We had started having big arguments when I'd finished in *Roughnecks*. I guess you can put a lot of it down to the fact that I'd been away for quite a bit. *Roughnecks* took up a long time away from home and like many other couples who have suffered similarly the time apart started taking its toll, no matter how much money was coming in.

I got this huge guilt feeling about not having been at home enough, but I was working, doing what people today call 'living the dream'. Everything was coming together for me after years of grafting on boilers, fitting pipes, putting out fires and all the other jobs I'd done to keep the money coming in. I was now doing what I had always wanted.

When I was home I would be like any other father. I would notice that the kids' bedrooms were a mess and try to make sure they sorted them out. I'm not stupid, I know it happens. I remembered, way back when I was a kid, that I would get bollocked off my mum if my bedroom was ever in anywhere near the state of some of our kids' bedrooms.

It was daft, stupid things like that which would set me off. Seconds later Sandra and I would be going at it against each other about all sorts of things which usually came back to how much I wasn't there. I couldn't take the arguments so I would clear off out of the house.

The first time Sandra and I split up must have been around 1996-1997 when I went to live in a flat for a while. We were apart for about twelve months then got back together when I landed the job of a lifetime in *Coronation Street*.

When you are being paid a lot of money, probably more money than you really deserve when you think about how much firemen, nurses and craftsmen are paid, you won't necessarily give it all away but you do feel guilty.

My head started ticking over when I would see other people. I'd look at them and think that used to be me. The guilt thing would kick in then. I'd ask fellers in a pub whether they were okay and we'd get talking. Some of them would say 'You're that guy off TV' but I never let it get in the way of our conversations. I'd get their life story and I'd be thinking f**k me, I lived like that. It wasn't that I was looking down on them. I don't know what it was. Maybe it had something to do with being proud of where I had come from to get where I now was.

One time I bought a pint for a guy who was down to his last shilling (for all of you below the age of 50, that's 5p). He'd just come in for a pint after work, only for the one, but I bought him another. We got talking. It turned out he was a pipefitter. I told him that's what I'd been. He'd recognised me from *Bob's Weekend* or *Roughnecks*. He told me that the money in the trade wasn't good at the time. He was having to budget his fish and chips for the family, working out how much he could afford and who would have to share. I'd done this myself.

I used to do what a lot of us did and what I'm sure a lot still do. I'd budget my money for the next day's work – my dinner money, fag money, enough for a pint or two at the end of the working day. I'm not trying to sound like some angel here but like I say I was feeling guilty. I ended up paying for fish and chips for all of his family so that they didn't have to share and I bought him another pint.

We got back to talking about life as a pipe fitter. I really was interested. He said that I wouldn't believe what was involved in the job now: 'You couldn't get back in. The tests you have to go through now are unbelievable. Every six months there's a new one to take.'

The thing is I don't know whether this guy was happy or not – maybe he was - but for all that I was enjoying my TV and movie status my home life probably wasn't as good as his. I wasn't wallowing in self pity either, I was more guilty than anything else. He was struggling to buy fish and chips, holding down a good job, whilst I was buying fitted kitchens just about every year!

I'm still a working class kid at heart. I've never forgotten my roots and I never will even though I did feel a bit guilty about what I earned in the nineties and up until *Coronation Street* ended for me.

I still feel more comfortable and more relaxed talking with people from my own kind of background. That's maybe why my relationship with Bob Hoskins was so good. It's also why I feel at home in a pub, a normal working man's pub, where I feel as though I can talk with real people – and hopefully not feel guilty.

CHAPTER TWENTY SIX

THE FULL MONTY

Cue Music:

'Je t'aime... mois non plus'

by Jane Birkin & Serge Gainsbourg

'I'm sorry... I'm sorry... Thought I'd give it a go... I got a bit desperate like, you know how it is... I can't even take me kit off properly can I ... '

'You're alright Reg... get you a cup of tea if you like...'

'No thanks, I've got the kids outside..'

'Bring 'em in..'

'..nah... this is no place for kids...'

That's it. That's my whole scene in The Full Monty. I played Reg and my whole performance lasted just over a minute of the film's 91 minutes, but it won me my second international award. It was released in August 1997 and I won a Screen Actor's Guild Award in the United States for outstanding performance by the whole cast, along with Robert Carlyle, Mark Addy, Paul Barber, Deidre Costello, Steve Huison, William Snape, Lesley Sharp, Hugo Speer, Tom Wilkinson and Emily Woof.

I don't suppose you need much reminding of the film, but my character Reg was the one who didn't make it into the dance team. My role was to play the awkward, embarrassed Reg who really wasn't cut out for the team but who was prepared to try anything. The scene was set in a disused warehouse in Sheffield.

The Full Monty came up whilst I was working on TwentyFour Seven and I was given two weeks off whilst I went up from Nottingham to Sheffield to make the movie. It had come about because Robbie Carlyle and I had met through Ken Loach and become good friends. It was Robbie who got me in.

It was the shortest part I've played in a movie but also, because of the film's massive success, the one that most people will know me for, especially as it was released just the month after I had made my first appearance in *Coronation Street* on 4 July 1997. For those who watched me in *The Full Monty* they would see quite a different character to Les.

The next 10 and a half years were to be some of the happiest of my life, times when I would work with a brilliant set of people that I still love today.

Are we ready? It doesn't matter how much you protest I know some of you have been itching to get to this bit. It's time for *Coronation Street*. Cue the music!

CHAPTER TWENTY SEVEN

CORONATION STREET

'No way! I'm not going to do that. I'll be the most hated person in Britain!'

You might think that any actor in the UK would jump at the chance of appearing in *Coronation Street* but believe me it's different when you're told what your character is going to be like.

Patrick (Nyland) had told me to be at Granada TV studios on the Friday night before I was to finish shooting the final scenes for *TwentyFour Seven*. Having already had two weeks out shooting *The Full Monty* I didn't want to upset anyone but Patrick arranged it that I would go up to Granada by train on the Friday evening, meet up with the casting director for this role they had in mind for me, and get back to Nottingham on Saturday morning to complete the film.

It turned out the meeting wasn't to be held at Granada after all but in the Victoria & Albert Hotel on Water Street close to the studios. I hadn't been told why I was to be here, all I knew was that I'd been up for an audition for a new series they had in mind which I think they were going to call *The Chain Gang*. I thought they might have called me up for that, but I really didn't know.

Sandwiches and a pint were brought to me and Judi Hayfield was there, one of the UK's leading casting directors, and a lovely lady who I already knew well; and Brian Park, the new producer of *Coronation Street*, who was looking to make an impact by bringing in a tougher and rougher family than they had there at the time.

I'd watched *Corrie* since it started in 1960. I'd watched it with my gran. When Judi and Brian told me they were considering me for a role in the programme you can imagine how I felt, when they told me that we were going to be the family from hell my reaction was very different.

So how did they convince me if I was so dead set against it? Well, Brian told me that he had watched *Raining Stones* and he had wanted me as Les from there. He could see through that film all the emotion and frustration I had felt as Bob and although Les was to be far louder and much more in your face – in fact closer to the character I had just been playing as Geoff in *TwentyFour Seven* – he had seen what I had in the tank.

I'm sure a lot of you reading this are probably also thinking that the other part that convinced me was the money. Well firstly I didn't know how much someone on *Coronation Street* was paid, although it wouldn't take Einstein to work out that playing a part in the nation's best loved TV series would not pay peanuts; and secondly I was of course flattered and honoured to have been thought of to play a role in it even though I didn't want to be hated. Thirdly, they buttered me up didn't they, telling me that they liked my work. Every actor is a sucker for that and I'm no different. We all want to be liked. And yes, the money was good but I left Patrick to sort that out. Another pint came for me. They knew what they were doing.

I signed up for 6 months thinking that would do. When they are bringing new characters in they're a bit cautious about offering long-term contracts. I was still more worried about how this character was going to be accepted or not.

TwentyFour Seven was completed and the deal was done for me to play the character of Les Battersby. All I needed now was my new family and it came in the shape of three wonderful actresses. First was the lovely, amazing and my favourite actress of all time Vicky Entwistle. They couldn't have found anyone better than Vicky and we will remain good friends no matter what life throws our way. The casting directors also came up with two terrific actresses who have gone on to great things both in and out of the Street – Jane Danson and Georgia Taylor.

Vicky had actually already appeared as her character, Janice, earlier in the year. Jane came in as Leanne, my daughter; and Georgia as Toyah, my step-daughter. The character of Toyah was originally going to be called Claire but I guess they wanted a punk kind of name for her. I remember Georgia being so worried that she wasn't going to get the part after her audition and the rest of us were trying to reassure her that she had nothing to worry about. She rang me the next day and she was so happy. She'd had a call to say that she had landed the role. It was one of those moments where 'I told you so' doesn't sound bad at all. The

Battersbys were good to go!

We knew the kind of reaction we were going to get from the viewers. You can't just bring a loud-mouthed, layabout, near-to-the-knuckle, mildly lawless family into *Coronation Street* and expect everyone to just accept it straight away – if at all – especially as we were offending some of the best loved names in the Street.

We were hated. Our fan mail was hate mail. Les assaulted Curly Watts and argued massively with Des Barnes in the early days. He always shouted the odds at anyone who took up a different view to his. I remember going into a pub called The Sawyers Arms in Deansgate in Manchester. There were 3 or 4 lads at the bar. I was just pleased the day's filming was over. I knew what we had filmed that day would annoy people because we had stolen some stuff from someone else in the Street. But in the episode that had just been shown I had head-butted Curly.

One of the guys in the pub came up to me and said: 'You want to get out of that street.' I wasn't ready for this and just begged his pardon. He said: 'You upset my f***ing grandmother. You want to get your f***ing arse out of the Street.' I was then threatened with a pool cue. I left the pub. It was a lesson for me early on, to learn just how the Street played such an important part of some people's lives.

When I went into work the next day I was wondering whether I could cope with not just being hated but the verbal and now close to physical abuse.

The next day someone else came up to me and said: 'Who do you think you are? You're making a t**t out of us (meaning guys like him I guess) in the Street. You're an arsehole.' I snapped and had a right go at him for that.

Vicky told me that she was getting abuse too, and so were the girls. Jane and Georgia coped with a lot at that time and I'm so glad that both have gone on to achieve what they have. To play the kind of characters they did, get the abuse they received, and still come out of the other side, as the lovely girls they always were at the start, isn't the easiest thing to do when you're playing in to millions of people's homes every night as the horrible family.

Vicky said she couldn't go shopping one day because when the store or supermarket saw her they just saw her as Janice Battersby. They didn't see her as a real person. That happens a lot when you're in a TV series. People can't differentiate between the character you're playing and the fact that you're an actor. They thought Vicky was going to attempt some shoplifting so she was refused entry. We had known things were going to be bad at first, but we weren't expecting things like this.

Viewers were ringing up radio stations to get us out of the Street. We really were what Brian Park had hoped for, or at least I think we were. Maybe he didn't even know just how much we would be hated.

As a group off-screen Vicky, Jane, Georgia and I all became very protective of each other. We didn't just have a great on-screen presence; we were strong for each other off-screen too. Vicky became like a mother to all three of us. Away from her screen character of Janice she is a beautiful, funny, lovely woman who is always up for a good night out.

Just a little note for all *Coronation Street* aficionados here, my character's full name was (and still is) Leslie Nelson Battersby; and Vicky's character's full name is Janice Bernadette Battersby. Our years of birth for the series are 1955 and 1968 respectively.

We went through a lot together, but that doesn't mean we didn't have a laugh. In fact we laughed a lot. We used to laugh at the daftest of things and we would corpse so many times, especially at serious moments in the script.

Vicky's a lot smaller than me (she's only 5ft nothing) and I have painful memories of the time she had to hit me with her handbag in the Rovers Return. She was supposed to hit me in the chest with it, but you can pretty much guess where it landed. No? Okay I'll give you a clue. There's one place where if a feller gets hit no-one ever gives you sympathy straight away because they're too busy going 'ooh' and smiling. That's right, Vicky had done me square on the bollocks! All I remember is hitting the floor with my knees, bent double, clutching my prize jewels! I had tears in my eyes and was muttering something unmentionable whilst everyone else on the set was in hysterics. No-one takes pity on the big guy in that kind of situation do they? They didn't with me.

She has one hell of a punch on her for a smaller woman as well. I can tell you, you don't want to be getting in her way when she's angry with you. She's not bad at throwing things other than punches as well. She threw a bag of spuds at me in one scene and this time when I caught it I was knocked right on my arse! In the scene below she hit me so many times my arm was black and blue by the end... I've just arrived home.

JANICE: Aww, there you are petal...

LES: Hello flower...

JANICE: Oh.. have you taken my keys?

LES: I don't think so... (both look at Les's keys and key ring)
Look how many times have I got to tell you... you've got
Phil Everly and I've got Don... can't you tell them
apart yet?

JANICE: Oh, well let me just go and have a little check...
(Janice moves towards kitchen, turns to Les who's watching telly)

JANICE: And I've got a lovely surprise for you...

LES: Yeah?
(Smiles, looks to the stairs thinking his luck is in - and by the time
he turns back Janice is moving towards him with a bin liner full
of Les's stuff)

JANICE: .... THAT!!!
(She throws it at him – and gets even more bags and throws them)

LES: What's this? What's that for!? What's going on?
(More bags, then Janice starts hitting Les)

JANICE: That's for lying to me about you and Charlie West (Thump!)
... and that's for getting done for drink driving... (grabs hold of Les)
...and that is for lying to me about what the doctor said... (punching)
... and this is for sleeping wi' Moira!

LES: I didn't I swear it!

JANICE: You lousy liar!

LES: Toyah, will you tell 'er? Get her off me...

JANICE: Liar... the whole flaming street knew except me didn't it!?

LES: I can explain it all Janice!

JANICE: Save your breath. You're gonna need it where you're going. It's cold in park at night... even in SUMMER!!!
(Janice continues beating up Les)

Charlie West (played by Keith Clifford), who Janice mentions in this scene, had plenty to answer for! Les had bought a camper van from him and together they got into a lot of scams and scrapes. He supplied the turkey for the Battersbys' Christmas dinner one year. The only thing was, if you remember, it was still alive!

It turned out to be one of my favourite scenes at No.5 Coronation Street with Janice and the family when Les ran over the turkey after it had escaped. The Battersbys had just decided they would keep it as a pet because Les couldn't face killing it, but since he'd run over it we still ate it for Christmas dinner.

When we got the script I was already in stitches. The scriptwriters really do make the programme. Just where they get all their ideas I really don't know but they do come up with some very funny stories. The funniest thing of this storyline was seeing the turkey still had rubber marks over it where the tyres had been!

Charlie also lent Les a Jag (car) to impress one of Les's previous loves, Moira Wood, who Janice mentions in the scene above. In one scene Les prangs the Jag into the back of a police car, gets arrested on suspicion of stealing it and that's when Janice finds out about Moira and throws him out. Not to worry though, Charlie comes to the rescue with the tattiest camper van you've ever seen!

Keith (Clifford) was really good fun to work with and the scriptwriters thought so too, so he kept popping in and out of the show. He went on to become one of the regulars in *Last of the Summer Wine*.

One of the scriptwriters' greatest ideas was for Charlie and Les to nick the cobbles off the Street. It worked brilliantly until one was dropped on to Les's foot! Charlie also managed to get hold of another camper van, amazingly probably even tattier than the first one, for Les and Janice's holiday in North Wales. We had seven days' filming at Conwy and I fell in love with the place. That's why Sandra and I bought a bungalow over there. It's a lovely little walled town.

Over the years we were playing as husband and wife both Les and Janice mellowed. They were still loud and Les was still someone you would rather steer clear of, but I think the viewers, ironically, started to love Les when they were about to split up. I think that's when they felt for him the most.

When Janice was having an affair with Dennis Stringer, played by Charles Dale, who was supposed to be Les's mate, I found myself feeling really hurt.

It was the writers who split us up and there was no return. I think Vicky was sad that Les and Janice were splitting. I know I was. I thought we had formed one of the Street's great feuding couples a bit like Jack and Vera. I would sit in my dressing room feeling quite emotional about what we were both having to go through not just as actors, but also as friends.

Later in the series, when I got together with Cilla (Wendi Peters) we were getting some great storylines that I felt Vicky and I should have been getting. I talked about it with Vicky off set and I think she felt the same. That doesn't mean I didn't enjoy working with Wendi, it's just that I missed Vicky not playing the part of my wife. But life, particularly in TV series, doesn't stay the same for long and you have to get on with the storylines you're given.

My own feeling is that Les really did love Janice. He might have struggled to show it whilst they were together. He did no favours to himself when he bought her a deep-fat fryer for their anniversary either. He was an idiot, but laying all that to one side he still fancied her.

That vulnerable, softer side to Les came near the end of Janice being with him. I think that's when the viewers really did get to see this different side to his character. It was a sad, lonely side that gave the audience a chance to feel for him, to sympathise. They hadn't seen that from him up until then, but they were about to see this raging male descend into a pit of despair.

When Les hits the wall and slides down it crying it was a special moment for me in the show. It's at that moment he knows he is losing Janice to his best mate and there's nothing he can do about it. Dennis and Janice are moving in together. These were proud moments for me in portraying this character because it gave Les depth as a person rather than a caricature.

In the New Year's Day episode of 2002 Les drives under a viaduct and sits in his car trying to commit suicide by drinking himself to death. Dennis rescues Les and drives him off to the hospital but we crash on the way and Dennis dies.

The suicide storyline was another massive challenge for me as an actor. I had been at the end of the North Pier in *Bob's Weekend*, but this was something more.

I was back in the method acting role as I had been for the scene with the priest in *Raining Stones*. I didn't speak to anyone during the filming of Les hitting the bottle. I went into my own space. I wanted to concentrate on the isolation, to make sure that I was playing the loneliness and desolation that Les feels.

If you're going into a sad situation, in your role, you really shouldn't speak to anyone, not the crew or the rest of the cast. You should just go and sit on your own somewhere and get it all into your head. When you do that's when I believe you move out of your own skin and you become this other character you are not just attempting to play. You are then – and only then – 100% in that character. This is when Bruce Jones became Les Battersby 100%.

Playing these kind of storylines and giving yourself totally does something to you inside. You are taking your brain into places that you wouldn't be going in your own normal life. That's the difference between real acting and simply playing a part without going there so deeply. When you're giving totally you are no longer you. That's when you are this fictitious character that you are making real.

Sometimes it is difficult, once that happens, to convince people that your character on screen is not you in real life, especially if you've performed well. I'm certain that's what happened to me many times whilst I was in the Street. It's tough to take but you have to accept it and get on with it. I've been made into a figure of ridicule over the years – and okay, I'll be the first to admit I've not helped myself in some ways, but I'm not all of what has been made out. I really am just this working class bloke who just so happens to have done okay out of acting.

I'm not looking for sympathy here, I'm just an actor trying to explain what it's like when you're being plastered all over the newspapers in a way that affects not just you but your family and friends. I know lots of other actors who have appeared in *Coronation Street* and other major TV series who could tell similar stories. Sometimes people don't realise just what we all go through in those really tough scenes. You should see what I come out like after going to those places in my head as Les.

The suicide scene really was one of the hardest scenes I ever did in the Street. I went there, to that place where my mind was Les's mind. You can't do it properly without sending your mind to think that way. These are dark places that you have to get to when you're going to perform. You have to think about making it real and once you're there you don't have to think about it at all, because you are then in that frame of mind. You think about how your suicide will affect others, not as an actor, but as Les taking over your body.

When I am that far into the character it's not a simple task of switching it on and off like a light bulb. It takes time to get into that zone and it takes quite a while to come out of it. Your head is full of this part you have been playing. If you've been doing it right you have not been thinking about anything to do with the life of Bruce Jones whilst you have gone.

It's difficult for a lot of actors and it has certainly been very difficult for me over the years. When you're in a TV series like *Coronation Street* it can be doubly or trebly difficult because your character could be in this particular frame of mind for weeks and months on end! That means that each day you're having to go back into this situation and, if you're giving 100%, it means more and more time is needed to get back in and come out of character.

Getting Les out of my head, particularly around the time of the break-up with Janice and the suicide attempt, became almost impossible. Splitting Les from real life became difficult for me, especially when I had been concentrating so hard on being him totally on set.

There were many times during scenes such as the suicide attempt and when Les hit the wall and slid down that I would just go for a pint on my own after we'd finished for the day. Don't get me wrong, I wasn't a total loner and I would have good times with other cast members who were going for a drink at the end of a day, but I just didn't want anything to do with where I'd just been. I wasn't on my own in a pub either. I was with blokes who had just finished their day's work, whatever they had been doing whether they were tradesmen or fellow actors.

I'd meet a couple of mates in Liz Dawn's pub The Old Grapes in Little Quay Street. It's my favourite pub in Manchester, well patronised and well liked by everyone. I used to have a drink with Craig Cash and Caroline Aherne from time to time. Caroline once told me she had written a TV series and I was in it. But I was in *Corrie* at the time. The series was *The Royle Family* and my character would have had the catchphrase 'My Arse'. Ricky and me again. Our paths just kept crossing at that time.

Normally though I'd chat with lads who worked in a factory, a pipe fitter, an electrician. I just found it easier to unwind that way and to get back to reality after a day in *Corrie*. All of a sudden I'd be back smiling again and I'd be back in the real world.

Les Battersby might well have been seen as this loud-mouthed, opinionated, but overall daft character by many who watched the show but you still have to act all of that. When I was in front of the camera I was Les and it didn't matter what the scene was, I wanted him to appear real to everyone. There were times when I wondered just how far the scriptwriters were going to take Les and how he would end up, because you don't get to know what's going to happen to you until you get each script.

After the suicide attempt Les definitely mellowed. I don't know what the scriptwriters thought at the time but my feeling is that when they saw how Les was during that time they probably felt they had taken him just as low as he could go.

I don't know whether the directors could see it as well, when they were in writers' meetings, but I think they must have thought they had to give Les his life back a little, let him have some happy stuff. He had gone to hell and back at that time.

Les didn't get back with Janice, but I did go to her wedding! Not Janice's but Vicky's. Andy (Andrew Chapman), who's now Vicky's husband, used to be the props man on the set. The pair of them had to keep their relationship quiet at work because you weren't supposed to have partners working together but I knew and so did Jane and Georgia. We all went to the wedding along with Denise Welch, Angela Lonsdale, Charles Dale, Gaynor Faye, Jacqueline Chadwick, Naomi Radcliffe, Julie Hesmondhalgh, Liz Dawn, Suranne Jones, Sue Cleaver, Jennie McAlpine, Naomi Russell & Tracy Shaw.

Les and Janice were together for four and a half years in *Coronation Street*. It was a great time and we all had fantastic storylines. Jane and Georgia did a great job with what Leanne and Toyah had to go through. Leanne eloped to Scotland to marry Nick Tilsley (played then by Adam Rickitt), became a pregnant teenager, had an abortion, was stalked by Brian Tilsley's killer, separated from Nick, and got hooked on cocaine! Toyah was raped, left for dead and found out that the rapist was someone who had later befriended her.

Really there's no wonder Les was in the state he got to sometimes! Jane is now developing into one of the top actresses in the programme. I can see her being one of the Barbara Knox's (Rita) of the future.

Georgia and I had a great time doing the *Sooty Show* together on TV in 1998. That was at least a little bit of lighter stuff.

Wendi Peters came into the Street as Cilla Brown in October 2003. I soon found out just what a joy she was to work with too, and very professional. She's from Blackburn. Wendi's a good head height taller than Vicky but still a lot smaller than me. It must have looked quite comical at times on screen.

Cilla was all tits and bum; as noisy as Les, and an absolute whirlwind. Her character was very busty and always seemed to wear clothing one size smaller than her actual size.

The two characters of Les and Cilla met for the first time in The Weatherfield Arms where she was working as a barmaid. Cilla lied about her name to Les, saying that she was called Lulu, but not before Les had already lied about who he was. Here's the chat-up lines in that very first scene that saw us get together:

LES: Worked here long?

CILLA: Not long, no...

LES: No, I would 'ave noticed... a looker like you... fancy a bit?

CILLA: No ta...

LES: So, err, what's your name darling?

CILLA: Is this the last point where I can go home empty-handed?

LES: Ey?

CILLA: I'm wondering whether I should ask the audience or phone a friend, all these questions, it's like being on a flipping quiz...

LES: I'm just trying to be friendly...

CILLA: I don't do free drinks you know, when the landlord's not looking...

LES: Hey, I'm no sponger... I can afford to buy me own drinks...

CILLA: Not like most round 'ere then...

LES: Well I'm not like most am I?

CILLA: Judging from your chat-up lines you're exactly like 'em...

(LES looks at 'karaoke nite' poster and gets an idea)

LES: That's because I'm trying to blend in, isn't it?

CILLA: And you wanna do that because?

LES: Well I don't know whether I should be saying...

CILLA: (sulkily) Fine...

LES: Oh, I'm with a record company aren't I?

CILLA: You what?

LES: ... under cover... scouting the karaoke evenings...

CILLA: (disbelieving) Right...

LES: Honest... hey... how do you think the undiscovered talent gets discovered?

CILLA: You!?

LES: Exactly... not just me mind... only this is my patch. There's been some great singers from these parts. I mean... Lisa Stansfield... she'd still be in Rochdale if it wasn't for me... I've found some of the best over the years... me and Quo for instance...

CILLA: So what are you doing in here?

LES: Well I'm checking it out before tonight aren't I? Don't say owt mind...

CILLA: So you'll be 'ere tonight?

LES: Might be, might be... only there's another place I...

CILLA: (jumping in) No, no, come in here... actually, I'm singing... I'm really a singer... just filling in 'ere...

LES: I could tell... I guessed... there's something about you... an Orca!

CILLA: You mean an aura?

LES: That 'n' all (holds out hand, shakes with Cilla) ...Clint!

CILLA: (incredulous) Clint!

LES: ... as in Eastwood!

CILLA: And I'm (thinking quickly) ... Lulu... They reckon I sound like her... big voice, husky...

LES: ... sexy...

CILLA: You know anybody else famous? How about Sting? I think he's gorgeous...

LES: Well actually... me and the police... we've got a bit of history...

This also brought about a new family for Les. Cilla was Fiz's mum. Fiz being played by Jennie McAlpine; and she also had Chesney, played by Sam Aston who I really took to like a son in real life. Sam is a cracking lad. He was only about eight years old when he came into the cast. He would come up to our house with his mum and dad and play with our grandkids on a weekend. He's a really normal young kid. He used to go to school every day, so when he wasn't on set he'd be in the classroom. Nothing ever seems to have affected him and he's had some good storylines as he's grown up in the show.

There was also the small matter, in fact quite a large one, in the shape of Schmeichel, the Great Dane who Chesney befriended. There have actually been a few Schmeichels along the way.

Here's the scene that has to be one of my all-time favourites. It involved Les, Cilla, Fiz, Chesney... and of course Schmeichel. And the worst planned Jacuzzi in history!

KIRK: (to Chesney) You mustn't go up there

(Schmeichel goes upstairs)

CILLA: (to Les) Well lover, here's to us then!

(Cilla hands Les a slice of pizza)

(Les laughs)

LES : Yes, haha...

(Schmeichel jumps into the Jacuzzi with Les and Cilla)

CILLA: (shrieks) What's he doing 'ere... get off... Les, stop 'im!

FIZ: (from kitchen) What the flippin' 'ecks that noise?

(the ceiling creaks)

And as they say the rest is *Coronation Street* history. The picture of Jennie with a sausage on her fork as Wendi, me and Schmeichel are by now in the living room, yet still in the Jacuzzi, must have been some joke at my expense – but let me assure you I was wearing my trunks!

That scene took two days to shoot and we were sat in that damned Jacuzzi for most of that time.

The problem was Schmeichel. The damned dog wouldn't jump in when it was meant to would it! In the end what you don't see is me grabbing it by the collar and pulling the dog in.

We started working on the scene early in the morning one day and finished it late the next day. The bath was lifted up using a hydraulic pump and we were sat in the bath all day – at least that's how it felt. We waited around long enough because the hydraulics failed – but it became one of those great Street moments so it was all worthwhile. You can watch a clip on YouTube. Whoever has put it on has also shown it in reverse which is also very funny.

Wendi had a flat in Manchester where she stayed whilst she was filming. I would walk her to her flat whilst chatting with her. She was good company. She'd have a drink now and again and come along to some of the social stuff the cast and crew were doing occasionally but she'd normally be off home early and with her family.

You would not believe that she played Cilla if you saw her off-screen. She's much more posh than Cilla would ever be. As I write this book she's currently touring in a John Godber play called *April in Paris* with the Hull Truck Theatre Company.

They split up a winning formula with Les and Janice and then it worked all over again with Les and Cilla. There are plenty who ask me when both Les and Cilla are coming back, and now that Vicky has gone

I'm sure they will soon be asking when Janice is coming back as well. All three proved very popular characters in the show. That's not bad is it, considering we were the family from hell when Les and Janice first appeared.

One of the things that happens in a show like *Coronation Street* is that the directors and scriptwriters will let you change things. They come up with great storylines, but sometimes they don't quite feel the lines the way the person who is playing the character feels.

Les was an explosive character and boy did he need to explode! There were times when I knew that what was written on the page wouldn't be what Les would say. I knew him. I knew how he would say things. He wouldn't mince his words because he was a very straight-talking guy. I also knew what his reaction would be to others' lines, how he would become this raging bull.

The Street's hierarchy let me play Les as I saw him, as I felt him. When I said something along the lines of 'Les wouldn't say that' they would tell me that I could say it my way. There would be a quick canter upstairs to get the new dialogue cleared and then off we would go.

I really was adamant about some of the lines that I was given. Lines that I felt Les would never say. I'd go out for a drink with some of the writers and I'd be telling them that what they had come up with as the storyline was great and largely what they had written was brilliant but there were some things Les would just draw the line at. Most of the time my problems with what had been written was that the words they had used seemed to me to make Les out to be a bit too nice.

John Stevenson and Peter Whalley are two of the best scriptwriters *Coronation Street* has ever had. They have both done loads of other things – John also wrote the TV comedy *Brass* starring Timothy West. John once told me after I'd left the show that no-one had questioned their dialogue and actions as much as I had. I was doing a concert in aid of victims of asbestosis and he'd come along. He said: 'You read it, questioned it. You know we can't get it right all the time as writers and you would say 'I wouldn't say that, or do this'. We respected that.'

It wasn't really the words that I changed, it was more the phrasing and the action that was needed. I just knew Les and how he would be if he was in real life which, as we all know, is what quite a lot of viewers think it is at times.

If Les was due to say something to Roy Cropper, for instance, it might be written in the script: 'Don't say that to me Roy.' By the time I'd got hold of it and charged it up to Les Battersby at full throttle the tone that I would give to the same, or similar, line would give the impression that I'd just said 'You f***ing say that to me again you little sh** and I'll f***ing well knock your lights out!' Of course I couldn't say that, not those words, but the way I conveyed it through slight tweaks to the script and all the pent-up anger and venom Les could muster is what would be seen on-screen. There was no sense in Les being seen as some pussyfooting bloke. When he had something to say he said it hard.

Another example of how Les would react in his very over-the-top manner was when Spider the Eco-Warrior was in the show. Toyah loved him and eventually went down to London to live with him. He was playing his didgeridoo. Martin Hancock played Spider Nugent and was in and out of the show, always creating some kind of mayhem. In the script this constant sound of Spider playing his didgeridoo got to Les. It was getting on his nerves, but in the script the writers had just put that Les was supposed to knock on the door.

Les doesn't do knocking, that was my thought. And Les certainly wouldn't just knock on a door if he was going out of his head with some incessant noise. I just thought there was no way Les would have any of that messing about when all that needed to happen was the noise was to be stopped. I felt Les would just kick the door down, so that's exactly what Les did. He always saw himself as a man of action, someone who would do something without any clutter of pleasantries getting in the way. He wouldn't ask someone to stop something he didn't want happening, he'd tell them to their face.

I remember my line was something along the lines of 'what the... is that?' and Spider simply said 'It's a didgeridoo Les'. I just said: 'Well from now on it's a didgeridon't!' And I got away with it with the writers because they liked where I'd taken the scene.

When you are a member of the cast of *Coronation Street* you soon realise just what a national treasure you are involved with. I don't think there is enough praise that can be given to the show. It is a great feeling to be a part of it all and fills you with pride, but it is also a factory in its own way. The hours can be long and arduous. Okay, it's not exactly a heavy, shifting and lifting kind of job, I'll grant you that, but it's the kind of job that takes its toll in other ways.

There were plenty of times when I didn't feel good enough to be there. That doesn't mean I ever felt my own performance was substandard, it's just that I was in awe. When I was sat next to members of the cast, as we went through our scripts in the Green Room, I would wonder whether I really belonged there. It's at times like those when you question your own ability. I asked myself several times during my stint in the show, 'Am I really good enough to be here?'

If you're looking for me to 'dish the dirt' about any of them in this book then you will be bitterly disappointed. What every cast member says about *Coronation Street* is absolutely true. It is one massive family right through from the scriptwriters, crew, cast, canteen and every other part of this show that celebrated 50 years on ITV in December 2010. Like every family it has its own share of falling out within, but I can't say that I ever suffered.

Whilst I had my own insecurities about whether I would ever measure up to actors such as Bill Roache and Barbara Knox I did play Les for a long while so I guess I must have been doing a few things right.

I did also get a few things wrong. One of my most spectacularly embarrassing moments involved Anne Kirkbride (Deirdre Barlow) and Bev Callard (Liz MacDonald). I was sat in a smoking room at the time. I think I was trying to get my head together for a scene and had a script with me. Anne and Bev were deep in conversation talking very naturally. I thought nothing of it at first, but then Bev said to Anne 'you don't look that old'. Anne sounded really upset with herself. She said to Bev, 'I do. They all think I'm that old.'

Anne sounded so upset that I really felt for her. I jumped in quickly, trying to help and offer words of comfort to reassure her, because she is a beautiful woman. I really had thought Anne was getting upset about her age. I said: 'You don't look that old at all Anne. In fact you look absolutely gorgeous for your age.'

That's when they both ran out laughing their heads off. I was thinking 'Oh God what have I done now? What have I said?' I needn't have worried, apart from the fact that I was going to be totally embarrassed by what they said when they came back. They were still smiling and trying hard not to laugh too much when they returned minutes later. And it didn't last long before they were howling with laughter again. Let's just say I'd misjudged the situation and hadn't quite grasped what was going on. You'd think I'd have known wouldn't you?

They were in hysterics. In between their laughter and tears, because they had been laughing so much, Anne managed to get out the words to say: 'O Bruce, thank you for that lovely comment, but we were just rehearsing.'

That's how good these people I worked with for over 10 years really are. They can be sat anywhere chatting and you honestly cannot tell where the line is sometimes between real life or acting.

Anne and Bev wouldn't let it go either. They had gone out of the room because they didn't want to laugh in front of me and embarrass me, but that didn't last. They couldn't stop themselves when they came back. They were like two giggling schoolgirls and they had told everyone else whilst they'd been out for a few minutes. When I walked through everyone started on at me. I saw the funny side of it though, once I'd overcome my embarrassment.

I hope they won't mind me saying but the great matriarchs of the Street are Barbara Knox (Rita), Eileen Derbyshire (Emily) and Betty Driver (Betty). I love all three of them dearly and I could talk with them all day about anything; but the one thing I didn't like to have to do was to say horrible things to them or about them in the script. To me there was something wrong with all that. I know it's only acting but these three ladies are women who deserve respect. I was always mindful of what they might think of me, but I was more concerned that they were ladies who should not be shouted at in the way Les would.

When I had a script that meant I had to rant and rave at them; and maybe say some words that I felt as Bruce Jones were unacceptable, I would go and apologise to them beforehand. I would tell them that what I had to say was terrible. I wanted them to know that I had respect for them.

Of course, as you would expect of three great actresses, as well as being wonderful women, they would say: 'What are you apologising for? You've got to say it? You're acting.' That's all very well, but when you have to call someone like Barbara, when she is playing Rita, a jumped up old tart, or whatever else the scriptwriters came up with I wanted to be careful. By having a word with them beforehand I always felt a little better.

Making every word and action come alive and count on screen is what everyone tries so hard to achieve. There are inevitably some who manage it better than others and more consistently.

This is where I want to pay my own personal tribute to Bill Roache. We all know he has appeared in the show from its beginning. Having spent a decade in the Street I know some of what it takes to maintain and develop the character you are playing, but to play a role into a sixth decade is a remarkable feat.

There was a time when his character was labelled as boring, and there was an implication that Bill was a boring man himself. It's a similar thing that happens to all of us. What I can tell you is that I have seen first-hand, on-set just how far Bill goes into his role. He goes in deep as I do and he constantly creates a performance that sets the standard for the show. I suppose there are those who would say that after you've been playing a part for over 50 years it must come naturally, but that's not the point. Bill becomes Ken every day as I became Les every day.

The mental effort it takes to put in the performance he has given year-in, year-out is outstanding. I've seen him give so many great performances. I've had tears in my eyes when he's finished it, because I know what it has taken out of him.

One of the scenes I most enjoyed with Bill was when Ken Barlow, Fred Elliott and Roy Cropper set up the Historical Society and we were all dressed up as either Roundheads or Royalists. It wasn't the deepest, darkest scene ever in the Street but it was a lot of fun. Bill also played in the *Coronation Street* cricket team that Charlie Lawson (Jim MacDonald) ran for a while. I did a spot of bowling every now and again but I was useless at batting.

The cheekiest of the funny scenes I had would have to be the loft scenes when I was going through from one loft to another in each of the terraced houses. This was a scream. It was a bit like going back to my childhood days when we would hide from the other kids during our games. In these scenes I had found out that you could get into the other houses and I was planting pornographic magazines under Emily Bishop's (Eileen Derbyshire) couch so that Norris or Emily would find them. They did give me some fun stories, as well as the loud, aggressive stuff.

I've seen many actors cry after they have completed a tough scene. I've also seen a number of actors weeping at the performances given by their colleagues. There are times when none of us want to come out of our dressing room for a long time because we need to re-emerge smiling and put ourselves back in the real world.

Kevin Kennedy (Curly Watts) is another fine actor who could fall apart on screen, in character; and also turn you into an emotional wreck watching him perform. He broke my heart watching him break down in one particular scene on camera. He went into that zone too, where he was no longer Kev, and I watched him go that day.

Kev is one of my favourite people and is a great friend. He went through some really bad experiences and has had to cope with a lot, but he's come through the other side. He was on the bottle whilst he was in the Street and ended up in hospital. It's all well documented; apart from this next bit.

The cast had been told not to go to the hospital to see him. I wanted to see him, to be there for him as a mate. I remember sneaking into Crumpsall (North Manchester General Hospital). After all, I'd been in and out of there for injuries over the years, so I knew my way around and how to get to most of the wards. I entered the hospital from the rear. The press were hanging around, presumably looking for their next *Corrie* story about Kev.

The reason why the guys who call the shots at the Street had told us not to go and see Kev was because they knew he was in a bad way. I knew I could get into trouble with them for going. Kev was just laid there shivering under the sheet and I held his hand. There's no wonder we had been told not to see him, he looked awful. His wife Clare and his mum came and they thanked me for being there.

Thankfully that's all way behind him now and he's in good shape. He's been dry for 13 years. When we last talked he was appearing in the Queen musical *We Will Rock You* in the West End. And just to prove he's now whiter than white, he appeared in one of those Daz commercials as well, where they use ex-soap stars. Kev's a very clever bloke. He's a good writer and has written and directed his own film.

When the character you are playing is involved in heavy, engaging storylines your workload increases massively. You may not be in front of the camera every second of the day, but you need to be there when you're needed and mentally you need to be prepared for when you are. The days in *Coronation Street* vary dependent upon what the scenes call for. You can work through the night; early in the morning; or the regular shift of getting in early and getting home late. There were times when I seemed to be there twenty four seven and that can sometimes take its toll.

Whilst I was with the show the cast was always involved in putting on charity shows for the Variety Club. We would play theatres in Manchester and at a number of other grand theatres throughout the area around Cheshire and Lancashire. We devised sketches and routines, and it was a rewarding diversion from the Street. It kept us all in touch with live audience work and the fans came out in their droves to support what we were doing for such a worthy cause. I would be going back in time a little, to when I was on stage with Eddie.

But you can take on too much and a combination of major storylines, concert and personal appearances started wearing me out. Fortunately my employers at Granada Studios realised the tremendous stress I was under in coping with everything and they checked me into The Priory centre at Altrincham in Cheshire in February 2000. This was where Kev Kennedy (Curly) had stayed for his alcoholism treatment after having been in North Manchester General; and I think the management must have thought they didn't want another cast member going the same way.

I was doing the day job to the best I could, but with trying to juggle everything else my life was totally packed out and I was left exhausted.

I was only there a few days, but it at least took me away from everything and had helped recharge my batteries.

As we all know, there's a time and a place for everything; and whilst Kev's experience was obviously a low point for everyone there were plenty of daft times when some of the *Coronation Street* family acted quite differently to what you see on screen. Some of our moments in the Green Room should have been filmed. I'm certain everyone who watches the show would have loved to have seen some of the things that happened off-camera.

When you get a lot of blokes and girls together – and steady now, before you go there, this is not what you're thinking – who are all up for a bit of a laugh things can sometimes get a bit out of hand! And there were plenty of pranksters and wind-up merchants around the team.

The chief wind-up merchants were Stevie Arnold (Ashley Peacock); Simon Gregson (Steve MacDonald); Alan Halshall (Tyrone Dobbs) and me. There were plenty of others too but we were the main ones. What happened was that we'd be sat learning lines, but after a while get a bit tired of it. Someone would start us off by flicking a rubber band at someone's head and it would kind of grow from there. You know the kind of thing that used to happen when you were kids. Before long it was all out war. It was like being back in primary school. The more mature members of the cast, and I'm not necessarily meaning by age but by nature, who might have been in the vicinity at the time, started getting out of the way. They would go off to their dressing rooms whilst the riot took place.

That only made us worse. Given the room to ourselves and with all the usual players it escalated from rubber bands! It was playful. We were just lads, grown men of course in my case, but lads winding each other up and enjoying it at the same time. There would be words thrown about such as: 'You f***ing do that again and I'm going to throw this f***ing settee at you!' They might just have been my words come to think of it. The settee was a challenge! And yes, the settee would be thrown. The whole room would by now be in uproar, but we'd be laughing about it at the same time.

Stevie Arnold got his comeuppance one day as a result of yet more winding up. Stevie had been messing me about, as usual, and so I got hold of him by the neck. Somehow or other he managed to get me on the floor and was sat on my chest. He had my arms well and truly pinned and said 'get out of that' obviously thinking there was no way I could. But what he hadn't banked on was that I would use any means I could to get him off and my mouth was still free! I won't tell you exactly what happened next, but picture the scene. What I can tell you is that my next move brought tears to his eyes and he said he'd never pin me down again!

There were others who were always great fun to be with too. I think a number of us clicked because our backgrounds were similar. Michael Le Vell (Kevin Webster) was always good to be around; Sue Cleaver (Eileen Grimshaw) was definitely in the wind-up category. She might not have thrown any settees, but she was as capable as anyone of enjoying herself at others' expense. I keep in touch with Kev Kennedy and Stevie Arnold; and Vicky phones now and again. I also see Bev Callard and Denise Welch regularly. I had some great times with Denise whilst she was in the show, although I didn't know she was getting up to what she was until I read her book.

Sean Wilson, who played Martin Platt for a long time, was another good mate. He's done really well away from television with his cheese business, The Saddleworth Cheese Company which he started 2 years ago. I love his catchphrase for it 'I bet you didn't know I made cheese'. He is a great lad and also a great chef. He likes mastering anything that's difficult and his cheeses have already won awards. I don't think he named one of them after me but there is one called 'Mouth Almighty'! He's also a great fly fisherman. He ties all of his own flies, whereas I just either button or zip mine up. Wa-hey! You can use that if you like! No? Okay. Anyway, I had the privilege of going fly fishing with Sean and we caught two big trout.

One of my great friends outside the show at the time was a man called Dougie Almond who ran a hotel in Marple. Dougie knew how much I wanted to learn how to cook so one night he presented me with my whites, my coat and chef's hat, and stuck me in the restaurant kitchen and started teaching me how to cook. When Sean and I had caught the trout we headed back to Dougie's hotel and he let me cook them. Because I wasn't a trained chef he couldn't sell them so we handed out portions for people to taste around the bar. Watch out for me in Gordon Ramsay's kitchen show one time. That would be something wouldn't it, if I came in as Les Battersby.

Dougie also had the Red Lion Inn in Marple before he had the hotel and he used to tell a funny tale about another *Coronation Street* legend Percy Sugden, who was played by Bill Waddington. Bill was never some shy, retiring type. He had been successful in music hall and he owned a 150 acre farm and horse stud in Cheshire where he bred racehorses until he died. The reason why I tell you that is he used to go into Dougie's pub and order half a bitter, then he'd ask for a couple of lettuce leaves or a tomato for his sandwich he was going to have back at home. Dougie once told me: 'That man owns 12 racehorses and can't afford lettuce!' He left the show a few months after I joined, but what a character in real life as well as the one he played on screen.

The Street also gave me the opportunity to work with two of the UK's most enduring actors. Sir Ian McKellen and the late Sir Norman Wisdom brightened up the cobbles with their characterisations of dodgy novelist Mel Hutchright and fitness fanatic Ernie Crabbe.

Whilst you've read plenty of words like lovely, wonderful, brilliant and great to describe nearly everyone I ever worked with on the Street inevitably there were some who failed to match up to the high standards the show needs. I'm not going to name their names here, mainly because I can't actually remember what their names were, but also because there's no sense in embarrassing them. Who knows, they might have gone on to achieve something bigger and better elsewhere.

The scriptwriters brought in a couple of lads who didn't last long. I was supposed to have this big fight scene with one of them. That morning I arrived at work and we were preparing for the scene. We had a stunt man who I had worked with on *Raining Stones*. I had done all my own stunts, but he had been there for advice. He was in the Street to offer his expertise again. Because he had worked with me previously he was telling this young lad that there would be nothing to worry about with me, and that he had taught me everything I knew about making stunt fighting look real on the screen.

If this lad had seen the fight I'd had with Bob (Hoskins) on *TwentyFour Seven* he might have realised just what was to come. The stunt man, who's really well respected on the Street and has taken part in loads of films, took this young lad out on to the cobbles. I think he was playing a character that was something to do with Leanne, maybe a drug pusher or a pimp.

He was full of himself and I just thought he didn't look right for what we were going to do. He certainly didn't look as though he was concentrating on what was going to happen. I asked him if he was alright with it. I still wasn't sure about him when he said he was okay, so I asked the director. The stunt man came out of the Green Room, where he was going to watch the action, and he reassured us. He said that he felt the lad would be alright. He'd spent two hours with him and that should have been more than enough.

'So why's he smiling all the time?' I said to anyone who wanted to hear. I was seriously concerned about this. He was just grinning from ear to ear. I didn't think he was taking any of it seriously. Fight scenes take a lot of co-ordinating to make sure that no-one actually gets hurt. They also need to look right and I just couldn't see that this was going to come out well. I couldn't get my head around why he was smiling all the time. He just said: 'It's fine. It'll be a doddle.'

That did it for me. I could see he wasn't switched on to what we were here for. I thought I'd better get him thinking the right way. There's nothing wrong with being full of yourself. God knows, I've been too full of myself at times but not on-set. I felt he just needed a little bit of guidance. So I tried to put him right:

'Listen mate, I've been here two and a half years my friend and it's never a doddle no matter what you do. Every day here is the hardest day's acting work you'll ever do, especially today. Now get your act together, wipe the smile off your face and let's get to work.'

When we shot the fight scene I smashed his nose, cut his cheek, blacked his eye. The director shouted 'cut' as though he was throwing in the towel in a heavyweight boxing match. The stunt man stepped in like a referee getting in before the next big blow sent the lad into next week. He didn't go with the punches.

I thought I was in trouble at first but the stunt man said 'Bruce, it's not your fault. He was fine on the stunts when we were rehearsing.' What a waste. It wasted my day, wasted theirs – and the lad ended up with a smashed up face. That's why when I'm on-screen I always concentrate hard on what I'm doing. You can have a laugh and a joke away from it all, but when you're there in front of a camera, that's when you have to be serious. You've 12 million people watching you.

I've seen actors come into *Coronation Street* for 6 months and not even last that long because they cannot cope with the shift you have to put in and the standard you have to keep up. That's what the viewers want and what they expect. Dedication is everything. All those actors currently playing in the Street, *Emmerdale*, *Eastenders* and *Hollyoaks* will know what I'm talking about.

It doesn't matter whether you use method acting or any other form of the profession, if you're going to give it your best shot you must give it 100%. That's how I was with Les and every other role I have ever played.

CHAPTER TWENTY EIGHT
QUO ON THE STREET

So here we are and here we are – and here we go! It's time for the Quo!

This had to be one of my favourite times in the Street, and I was responsible for setting the ball rolling to make it happen, for my favourite band Status Quo to appear on the show.

I've always loved them, right back to the early 70s, so it was great that the scriptwriters wrote that Les was their 'greatest fan'. Tony Wood had taken over as producer. He told *Music Week* magazine, when they were writing a piece about Francis (Rossi) and Ricky (Parfitt) coming on the show, that Les's liking of Quo had emerged in the storylines over the years. He felt that Quo were the right kind of music for Les to be into in the show, and that he could imagine Francis and Ricky drinking in the same kind of pub as Les.

I had been to see them a number of times over the years but I'd never met them. Filming schedules had restricted me from seeing them play live when I was in the Street but I was made-up when my tickets arrived to see them at Manchester Apollo on a night when I was free. I'd rehearsed my script for the following day, left the studio, got home, showered, suited and booted. Sandra looked fantastic as ever. We were on our way. This was to be another one of those really special moments that you could never believe would happen.

We arrived early at the Apollo, bought a programme and were shown to our seats. We'd been sat there for about 10 minutes when a hand tapped my shoulder. The owner of the hand said: 'Mr Jones, the band is Backstage and heard you were in. They'd like to meet you.'

Sandra and I were ushered backstage by this 'man with the hand' who turned out to be their manager, Simon Porter. There were people busy everywhere, running around, sorting lights and sound, organising sound checks and tuning masses of guitars. As soon as we saw them and they saw us Francis and Ricky clapped their hands and cheered. I was being applauded and welcomed by these guys who were Rock Gods so far as I was concerned. I should have been applauding them.

We were offered food and drink. It looked as though they had enough for a wedding reception. They were on good form and we talked about music, acting and show business. I was having a great time meeting my idols. But then it all came to an abrupt end. It was getting close to 7.30pm and I just thought maybe they were getting ready to go on stage and wanted a few minutes to get themselves together. As Sandra and I were starting to make our way back to the auditorium Francis and Ricky said we should come backstage later to talk again and have a drink.

As we were going back to our seats I asked Simon if the band was about to start, but he rolled his eyes as if I was some kind of idiot: 'It's nearly 7.30,' he said, 'and you know what that means!' I still wasn't on his wavelength, all I was thinking was that I'd come to watch Status Quo. He tried again: '*Coronation Street*?' I still wasn't there. That's when he told me something that amazed me and led to another great experience and a wonderful few weeks in the show.

'The boys never miss an episode of *Coronation Street*. They won't go on stage until it's over; and they always watch the current episode because they keep right up to date. They are massive fans.'

Because the boys are from London, you would probably think *Eastenders* would be more up their street than the Street but not so.

When Francis, Ricky and the rest of the boys hit the stage that night they rocked the Apollo for two solid hours. They did everything from *Rockin All Over The World* to *Down Down*; *Whatever You Want*; *Caroline*; *Paper Plane*; *Marguerita Time*; *Break The Rules*; *What You're Proposing*. They did the lot, every hit they'd ever had. The place was full of fans wearing denim, just as I did in the Street as Les. It was a brilliant night and they even mentioned that I was in the audience. The place erupted when the spotlight was turned on to me. I was stunned. I was very nearly a rock star. At the end of the show I was mobbed by fans. Everyone wanted an autograph. Simon managed to push his way through to save me and Sandra.

Backstage again Francis and Ricky confirmed what Simon had said was true: 'Yeah, we never miss an episode,' said Ricky. 'But don't tell anybody because we've an image to live up to,' said Francis. Then something clicked in my brain and I just came out with it. I asked them whether they would like to be in the Street, to appear in the show. It wasn't something I thought would ever happen, and obviously it wasn't up to me, but I said I could at least put in a word with the people that mattered. You don't get anywhere if you don't ask.

I'd been playing air guitar to their records in the show; and I was excited about the prospect of them appearing. I had no idea how they might be written into the show or whether the producers would be interested. We exchanged telephone numbers. I told them I would give it a try. I said I'd have a chat at work but couldn't promise anything.

The following Monday morning I went to see Kieran Roberts, who was our producer prior to Tony Wood, and told him all about our night with the boys. When I told Kieran how keen they were in coming on to the Street, I think he was as stunned and surprised as I had been. This was one of the UK's best-loved bands and they were offering themselves to the show.

I didn't hear anything for a while, but just when I was thinking what I had said had fallen on deaf ears I got a call to visit the producer's office. Tony had taken over as producer. I'd been hanging around a bit saying that Francis had been ringing again to ask whether there had been a decision yet about them coming on. The boys really wanted it. They'd got Simon to email Tony, so there was some pressure being put on.

Tony's major concern was bringing in existing stars as cameo appearances, playing themselves. He worried that this would mean that *Coronation Street* might lose its way a little. Bringing in celebrities to act as themselves is difficult in soaps. This fictitious area called Weatherfield wouldn't be such a magnet that a star of TV or films would appear every week.

We'd had a few celebrities in the show and I can understand what he was bothered about. Nobody wanted the show to become another celebrity-based programme.

In the end it was the scriptwriters that came up with this wonderful storyline that saw them beat me up, call me the 'ginger berk' and provide me with one of my greatest moments ever on the Street. Stephen Russell wrote the script.

Ricky and Francis are drinking in the Rovers because Francis has a

20-year-old whiplash injury from a fan coming on stage in Doncaster. The fan tries to grab the leather thong he wears on his wrist and then stage-dive off with it. Unfortunately Francis was still attached to it. He has borne this grudge against this idiot for the past two decades and the line goes: 'If I ever see that ginger berk again...' It goes from there... They're in the pub to get a brandy to help with the pain Francis still feels constantly.

It's Chesney (Sam Allen) who sees them before I do in the show. He just mouths the words: 'Francis Rossi...' Chesney tells Kirk that Uncle Les's favourite band Status Quo are in the Rovers and Kirk says they need to find Les and tell him. Unfortunately Les is out in his taxi. They try him on the radio but he's skiving as usual and doesn't answer the call.

Chesney worships his Uncle Les and sees this as a chance to do something nice. He goes to get Les's denim jacket for Francis and Ricky to sign it, but when Les sees it he thinks Chesney's forged it. The storyline at the time was that Chesney was telling lots of lies; and Les had got to the stage where he didn't believe a word he said. Both Francis and Ricky were taken with Sam's confidence. They were so blown away, by how well he went in and out of character, that they gave him a signed guitar – a Squier Fender Telecaster.

When Les relents and thinks that maybe Quo might have been in his boozer after all, it's nearly too late. They are getting in the van to leave. The van gets under way. Les is running down the street telling them not to go; and that's when they realise this is the guy – the ginger berk – who was responsible for Francis's neck injury 20 years ago.

Francis is first out of the van. He goes straight for Les and knocks him out. Then Les gets up and Ricky knocks Les out. Stewart St Paul co-ordinated the fight scene and I think the boys were a bit more worried about it than me. But they're always good with one-liners. I said: 'Have you shown them how to hit me?' and Ricky just came straight out with: 'It'll come naturally!'

What didn't come naturally, and you don't see it in the show, was the opening of the side doors to the van when Francis and Ricky were supposed to get out. It was comical really, being sat on the pavement waiting to be beaten up by rock stars who couldn't even get out of their own van! I guess Charlie West must have sold them it.

Here's pretty much how that scene played:

(Les comes out clutching his old Status Quo LPs)
(Status Quo's van is on the move)
(Les runs, shouting)
LES: Francis!! Rick!!
(Les bangs on van at junction to the Street)
LES: Hey... ey! I'm you're Number 1 fan! Come back!
(The boys see Les running just behind the van, then nearly alongside)
FRANCIS (to RICK): It's him isn't it? The ginger berk...
(The boys realise who it is, they come back, by now Les is on
the pavement in tears that he's missed the chance of seeing them)
LES: They've come back. The boys! Wa-hey!!!
(They get out of the van)
                    (Les holds up the leather thong!)
LES: I took that off you at Doncaster, the Alhambra ...!
(Francis does not look happy)
LES: ... I think... 1980-summat...
RICKY: Francis don't...
FRANCIS: 20 years of pain...
(Francis wallops Les – Ricky picks Les up to knock him down again
Les starts crawling away and Ricky picks Les up again, Francis hits Les again
Then it's Ricky again – they scoot off back into their van and disappear)

Cilla realises there's potential for a bit of compensation to be got out of this situation since the band are rock stars. She and Les are going to get married and she sees this as another perfect scam. First, she wants to get married to Les for the wedding presents they'll get, then she reckons Les and she will get loads of money by suing the band. But Les comes home after going to the solicitors and doing a deal with their manager telling her: 'there's something far better than money. The Quo are going to play at their wedding.' She's not impressed!

As a result of the beating Les had been given he ended up in a neck collar too, as well as Ricky and Francis. I'm making a wild guess that this was the first UK TV show featuring three neck collars in the same scene.

The boys really were taken aback by Wendi's performance. They thought she was frightening. When Les decided to be a proper rock God, by trashing the room, what he hadn't realised was that he was trashing their own wedding. Cilla decided to trash him.

Here's how it went:

(In the hotel room – Les, Francis & Ricky are all in their head collars – Barney their roadie is there too)

LES: Let's let bygones be bygones eh?

We can be mates – start again!!!

(Les goes towards them – arms outstretched – he's happy)

(Francis goes as if to hit Les again)

LES: I tell you what, times have changed... I didn't think you'd have a dressing room as smart as this in the old days...

(Barney tries to get Les out of their room, they don't want Les with them)

BARNEY: Les, can you come outside please...

(Les carries on oblivious)

LES: It's like an army barracks... I thought you two were dirty rock 'n' rollers!

BARNEY: Les...

LES: The Quo have gone posh!

FRANCIS: Barney...

BARNEY: Come on outside...

LES: Some of us are still young at heart thanks to you lot. You know you're one of the most important things in my life…. Straight up...

BARNEY: This way Les...

(Barney tries to usher Les out, Les skirts around him)

LES: Ey,ey,ey... I can 'elp you reclaim your youth... if you can't do it, I can do it for you... there's one thing I've always wanted to do... is trash a room like this... hey, hey!

(Les starts throwing things off the dresser)

RICKY: What are you doing?

LES: You spoke!... Come on lads, join in, trash the place!!!

(Les pushes everything off the dresser on to the floor, smashing all the wedding presents)

LES: Live a little... come on join in... wa-hey!

(Les throws a lamp stand and Francis dodges it)

LES: One last ambition... a TV out the window.!!!

(Les picks up the new flat screen TV)

LES: Do the honours lads!!

(Ricky opens the window)

RICKY: There you are then...

LES: This one's for Keith Moon!

(Les lets it go)

LES: Wa-hey! ... Now that is what the Quo's dressing room should look like!

Do you feel at home?

FRANCIS: Well not really... it's not our dressing room...

(ENTER Cilla, with Kirk in tow)

CILLA: No ..!

LES: Whose room is it then?

KIRK: It's the present room Les...

LES: (incredulous) The present room?

CILLA: Our Present Room... Our presents!

(Cilla grabs a black bag)

LES: I've trashed our presents? ... I don't believe it, why didn't you stop me?

CILLA: I'll tell you for why shall I?

LES: Cilla... honeypot... I wasn't to know!

CILLA: Because no-one could expect you to be that stupid and useless. You've ruined everything you brainless pillock!

We only got married for this... and you're stupid, stupid, stupid...

I hate you...I detest your very bones!

You're half a man... you're gonna wish you'd never married me!

Your life will be hell on earth Battersby... you think you're going

near me, think again... a burning pit of agony that's our marriage!
Worst mistake of your life!

(Cilla throws black bag at Les as she leaves)

LES: How was I supposed to know!! This stuff looked too good for us...

(Ricky is laughing)

(Les goes in search of Cilla)

(Ricky, Francis & Barney all exhale together)

BARNEY: I don't fancy his much

FRANCIS: He's married that!

RICKY: Poor sod!

BARNEY: Look lads, you've got to do a full set haven't you? 4 songs ain't enough...

FRANCIS: Nah, it's plenty...

BARNEY: Come on, it's no skin off your wattles...

(RICKY turns to FRANCIS)

RICKY: Well it's up to you, my neck'll get better...

FRANCIS: Compared to him I got off lightly, she's a life sentence.

Ricky and Francis told me they had loved every minute of their time on the Street. Having them on the set was like a dream come true for both me and Les. Everyone made a fuss of them.

During their time on the Street I told Francis about a rare guitar I had called a Fender Flame. I didn't play it any more because when I'd had that accident to my wrist, with the cowling, at the factory years ago it had stopped me from playing it. He said he'd heard of it but he'd never seen one before, so I brought it in for him and gave it to him as a gift.

About a week later Francis called me to let me know that he thought the guitar I'd given him was awesome. He'd heard the Flame was a great sounding guitar but now he knew how good it was. A few weeks later I got a call from the *Coronation Street* office. A parcel had arrived for me at the gatehouse. The parcel contained a white Fender guitar, the exact same model that Ricky plays, signed by him.

The next day I got another call from the *Coronation Street* office. Another parcel had arrived for me at the gatehouse. This time it contained a handmade replica, in exactly the colours that Francis has, of his special edition Fender. Both guitars were thank-yous from the boys for my part in getting them on the show.

The songs Francis and Ricky played as Status Quo in the Les and Cilla wedding party scenes were recorded at a local recording studio. The location used for the party was one of the bars in the studio where we could go after work on the set.

CHAPTER TWENTY NINE
KIRKY & ME

The funniest scene I ever played in the Street is when Les and Kirky (Andy Whyment) pretended to be gay. The thing is it's not just the storyline that was funny. What made it at times hilarious in filming were Andy's reactions. The scene revolves around Les and Kirk convincing the council woman they are a couple.

Andy is usually a very funny guy and very dry, but he wasn't at all happy on this day. The writers, God bless them, had come up with this brilliant scene where we had to be very touchy-feely. I thought it was going to be very funny but Andy didn't want to do it. I think he even complained 'upstairs' about the script. He just didn't want to do the scene and I said to him 'Look it's only acting'.

As part of their plan Kirk and Les had photographs of them taken together. They had positioned them so that the council woman, who was interviewing them, would see that they were to all intents and purposes a settled couple. They wouldn't have been allowed to continue living there if we weren't. It was one of those scenes that you just knew the scriptwriters had already laughed their socks off whilst writing.

What offended Andy most of all was that in the script I had to put my hand on his leg. I knew he was really annoyed with the scriptwriters and when I did it the first time he moved it away and said 'cut'. Then he turned to me and said 'You see he can't stand anything like that.' I knew. We all knew. And I think even those dastardly scriptwriters had an inkling.

We tried again. The same thing happened. And again. And again. Andy's face was a picture. He really didn't want to go through with it on screen. He wouldn't let me do it. This was by now going more than just pear-shaped. We got a bollocking from the director who came downstairs and said 'What are you doing?'

Andy would just say: 'He put his hand on my leg... Don't put your hand on my leg (to me)... Do something else, but don't put it on my ****ing leg.'

We started again. This time I touched his hand.

'Cut! ... He touched my hand!'

It took the longest time to get that scene. The crew were falling apart. Andy was getting more and more annoyed. I just said: 'Andy you're a ****ing actor for crying out loud, get on with it. Whatever happens here you're alright. You're not gay, I'm not gay. Let's just do it.' Then I went to the director and told him that I was going to kiss him, right on the lips!

By now we all just wanted to nail it, so I said to Andy that the producer was on his way. We had taken four hours doing this one scene and it wasn't a long scene at all. We had to get it over with. Andy finally agreed. He'd go with whatever I did! Little did he know what was coming!

Knock on the door – bang, bang, in walks the council officer and off we go. We love each other don't we? Yeah. I put my hand on his leg; then I started rubbing it up and down his thigh. He couldn't move! He knows he's in for a bollocking otherwise. I'm saying 'Kirky' to him in as effeminate way as I can muster. I put my arm around him. It goes on. I hold his hand and pull him close. She said: 'Well I can see you're both in love.' I said 'We are'. At this point I pulled him to me and kissed him full on the lips!

The following minutes were so funny. He shook his way out from me and I saw the way he was looking. I was off!

He chased me down the street shouting: 'Come here you ******** (too many words to put in here, make up your own!) I'll ******* kill you!'

The place erupted. It was like I'd upset someone at school and they had been waiting outside to get me. The actors in the Green Room were all howling with laughter. They had all been watching this unfold on the monitor, but at least we finally got the scene.

I loved that scene so much – and how Andy reacted – that I re-enact it on stage as part of my own show. I get someone up from the audience and watch their reaction. Of course you have to choose the right one. I don't think I'll be asking Andy to do it with me if he ever comes along – but then you never know!

CHAPTER THIRTY

LOOKALIKES, BOOTS, ONIONS... and DYING

There are now hundreds of people who pose as lookalikes of celebrities, whether they are actors, singers, politicians or footballers. You can always tell when you've become reasonably famous, because there will be a lookalike of you. There's nothing wrong with them earning their own money from posing as the character, so long as it is done in a law-abiding way.

Sometimes though I wonder how people get away with even being called a lookalike. When you look at someone who is supposed to be Michael Jackson or Elvis you do wonder what kind of mirror they have at home.

I had a few Les Battersby lookalikes around the country, there may still be a few today, but I had a real problem one time. This particular lookalike must have been close to how I looked, because he had posed as me in a restaurant and had racked up a bill of £1200 before doing a runner. The restaurant contacted the *Coronation Street* office and I was hauled in. They asked what I had been doing that night. I didn't like the way things were heading so I got Stuart, the press officer, to sit in on the conversation and we showed everyone that I couldn't have been there. I don't think they ever caught up with the imposter. So beware fake Les Battersbys wherever you are.

Product placement has always been something that TV shows have had to be very careful about, but I had two instances where I did quite well out of 'inadvertently' promoting products through my time with *Coronation Street*. Companies are always looking to save money on massive advertising campaigns by getting their products on display in TV programmes and films. If they can get their products placed on the soaps it is even better for them. It's a subtle technique. They supply the product they think would suit a character, so that it doesn't look out of place and won't arouse suspicion. You wear it or use it on screen but with no guarantee it will be shown. Somewhere on the way it appears on screen and they've saved thousands of pounds on advertising and you've received some free gear. I believe that's how it works.

I had a man from a boot company who liked me very much. He had good reason. He gave me a pair of his company's boots and said if I got them on to *Coronation Street* I could have boots for free for life. I started wearing them as they fitted in with Les's image. The sound crew loved the boots and so I went to my mate who'd supplied them and he got pairs for all the crew. Soon the whole camera and sound crews were walking around in the same boots. In fact that was the reason they found me out, but not before these boots had been on TV for ages.

Then there was the pickled onions moment. This wasn't whilst I was on the *Coronation Street* set but when I was appearing on *Ready Steady Cook* with Vicky (Entwistle). On the programme you have to supply your own ingredients and I'd taken two cans of Guinness, no surprise there; a piece of beef and a jar of Maynards onions. I even showed the jar to the camera and said I loved them. It was as big an advertisement as you can get. I'd started my professional career in commercials so maybe it was rubbing off.

It was the last week before Christmas when they broadcast the show and the next day I received six boxes of 20 jars of pickled onions. That's 120 jars. I know there are a few people who probably think I'm a bit pickled. Maybe this is why.

They arrived at the studios, so I took them up to my dressing room and piled them up in one corner. Charlie Lawson (Jim McDonald) was one of the first to get a jar. I think most of the cast and crew ended up getting their share. At least that's one time when I was in a right pickle for the right reason.

Instead of being in a pickle, try nearly being at death's door. Many actors will tell you how far they will go to land a part, but I guess not many will have nearly lost their lives on the set. That's how it looked one day when Wendi (Peters) and I were filming a scene. All I had to do was open the door to No. 5 but as I reached out for the door a pain shot through my arm and chest. I fell. The pain came again. I didn't know what was going on. Everyone thought I was having a heart attack. A doctor from Granada studios came. He sent for an ambulance. Members of the cast and crew were crying and I could hear someone saying 'we're going to lose him'.

By the time I arrived at Manchester Royal Infirmary the pain had increased. A nurse stayed with me. I had six ECGs, but it hadn't been a heart attack. They found that all I had been suffering from was dehydration. I survived, but unfortunately I wasn't to survive in the show.

CHAPTER THIRTY ONE

GEORGE, ALEX & CONWY UNITED FC

Appearing in *Corrie* means that you are privileged to meet and become friends with famous people. You might never have had the opportunity to come into contact with them otherwise, and I was extremely fortunate to count the great George Best amongst my close friends.

I've always loved football, and although I'm a Manchester City diehard there is one footballer from my generation who everyone loved. He was the kind of footballer we all wanted to be and it didn't matter at all that he played for the other lot.

George was a regular at the Midland Hotel in Peter Street. It's a big pub and was built to serve Manchester Central Railway Station. The two of us would sit and talk over in a quiet corner every Friday night. I chatted with him about his great times in the 60s and 70s and about the women he'd been with. It was lads' talk and I just loved it. He was great company.

We were generally left alone. The waitresses in the hotel knew who we both were so they managed to keep people away from us, although we both signed autographs when fans of the Street and football came over. There I was each week chatting with the world's greatest ever footballer.

One time we were joined by Alex 'Hurricane' Higgins. He and Georgie were both from Northern Ireland and knew each other well, but Alex was going through a bad time. Alex had met me before and he was always saying 'Brucie, Brucie... any chance of a drink?'

I got to know Alex really well, but it wasn't the same as when Georgie and me were together on our own. That was special. I remember one time getting up to go home. I think it was the first time Alex had come over. George mouthed: 'Next Friday, if...?' His actions were meaning if Alex wasn't with us. We enjoyed our time when it was just me and him together, but Alex stuck around and the group became the three of us. It still ended up being a good trio. George, me and Alex! The world's greatest footballer, the world's greatest snooker player and me, not exactly the world's greatest anything. Don't go 'aww' whatever you do. Sadly they have both passed away now.

If only George had been a bit younger I could have brought him back out of retirement to play for Conwy United. I was chairman of the club for two years and did my best to help when the club was in financial trouble in 2004. Neville Southall, the Everton and Wales goalkeeper started his playing career with them. I had been approached by a guy on the board. The previous chairman was leaving. I paid for things like the interior of the club premises to be redone with stage and new lighting. I bought lawnmowers and things like that for the ground. There have been all sorts of reports that I put in huge amounts of money. I did help out when they were in dire straits but it was only a couple of thousand pounds or so.

CHAPTER THIRTY TWO

DEANO & DIANA ROSS & NEIL DIAMOND

One of the nicest things that happens when you're on a show like *Coronation Street* is that you occasionally get invited to go along to see someone you really would have paid to see anyway.

The whole cast and our partners were offered the chance to be in the audience to see Diana Ross. It was one of those *An Audience with...* programmes.

Half way through the filming, although I don't think it ended up getting used, Diana Ross said 'Where's Bruce Jones?' I couldn't speak. I just couldn't believe she'd said my name. I went on stage and not only had I lost the power of speech, I just stood there gawping at this beautiful woman with the most fantastic hair. She said she'd heard a lot about me and that I was very funny.

I'm now on stage with Diana Ross who I've danced to for years at discos. She also brought H from Steps (Ian Watkins) on stage and said she was going to dance with the two of us. I still couldn't move. I was transfixed. I've got Diana Ross next to me and all I can do is look at her. I totally froze for the first time in my life on stage or in front of a camera. Bless him, H managed to snap me out of it. What an embarrassment, everyone could see me there just with my mouth open. Fortunately I don't think either H or me made it through the editing stage of the show. Thankfully we must have been left on the cutting room floor. It was the one moment when I was grateful for editing equipment.

Before the celebrity reality programmes started the only other TV shows featuring celebrities were either game shows or *Celebrity Stars in Their Eyes*. In 2002 I got the chance to perform as one of my idols on that show.

I've always loved Dean Martin's voice. I prefer him to Frank Sinatra. There had already been one *Coronation Street* Special of the show in 2001 and due to its success they came back for a second go at us. This time it was my turn, along with Sue Cleaver (Eileen) who sang as Judith Durham of The Seekers; Jennifer James (Geena Gregory) as Shania Twain; Kev Kennedy (Curly) as Bryan Adams; and Nikki Sanderson (Candice Stowe) as LeAnn Rimes.

The press were always making a big thing about my drinking, so when it came to thinking about which Dean Martin song to choose I thought of *Little Ol' Wine Drinker Me*. I didn't just practice, I had a voice coach to help with phrasing and singing. I'd never sung on TV before and I had to sing the song four times. I was more nervous performing on *Stars in Their Eyes* than anything I had done before. Matthew Kelly presented the show.

The show made me a suit fitted out exactly like Dean Martin's which cost about £1000 so I was told. They bought two pairs of patent black shoes, the shirt and gave me a black wig. I was sat on a bar stool singing with a barman in the background. I was shaking all over. Hold on, I think that's a cue for a very different song.

Nikki won with *Can't Fight The Moonlight* and rightly so. I was happy to have been in the show and they let me keep the specially-made Dean Martin suit which I still wear. If I hadn't been Deano my second choice was going to be Kenny Rogers singing *Ruby, Don't Take Your Love to Town*. What the experience taught me though was that singers should sing and actors should act – and never the 'Shania' twain should meet.

One of my favourite singers and also Sandra's is Neil Diamond. I met him when I was recording a show for ITV with Paul O'Grady. Neil Diamond was in studio for the *Parkinson* show. I asked the producer if I could say hello, never thinking I would get chance to talk with him. We spoke for a few minutes and I told him Sandra had all his albums. That's when he told me she hadn't got all of them. He then pulled out a CD from his bag. It was his new album which was due out the following month. He signed it and gave it to me saying: 'Now she has all my albums.'

CHAPTER THIRTY THREE

KICKED OUT OF CORRIE

LES BATTERSBY
Coronation Street
1997 – 2007
First appearance: 4 July 1997
Last appearance: 6 May 2007

It reads a bit like a headstone doesn't it? Right, are you sitting comfortably? I'd like to get something straight here. Why did I leave the show? As many actors have said before, and my story is similar, I didn't just leave, I was pushed. I wasn't officially sacked, but I might just as well have been because the way in which circumstances led to my departure left me with a great deal of sadness. In official lingo my contract wasn't renewed

You know the saying 'all good things come to an end?' Well this was it. Now I'm not stupid, even though I've done some pretty stupid things as Sandra will tell you, but you just know when you're not wanted, you get a feel for it. It feels like the whole world is against you, it feels like everything you've worked so hard for is slipping away. And no matter what you do it seems as though you're hitting your head against a brick wall.

I know that characters in *Coronation Street* generally only last for a certain length of time and I had done quite a spell, but it was still hard to take. I thought Les had become one of the most popular characters at one time, but things change. What was harder to take though was the way it was done. It was as though everything just slotted nicely into place for me to be given the boot. I can't say there was a conspiracy because I never saw anything like that, but when you get paranoid about everything going against you that's what you tend to start thinking.

Liz Dawn and me at one of her great charity nights.

The BAFTA award we won for *Coronation Street*.

Sandra and myself at an awards evening.

Two great wives – Janice Battersby and Cilla Battersby-Brown – getting to grips with each other. Two great actresses too – Vicky Entwistle and Wendi Peters.

Samia Smith (Maria) and Georgia Taylor with me at another big night.

Wendi Peters played
Cilla brilliantly and is
such a nice lady.

Here I am lining up as the next Ricky Hatton for a charity show, in a sketch devised by Roy Hudd who was in the cast of *Coronation Street* at the time.

Just like me – my mum took a shine to Sam Aston (Chesney).

My *Stars in Their Eyes* appearance as Dean Martin singing *Little Ol' Wine Drinker Me.*

Steven Lloyd, who organised everything behind the scenes for this book and looks after a number of bookings for me. Thanks Steven.

I used to be a striker! Here I am displaying my talents warming up for a charity match.

A press shot of me in *Coronation Street.*

Status Quo on the Street. Francis Rossi and Ricky Parfitt are great guys.

John Stapleton presented the TV programme *My Favourite Hymns* and I chose mine.

You see just how much I knew how to bow to HRH Prince Charles. Steve Arnold (Ashley Peacock) looks as though he's about to burst out laughing at how low I've gone.

The FA Cup – it's ours,
Manchester City's, this year.

Another charity event – this time
I turned salesman, selling flags for
£20 each.

"PUT HIM DOWN, LES, I'M NOT HAVING AN AFFAIR WITH PRINCE CHARLES"

Fantastic newspaper cartoon of me and HRH Prince Charles. It does both of us justice, but not Vicky (Janice).

Visiting the Armed Forces in Cyprus.

Poster from one of our many charity nights. This one at the Plaza Theatre, Stockport.

In Pantomime as Fleshcreep in *Jack & The Beanstalk* – Winter 2007-08 at The Playhouse Theatre, Weston-super-Mare.

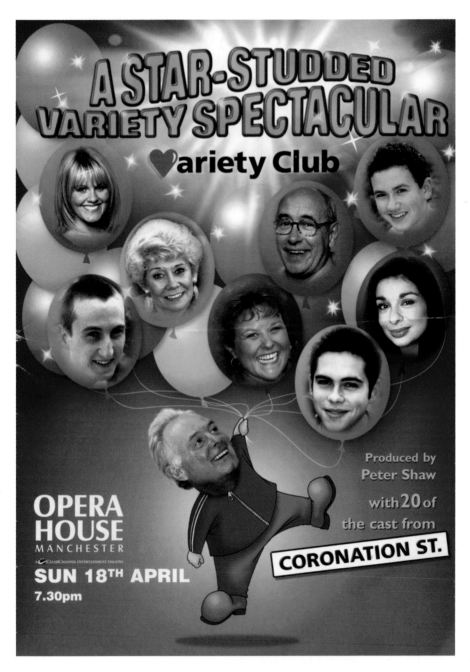

Variety Club Spectacular at The Opera House in Manchester.

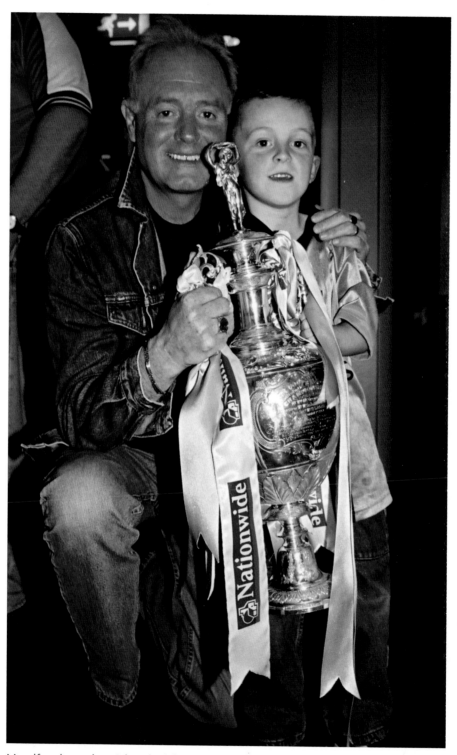

Myself and grandson Jake – look how good he is, he's already won a cup!

Sandra and me at home in our garden.

I love the North East and here I am with two of my greatest friends – Steven Lloyd (far left) and Ronnie Oliver (far right). Ronnie started me off with writing the book before handing over to Chris Berry. Ronnie is one of the best funny men around.

The man who got the whole story out of me. My good friend and great writer Chris Berry.

Little Charlotte Speddy - she needed lots of money raising to help her and we as a team of friends managed to get her the help she needed. We won a team award in the local newspaper.

Come Dine With Me – with Natasha Hamilton from Atomic Kitten; Roy 'The Legend' Walker; and Yvette Fielding.

Sinitta and me – enough said!

In May 2007 this is how the *Daily Mail* reported what had happened.

CORONATION STREET'S LES AXED FROM SOAP

Coronation Street actor Bruce Jones, who plays resident layabout Les Battersby is to leave the show, ITV has announced. Jones, 54, is currently suspended from the soap over allegations of drunken antics in a family restaurant. Les will not be making a return to *Coronation Street*. Playing the head of the family from hell, the Battersbys, he arrived on the Street in June 1997 with loud-mouth wife Janice, daughter Leanne and step-daughter Toyah. Les quickly became a popular character on the Street for the past 10 years, until his suspension in March. *The News of the World* reported that the 54-year-old launched into a foul-mouth tirade at The Old Rectory restaurant in Stockport, Greater Manchester. It was claimed he insulted fans and discussed forthcoming *Coronation Street* storylines - including the outcome of the on-going Tracy Barlow trial. Jones is understood to deny the newspaper allegations strenuously. While Jones is out, the Street would be welcoming back Danny Baldwin, played by Bradley Walsh with the actor said to be discussing a comeback with the show's producers. Les's character is currently written out of the soap - he is currently a roadie in a band – and will not be appearing again, ITV said. The news was released in a brief statement from ITV:

'ITV today announced that Bruce Jones will not be returning to his role of Les Battersby on *Coronation Street*. Bruce's current contract will not be renewed when it ends in September of this year. The character of Les will not be seen back on screen. His absence is currently explained by nature of the fact that Les is travelling as a roadie for a tribute band. A decision is yet to be made as to how the character will be written out. It is likely to be linked to the departure of his new wife Cilla – actress Wendi Peters had already decided to leave the show in September at the end of her current contract.' Producer Steve Frost said: 'Bruce's portrayal of Les Battersby meant that Les quickly became a classic *Coronation Street* character who will be remembered for many years to come. However, after 10 great years we feel we have reached the end of the road with storylines for Les. We wish Bruce all the best for the future.'

The statement also included a quote from the actor. It said, 'I have had a fantastic time at *Coronation Street*, but the time has come to move on and try my hand at other things. I have already had some very exciting offers and I am looking forward to what the future holds.'

And this is how the *Manchester Evening News* reported it:

CORRIE SACK BRUCE JONES

Coronation Street star Bruce Jones has been axed from the soap. The actor, who had been suspended from his role as Weatherfield layabout Les Battersby, will not be seen on screen again. Earlier this month Bruce, 54, had his six week suspension extended by a further four weeks as soap bosses investigated allegations that he launched a foul-mouthed rant about his co-stars. He was originally suspended after allegedly downing several pints of Guinness and revealing the top secret outcome of the Tracy Barlow murder trial. The former soap favourite was called in to see Street producer Steve Frost at ITV Granada's Quay Street HQ in Manchester today and given the news.

Pick the bones out of that lot eh? I think you get the general idea. They wanted rid of me. Like I said, that wasn't really the problem. All roles come to an end eventually, it's just a matter of how it's handled. Different producers have their own ideas and Steve, as he pointed out in the press releases, just didn't want me. I could handle that. It had been getting trickier for a while because when you know that the main man doesn't really have faith in your character any longer you feel so powerless.

You want to do something to prove that your character can still play a part in the show, but then you can't do it if you're not given the storylines. It happens to every actor in a soap at some time or other. Even Bill Roache had only anticipated being in the show for a few weeks back in 1960. We all live from one contract to the next, nothing is ever infinite.

I think Steve saw Les and Cilla as pantomime characters, which they were to an extent, but funnily enough he'd been at Emmerdale when the

Dingles were brought in as a farming version of the Battersbys. Pantomime was the way the scriptwriters had taken Les, and how Cilla had come in.

I honestly don't have any hard feelings about the decision to finish with Les because at the end of the day it's a business decision. The programme makers have got to do what they feel is right.

My problem was the way it all came about and the way I feel they seized an opportunity to get rid of me through unsubstantiated newspaper talk.

Since I've been gone from *Coronation Street* the general feeling I get from viewers I meet is that I'd left because of a drink problem. Hold on a sec! Barman! I'll just have another pint! Joke, folks, joke! But as you can see that wasn't the case at all through the statement from *Corrie*. And they didn't put any of it down to anything else. One newspaper had said that: 'During a 19 pint session at The Old Rectory in Stockport, Cheshire, Bruce was said to have cracked jokes about Pakistanis, made sexual jibes about Wendi Peters and called other stars w***ers.'

The *Daily Mirror* interviewed me properly and they printed my reply which was: 'They said I slagged all these people off when I didn't. That cast to me is like a family so I wouldn't call anyone a w***er. I never swore. The manager of the hotel would have thrown me out.'

So what did actually happen around this time? Well this is how it went, the whole sorry saga that was used as a way of levering me out of *Coronation Street* in my own words for the very first time.

Sandra and I had been over in Spain on holiday. I had met this guy in the airport at Malaga and we had got talking. He was sat at the opposite table to us with a friend. He tried talking to us but Sandra could smell the alcohol on his breath, so could I. We tried to ignore him. I went to the toilet and when he came back he said he recognised me. He started talking and said he'd been doing some work with Gary Lineker.

He said he was involved with people who often booked TV celebrities abroad and that he knew someone in Dubai that might be interested in me going over. This Arab guy he worked with had clubs there and would probably offer me a lot of good work.

He contacted me a few weeks later. He reckoned that I had a great chance of being offered a job in Dubai worth £10K. I was on £120,000 a year in the Street, but at least this might have gone towards another new kitchen for Sandra!

And it was Dubai. I'd not been there before so it sounded like a good place to go, the money sounded good and it would be a nice holiday.

This bloke said he'd set up a meeting where I could meet the other guy, from the company who were going to book me. He said they would come to meet me at a hotel somewhere close to where I lived and they would pick me up.

I didn't know it at the time of course but I was being set up by the *News of the World*. As we've found out whilst writing this book I certainly wasn't alone in suffering at the hands of this thankfully now defunct newspaper. The *News of the World* ended up costing me my job and these two guys were both in on it together, probably both journalists.

Now look, I'm a bloke who likes a drink. Everyone who has ever known me knows that I enjoy drinking and talking with people. Yes, sometimes I get loud and oafish when I've had more than I really should, but I just couldn't have drunk what they reported I had. In fact I was nowhere near it. I remember everything about that day. I wasn't drunk at all even if I did have a few.

I met with these two arseholes, there's no other word for them and what they did to my career, at The Old Rectory in Stockport. It's a nice place, very handy for business meetings. We had a drink and some lunch. I had gammon, egg and chips. I didn't finish the meal, I don't eat much. They said they'd get a bottle of wine. I only drink wine occasionally and I didn't want any that day. I went through to the bar area for a smoke, then came back in.

They started talking to me about Bernard Manning. There was no talk of the job in Dubai, but I just thought they'd get around to it in the end. Being sociable I said that I knew Bernard Manning well and his family, and that our families knew each other from my days in Collyhurst; and of course I'd been on the variety club circuit with Clarke & Jones and had played in Bernard's club. They asked me if I thought Bernard was racist. It didn't floor me as a question because I just thought they were making small-talk. One of the two blokes, not the one I'd met on holiday but the guy who turned out to be the reporter was of Pakistani origin. I'd just thought he was asking me about Bernard because of that. Maybe this guy had a chip on his shoulder about him.

If I'd thought for one minute they were from the *News of the World* I would have been out of there like a shot at this point. I told them that they'd have to ask Bernard himself. They started pestering me to give an example of Bernard's humour so I did. The bloke of Pakistani origin said he didn't think what I'd said was very racist.

Maybe I'm a bit naïve. Yes, I can see you nodding your head. You're thinking how could I have been so stupid and so gullible? All I was doing was chatting with people in a hotel, like I do. I really didn't think much of it. I was a bit fed up with questions about Bernard Manning but it didn't make me ask why they were asking me about him. I just accepted their questions without thinking where anything would lead.

We'd had the meal by now. I'd had another drink. I was having another smoke when these two women came up to me. They looked a bit like mother and daughter and they were dog-rough. They said the usual thing: 'You're Les Battersby aren't you?' and we had a brief chat and a laugh when one of the women said her boyfriend lived in Norfolk, bred pigs and was a pig tickler for a living. She explained what one of those was; that he made sure the male pigs ejaculated, so then we got on to the subject of wankers. It was all just pub chatter whilst I had my cigarette. I told them that I needed to go back to my meeting but the *News of the World* bloke saw them and invited them to join us.

Yes I know, it doesn't sound very businesslike does it. Why invite two total strangers to a meeting when you are supposed to be talking about a £10K contract in Dubai. Except they weren't strangers were they? At least they weren't to these other two blokes. That's what I surmised afterwards. And still the Dubai job hadn't been mentioned.

I'm not a businessman, I don't sit around in meetings watching how people get shafted by others. I'm just a guy who enjoys a pint, likes chatting with different people and doesn't see things coming, obviously. Well I was going to find out exactly what was coming my way wasn't I? Although not yet; not until after this day was over.

More wine appeared. There must have been that many bottles of wine on the table and I didn't touch one!

Actually I did touch two bottles, but not to get a drink. An elderly couple had walked in and they were celebrating their 60th wedding anniversary, so I went over and gave them a bottle of red and bottle of white and wished them a happy anniversary. They were very grateful and thanked me for being considerate.

What happened next might have saved me a lot of grief and who knows, may have also saved my role in *Coronation Street*.

Sandra arrived. My God if only I had gone home with her. Sandra had come in with our granddaughter Sophie and asked if I was okay. She also asked whether we had finished. It was after 6 o'clock by now. Any normal business meeting would probably have been over hours ago, but I'm not a business man am I? We hadn't even talked about Dubai in all the time we had been there.

I think Sandra thought the situation was odd. She and Sophie had come to the hotel in Stockport to pick me up. She saw the journalist there, not that either of us knew he was a journalist at that point. She saw his driver, the guy we'd met in Malaga who had arranged the interview, and these two women. Sandra describes the two women as a big fat woman with dark hair who called herself something like Mrs Popadopolous and who just didn't look as though she was made to be in the hotel at all; and that the other girl looked about 16-17 but was very plain and simple, with a strapless dress, a little necklace and her hair curled in ringlets. Sandra said she thought it was a bit strange that this girl was sat in a pub in Stockport in a restaurant on a Wednesday afternoon or whatever day it was. She remembers that they were meant to be aunt and niece and wondered how they could possibly be related because they didn't look anything like each other.

All I'd done was eat, drink, smoke, answer a few daft questions about Bernard Manning and make general chat. Because we hadn't even discussed Dubai as yet I said I was okay, that I'd stay. Sandra was used to that anyway. She's turned up for me so many times to help me get home, and also to save me from myself, but most times I've just turned her away. What a fool. And more particularly, what a fool I was not asking about Dubai beforehand, not smelling a rat, and not going home with Sandra. I've made some big mistakes in my life. At this stage I wasn't aware how big a mistake I was making here.

But the set-up they had planned was about to go wrong for them, even though in the end they inflicted enough damage.

Once Sandra had gone the journalist (remember that I didn't know he was a journalist at this point) told me he'd booked a room at the hotel and I could use it if I wanted. It was one of those nudge-nudge, wink-wink moments as he clearly gave me the impression that he was talking about me using his room with the two women who were with us! I still didn't smell a rat in terms of some kind of newspaper set-up, but I was now very annoyed about what he'd intimated. I went off the deep end at him.

'My f***ing wife's just been here. She's just gone. I'm a happily married man, me. If you want to take them upstairs you take them and I'll f*** off.' The manager of the hotel was stood right next to me when I said that.

I'd had enough now and was about to leave, but before I did this bastard journalist asked me the question that condemned me. I didn't answer it the way he wanted but it condemned me anyway. He said in a conversational way that he had heard there had been three endings filmed to Tracy Barlow's court case, so was she going to get sent down or not?

I said if he'd heard there were three endings to the storyline then he should go and put £1 on each one and then he'd at least get £1 back. I didn't know what was going to happen. I never knew what was going to happen to Les next, let alone what was going on with other actors' roles. Apparently this journalist knew the ending to the storyline, but I didn't.

When I left the hotel I went to the White Hart pub in the centre of Stockport, but the two women followed me there. I guess they were getting me to think they were just fans. They came over for a photograph and an autograph. I got a taxi home, on my own!

The manager of the hotel told me later that the bedroom the journalist had booked had been bugged. These two scum had set up CCTV and voice recording equipment so that the whole room was wired. These gentlemen, and I'm being very diplomatic with that wording, wanted me to go up there and they had hoped I might go up with the two women they had planted as part of their team. I wouldn't have gone if they had even been anywhere near attractive, but they weren't.

So you see all those elements that were contained in the report about what I am supposed to have done wrong that day were all twisted. I never gave away a storyline at all.

Later, when *Coronation Street* suspended me, saying I'd leaked the story about Tracy Barlow, Sandra found out some interesting information. If there's a crime committed in a soap you can't be seen as having got away with the crime, so it wouldn't have taken the journalist long to find out that she was to be convicted anyway and say that I had told him. There was absolutely no doubt in my mind that what I had been through was a set-up. If only the *News of the World's* demise had occurred four years earlier!

So here are the six things that the media said – and how that meeting led to my downfall:

First, I was supposed to have cracked jokes about Pakistanis: I wasn't cracking jokes about Pakistanis, I was with one and he was trying to get me to say something racist by mentioning Bernard Manning and his jokes. As I told the *Daily Mirror*: 'I am not a racist. I've got lots of black and Asian friends. Jimmi Harkishin, who plays Dev Alahan on the Street said that if I was racist he'd show his backside.' Thanks Jimi, but no thanks!

Second, sexual jibes about Wendi (Peters): I don't know where the journalist got that from but I'm guessing it was something to do with the two women who were there and his invitation to go upstairs with them.

Third, w**kers: I think we know where that came from. I was set up there by the two women wasn't I? I mean why else would one of them have mentioned a story like pig tickling?

Fourth, insulting fans: I guess the journalist wrote that because I didn't go upstairs with his dog-rough women and since he'd posed them as 'fans' that's how he justified it.

Fifth, my foul-mouthed tirade: I can't deny that I got annoyed and said the words I did, but they were when I was being propositioned by this journalist acting as a pimp.

Sixth, the Tracy Barlow storyline: I gave nothing away. Sure, I was asked questions but I had no answers.

I guess until you're set-up you never believe that set-ups like this really happen, and that they're only what you read in books or see in TV programmes and films. But this really happened to me and it gave someone who I felt wanted rid of me the opportunity to do just that. I could still have been written out but who knows, if this hadn't happened maybe I'd be on the Street now.

I was suspended from *Coronation Street* for allegedly giving away storylines. Steve Frost suspended me whilst they 'checked it out'. I told him that what he'd read in the newspapers was a load of bullshit, but deep down I knew he didn't want me back. If you're liked and wanted people will stand by you immediately, and if you're not they will 'check it out'. Eventually, to be fair to him, he did tell me: 'You're not sacked, but I want you to leave.'

There was no chance of staying. I was out. When you get to that stage you have to say things like I did such as 'I'd had enough'; 'I'm looking forward to new challenges'. But I didn't mean it. I was gutted. After ten and a half years in this wonderful show I was gone.

I hope Les returns to the Street one day – and I hope it's me that plays him again.

CHAPTER THIRTY FOUR

OH YES I DID!

What do you do after you've been dumped by the top-rated TV show in the UK, and the character you played is associated with you wherever you go? There are a number of producers who won't touch you because of that. You are too well-known as that character.

What you need is a really good agent and I always consider myself to have been very lucky. When Patrick (Nyland) retired from the agency business Tony took over and it was him who started getting me new work. Tony has his own band Zingari Swing and has regularly backed me on charity nights over the years. That's when the Dean Martin suit comes out again.

My first job since the Street was back treading the boards, on stage in pantomime at Weston-super-Mare. The Playhouse Theatre is a really warm, friendly place just like the people from the town and I was playing the bad guy.

The panto was *Jack & The Beanstalk* and I was the giant's evil henchman. The panto villain and I milked it for all it was worth. It was produced by Paul Holman Associates and played for a four week run from mid-December to mid-January. Sue Hodge who played Mimi in *Allo Allo* was brilliant as Fairy Organic aka Katy Cucumber.

I played Fleshcreep and *The Stage* said 'Bruce Jones uses all his experience to make his Fleshcreep as horrible a baddie as they come.' The local paper said: 'Excited youngsters were leaping out of their seats and booing to the tops of their voices whenever the show's star, ex-*Coronation Street* actor Bruce Jones shouted and rasped his lines as baddie Fleshcreep.'

I was at last getting the type of press coverage an actor likes, glowing reviews. The national press were leaving me alone at last because I was playing a provincial theatre and not on the TV every night.

I was hoping they had moved on and I was certainly trying to. It was working well. It was hard work and I was loving every minute of it. I was back to being an actor, doing what I had always wanted to do.

This was my first professional panto. In fact it was my first ever professional appearance in a stage production, other than some of the *Coronation Street* charity concerts. I'd been in front of the camera for all of my professional acting life. I found that playing the villain was fantastic. I was basically the giant's 'lackie' doing all his bad work.

I kidnapped the princess and made sure I was booed as noisily and excitedly as the kids – and their parents – could manage. It was all good fun and in the end Fleshcreep was tamed and magically put right again.

The house nearly came down every night when I threatened to take Daisy the Cow to slaughter. Remember that one of my jobs when I was younger was working as a butcher. I would kick Daisy's arse during every show. In fact I did it so much that the front end had to swap with the back end after every other show.

Fleshcreep was an ideal role for me to make my reappearance on stage and two years later I did panto again when I appeared as King Rat in *Dick Whittington* at the Contemporary Urban Centre Theatre in Liverpool. My other name in that show was Rattersby – now I wonder what gave them that idea?

CHAPTER THIRTY FIVE

SINITTA

It wasn't long after I'd finished at The Playhouse in Weston-super-Mare that I was offered the first of a number of 'reality' programmes, *Celebrity Wife Swap*. This was one TV programme I wasn't sure about doing. I'd only seen one episode before and at the time I had thought Christ, I wouldn't like anybody coming into my house and taking over from Sandra, telling me not to do this, that and the other. I wouldn't stand that.

I'd rather have been working, playing roles either on stage or in front of the camera, but as most out-of-work actors will tell you, when the work comes you should take it unless you're in the fortunate position of having enough money to be able to say 'no'. I wasn't one of those people, I was 'between jobs' as they say. We had a huge mortgage and I was no longer earning the money I had whilst I was in the Street; but money isn't everything and I was still not convinced this was something I should do. I didn't feel I was quite that desperate for money that I had to do it.

I'd left the Street officially in September 2007, even though I'd not been on screen since May 2007, and we were now into early 2008. The panto job had come up at the right time and although there were other jobs being mentioned there was nothing definite. I started to think that maybe I should do the show.

Tony (Nyland) had made the call to let me know that RDF Media had been in touch to ask whether Sandra and I would be interested in taking part. Another reason I wasn't keen on doing it was because it meant that both Sandra and I would have to live with someone else for a week. Sandra has often said it's bad enough living with me, someone she knows, rather than someone she doesn't, but she agreed to give it a go.

The first thing that Sandra says on the show should have been a warning to whoever was to become my wife for a week. She said that I was quite like Les Battersby: 'I think he wrote quite a few of the scripts in *Coronation Street*. He wasn't acting.'

When I took another look at the show on television, before we signed up for it, I thought, 'What will we be signing up for here?' I didn't realise that you don't know who you're going to get as your 'swap' until they knock on your door. Everything is kept hush-hush, so you could be faced with a nightmare from hell.

Sophie, my granddaughter, had lived with us for a number of years by then and was with me on the day I found out who I was going to have to live with for a week. Our kids are grown up now and have children of their own, but the grandkids are always around. We've never seemed to be without children.

Sandra had travelled down to London ready to meet the woman's husband Andy Willner. I'm saying 'the woman' because I didn't know who I was going to have to live with.

When I opened the door there she was - Sinitta. That's what they do with the show. Your new 'wife' is already in your house when you come home. If you see the show, which is still on YouTube you'll hear me say 'hey-hey-hey!' with a big smile on my face and I do an 'X' with my arms for *The X Factor*. It all started pleasantly enough. I came in with Sophie (she was 15 at the time). Sophie and Sinitta seemed to hit it off straight away. I was a bit wary but it can't have shown because in the show Sinitta says some nice things about first seeing me: 'He's really sweet, he's really soft and warm and friendly and he hugged me a lot.' Those feelings for me didn't last very long.

My first thought when I saw her was what a gorgeous, beautiful, attractive woman – and I remembered her hit single *So Macho*. I thought she'd been a one hit wonder but I found out during writing this book that she actually had four Top 10 hits. One of her others was called *Toy Boy* but I don't think I qualified for that. I thought yes, great, Simon Cowell and all that. But the next week was a nightmare right the way through – for me and for her.

Each wife gets a manual written by the other wife, explaining how they run their homes. Sinitta was given a manual for the Jones household and Sandra received one when she arrived at Sinitta's place in London. She unpacked and then proceeded to look around our home. She seemed to be looking up and down it as though she were looking for cobwebs or a little bit of dust. That's when I really started thinking this wasn't going to work. There was something about her.

She read through the manual and seemed to be mumbling 'housework' to herself. I don't think she was used to this. She was married to a millionaire and had the lifestyle to suit. She has a housekeeper to look after things at home.

What happened during the week was Sinitta tried to change my life. You can't do that to a guy like me. My wife's tried to do it for 30 years and never changed me. Sinitta had no chance, or that's what I thought at the time.

I just thought: 'No, this isn't happening.'

The producers of *Celebrity Wife Swap* tell you to do things because they want reaction. They want things to kick off. They would say to me that Sinitta doesn't like this or doesn't like that, so do it. They knew it would wind her up. If they don't do things like that you haven't got a show, so you're being railroaded into these situations. You're getting paid for it so you accept it. She probably had the producers say the same kind of things to her, I don't know for definite of course, but it wouldn't surprise me.

If you've watched the series you will know the way it works, but for those who haven't it goes like this. For the first three days your new 'wife' has to live under your ways. The second three days are then under the new rules the new 'wife' comes up with.

The first full day Sinitta got up early, made breakfast and made sure Sophie got off to school on time. It's a 2 hour round trip getting Sophie to and from school each day. She did the washing up, vacuuming, dusting and ironing. I would come down and watch my favourite TV programme at the time *Stargate*. I never missed an episode of it. I was in my dressing gown and I could hear Sinitta mumbling something about whether I was going to stay in my dressing gown all day.

I thought our first three days together went okay, not brilliant because I knew Sinitta didn't like any of them. They weren't a great time but they were at least under the conditions I normally live. She didn't like me going to the pub; she didn't like me watching television and she didn't like me smoking.

I've smoked since I was 14. I started off with Park Drive Fives tipped. When I was at school they were 7d a packet. I smoked about three a day and pinched one of my mum's now and again if she wasn't looking. So I'd been smoking a long time. I wasn't going to change. Or was I?

There were plenty of things they didn't show in the programme because they're looking for extremes. I took Sinitta to the pub a few times during my three days. We went to the Bird in Hand at Knolls Green, near Alderley Edge. One of the things they didn't show was when Sinitta got hungry one night and she asked me to order her a Chinese meal from a local takeaway. I asked the landlord whether it was okay to have it delivered to the pub thinking we'd take it home for her to eat. She surprised me by opening it up and eating it in the pub. Everyone just looked and wondered what we should do about it as it's not the done thing to bring food into a pub and eat without getting permission, but the landlord let it be.

In the programme they showed Sinitta coming to pick me up from the pub one night; and then coming out with me and Sophie another night when I was singing with a local band. I thought it was going to be a really good night for everybody. Sophie had invited her friend along, I had checked with the landlord that it was okay for them to come with them being under age. I thought Sinitta might even give us a rendition of *So Macho*. The band could have played it for her to sing along to. We could have even sung together.

But Sinitta took the girls home before we even started. We had only been there about 20 minutes when she said she was taking the girls home because a drink that one of my friends had bought for Sophie contained Malibu. I could understand her concern because of under-age drinking, but I think she used it as an excuse to get out of the pub. I could tell that she didn't want to be there. She seemed very uncomfortable.

Things started getting heated after the first day. The next morning I woke up to the sound of Sinitta doing the housework and making as much noise as possible in order to wake me up. I headed down the stairs to the kitchen for my morning cuppa to be greeted with 'half the day's gone now'. I knew things were going to get worse and I was dreading her rules.

When the rules came in Sinitta called me selfish before giving me the rules she'd come up with. Here's what she said:

'TV is banned for the next few days; smoking is also banned; I have a list of chores for you from Sandra's schedule that you will be taking care of, starting with the school run tomorrow. This will give time to find out more about Sophie. Spending so much time in front of the TV and being down at the pub is a waste of your talent. I've also arranged a workshop at a local theatre college with some young actors who are excited and privileged to be meeting you.'

It was like being read the riot act. She also said that going to the pub was banned; fish and chips was banned; bacon and eggs, banned; all the stuff I like was banned, hidden, unplugged; she wanted me to get up earlier in the morning to go for a walk or find a gymnasium. I moaned but said I would try, but as far as the gymnasium was concerned she could count me out. I ended up going but they didn't show it.

The next morning I took Sophie to school and I know she wasn't happy because I needed to have a cigarette. By that time I would normally have had eight or nine so I thought I was doing well having survived until then. People who don't smoke don't realise how difficult it is to go without one. It drives you around the bend. With Sophie safe at school I headed back home.

You're not allowed to have contact with your real wife whilst you're living with your 'swap' but I wanted to find out how it was going for her. I was hoping that Sandra was having a better time than I was.

When I got back home from taking Sophie to school the first thing Sinitta did was to sniff me. She smelt the tobacco on my breath. I owned up straight away. I told her I'd had a cigarette and that normally by now I would have had a lot more. I felt that was progress, but for Sinitta it was a case of no cigarettes at all. When she had said no smoking there was to be no leeway.

I got on well with the housework chores she had given me. In the show you see me cleaning the toilet; filling the dishwasher; and Sinitta enjoying herself telling me to vacuum; and wipe the TV screen. I knew what she was doing. She was playing a game with me, putting me into Sandra's shoes and getting me to clean a TV screen, when I wasn't allowed to watch the TV, was Sinitta's idea of a joke at my expense.

Sinitta had frightened the living daylights out of me when she said she had arranged the workshop. I'd never done anything like that before. It was bad enough learning at school let alone teaching others. But I have to take my hat off to Sinitta on that one. I loved doing it and it certainly was better than sitting at home watching an episode of *Stargate*, she was right.

They were really interested in my experiences and what I had to say. I told them that in a show like *Coronation Street* if the writers can see that you are working on your character they will write even better for you. I explained the ups and downs of show business to make sure they understood that acting is not about being famous and appearing on television. It's about playing that character, getting into that role and being that person. The students were really attentive and they were genuinely interested in my comments about the acting industry.

I think Sinitta was impressed with the way I took to it. I had been nervous leading up to talking with the group, but it had gone well. Sinitta had also arranged for us to go ballroom dancing after the drama group session. I think she arranged it because I'd originally said no to the gymnasium. We never did get to ballroom dance.

If Sinitta had been impressed by what had happened with the group then she was absolutely livid when I went outside and lit up a cigarette. This was when she showed me just how disappointed she was, but in my defence I'd gone down in two days from 30 a day to two. To me that was a result. Not to Sinitta, it seemed to me that going down to zero straight away was the only result she would tolerate.

After having had a day of it I decided I needed to go for a walk. At home I just said I needed some air but it appeared Sinitta knew where I was really going. She asked whether she could come. I think she only said this so she could check up where I was going and to make sure I didn't. I told her I wanted to be on my own and then she came to find me. I was in the Horse & Jockey pub.

I ordered a pint and sat down. I'd only had a couple of sips and in she walked. She wasn't happy. What you see and hear in the programme is only a very small part of what actually happened. We went outside and I told her she had been out of order following me.

I couldn't believe she had come to get me. I'd only been gone 20 minutes. She said: 'If you can't do something like this for a few days you might find you're on your own for the rest of your life. Your wife's unhappy with your lifestyle and I'm trying to help you.'

I stormed off. When I came back home I told her that Sandra would never have treated me the way she had. All I wanted was a bit of peace and quiet. But later her words did make me think about what I was doing. I thought about Sandra and about our relationship. So maybe she did do me some good there.

What also affected me was that Sophie ran off to her room crying when I came home. At first I thought she was upset with me going to the pub because Sinitta had banned it, but that wasn't the main reason she was upset. I went to see Sophie and realised that she was worried about me. She had never said anything before about my drinking, but from what she told me she must have sat with Sandra on a night watching telly while I was down at the pub and wondered why I was drinking so much.

To my mind I was just having a pint with my mates, the way any normal bloke does, but the way Sophie told me I realised that perhaps I'd gone too far at times. So again, maybe Sinitta had helped in her own way.

I knew that what Sophie told me was for my own good, so when I went downstairs I told Sinitta that what she had been saying was right. My life wasn't fine, it was a mess. I thanked her for teaching me how much I had taken Sandra for granted and that I'd taken my kids and grandkids for granted as well. I told her that I loved my wife more than anything in the world. Sophie's tears had brought that all home to me. I didn't like myself one bit for hurting her or Sandra.

One thing RDF recorded but didn't show was the meal Sinitta and I shared at a restaurant together. We went to this Italian restaurant and the TV company had set it all upstairs so there was just me and Sinitta. Downstairs in the main part of the restaurant were my football idols, Manchester City legends Mike Summerbee and Peter Barnes. When I came downstairs one time Mike called me over and asked what I was doing. I told him what I was up to and that we were only drinking water with our meal as Sinitta didn't want us to have alcohol.

Mike slipped me a glass of wine and I went back upstairs; had a chat with Sintta in front of the camera again and came back down the stairs to go to the toilet. I ended up going up and down those stairs a few times. Sinitta then asked where I was going and I told her I had some friends downstairs, the Manchester City legends. The crew then came downstairs and Peter (Barnes) asked if I wanted a glass of wine. I told him I didn't drink wine – even though I'd had the best part of a bottle by now.

In the meeting that the TV company recorded, when the four partners come together at the end of the week, Andy told Sinitta that he had seen what she had tried to make me give up. They didn't show what he said in the final cut, but he said that trying to make me stop smoking and change my diet there and then was out of order.

. I don't know whether it was meant to, but the show did help me. I now knew, as a result of Sinitta being with me and from what Sandra said when she came back, that I had to change things for the sake of our marriage. I felt that I had learned more about myself and Sandra. I was starting to feel that my time with Sinitta hadn't been wasted.

What happened in the days leading up to the programme being broadcast were not good for me. I wasn't happy with the way Sinitta talked about me on a breakfast television programme to publicise the show. Sandra wasn't happy either but we couldn't do anything about it.

That wasn't all. It had been reported in the media that Sinitta had put on 10 pounds in weight whilst being in our house, but there's no way it could have happened. I wasn't blaming Sinitta for the story at all because I know only too well how things can sometimes be reported. The media said she had eaten a diet of fish and chips and Guinness.

We had fish and chips only once whilst I was with Sinitta. It must have been a bloody big fish and we must have had a mountain of chips! As for the Guinness, she didn't drink any, she doesn't drink alcohol, and we only ate for three days under my rules.

The three days we ate under Sinitta's rules all we ate was rabbit food!

Sinitta then appeared on ITV's *Loose Women*. I don't think she liked me very much. Even so I was still sorry to hear that she and Andy had split up and have since divorced. We might not have seen eye to eye but I knew that in her own way she had been actually trying to help me.

Sinitta has her ways and I have mine. Good luck to her. I've no axe to grind. The one thing I can thank her for is telling me that I was taking my wife and family for granted. Sometimes in life it takes someone else to tell you something like that because you just live your life as you think normal. You ignore the most precious things. The show was good for me in that way, so thank you Sinitta.

CHAPTER THIRTY SIX
PIERS MORGAN & GAY BYRNE

I've appeared on quite a few chat shows over the years, but the two that had the greatest effect on me were being interviewed by Piers Morgan in his *The Dark Side of Fame* series and when I was on *The Late Late Show* presented by Gay Byrne in Ireland. These two programmes were to show me just how much fascination people still have about the Yorkshire Ripper, because both interviewers went there with their questioning. The only thing is that one of them didn't let me know beforehand that he was going to do it.

I appeared on Gay Byrne's show in the 90s. He was Ireland's leading interviewer, the Michael Parkinson of the Emerald Isle. He interviewed everybody and he had some style. He was noted for being controversial and raising issues. The show was the longest running chat show in the world at one time and probably still holds the record although Gay retired back in 1999.

When you're on most chat shows, like *Parkinson*, Des O'Connor's shows and *Loose Women* you're prepped beforehand so that you know what questions to expect and the areas the interviewer is going to go to. With Gay there was none of that.

I had been given the impression that all Gay wanted from me was to know about *Coronation Street* and whether there was any behind the scenes conflict and shenanigans, to use an Irish expression, between the cast. I was happy talking about the show but never commented on the cast other than to say we all worked very hard and we were one big family.

One or two people had warned me about Gay. They'd not been very complimentary about him, but I always try and judge people for myself. By the end of the show I knew what they meant.

It all started well. He introduced me as *Corrie* Bad Boy, Les Battersby alias Bruce Jones and I walked out to a fantastic reception from the Irish audience in the studio. The interview took the course I'd pretty much expected. Gay ran through questions about how I had made it into the

'Number 1 Soap' to become a household name. I was quite pleased with the result given that there was no prepping beforehand. The audience gave me a standing ovation, which was really nice of them and then Gay thanked me for coming over to Ireland to appear on the show. I stood up to leave.

That was the moment when the night turned sour and the air went blue.

As I stood he then asked me: 'Ah before you go Bruce, is it true that you found the body of Jean Jordan, one of the Yorkshire Ripper's victims? Could you tell us what it was like?'

I turned, with a look as though I had just looked at Medusa and turned to stone. I forgot all about the show being live, glared at him and called him a bastard. The studio fell silent. I walked over to him and said 'You want to know about the Ripper?' He could see that I was fuming about being asked this question. Of all the times not to have been prepped this was it, but then maybe that's what the warnings had been about, that this was the kind of thing Gay tried for. He wanted instant reaction. Well he got it.

As you know if you read the earlier chapters finding Jean Jordan's body has been something I have been trying to put out of my mind for many years. Yet here it was again and Gay had brought it, with one swift question, flooding back.

I sat back down and told the tale once again of finding the body. Gay and the whole audience were completely still and silent throughout. I finished and walked off the set and the show ended. Then I waited for Gay to come off the set. I was still upset but I apologised for swearing at him. He had taken me by surprise by his question, as he had probably intended.

Fortunately for me Sandra was there too. I was still fuming about the way Gay had brought up the Ripper and that I hadn't been told he was even going to ask. Back in my dressing room Sandra tried to calm me down. She gave me a reassuring hug and handed me a drink. But still it wasn't over.

As I started to wash off the make-up there was a knock on the door. Sandra opened it and one of the producers came in telling me the phone lines were jammed with the number of people calling in about the show and feeling sympathy for me.

My first thought then was 'shit I've done it here, swearing and having a go at Gay Byrne on Irish television'. But I hadn't done anything wrong. No-one cared about that. Instead I was told that the Irish Prime Minister at that time Bertie Ahern wanted to speak to me.

I answered the phone as calmly as possible and Mr Ahern said he thought I had brought Ireland to a standstill with the interview. Would I meet him for lunch the following day. I told him that we had a flight to catch in under two hours and he said he would book and pay for another flight, as well as booking us into a first class hotel.

I couldn't sleep much that night. The next morning Sandra and I went down for breakfast and the headlines on the *Irish News of the World* were staring at us. It was all about last night's show. There were reporters hanging around the hotel and cameras flashing here, there and everywhere. I just thought I was still going to be in so much trouble, but that wasn't the case at all.

Everyone seemed genuinely interested about the story and wanted to read about it. For once I found the newspapers were on my side. Sandra and I were told a car would be sent for us, along with an escort.

When we met Mr Ahern we sat and talked about television and politics and various other interests, then he asked me if I wanted to talk about the Ripper case. The way in which he asked made a big difference to me. This way it made me feel easier and we chatted for a while. Imagine that, being summoned by a prime minister and not being told off!

The Gay Byrne interview had been a decade before I was asked to appear on Piers Morgan's *The Dark Side of Fame* series which was broadcast in October 2008. Once again I had similar warnings about Piers that I'd had when I was going to appear on Gay's show.

But this was going to be different. There was to be no audience. It would be a one-to-one. Tony (Nyland) went down to London with me and we arrived at this restaurant-cum-club in London. We talked with the production team who told me what was going to happen. This was far more professional than the Gay Byrne interview already.

I was introduced to Piers Morgan, who immediately said to just call him Piers. I'd heard stories about him upsetting people but I found him a fantastic bloke. I spent 20 minutes with him before make-up and even though I was still worried about what he was going to ask me he put me at my ease.

Piers was one of the most relaxing interviewers I have ever had. I felt so easy in his company even though I was very nervous at first. He could have turned me over, and he did get into me with the questions, but he was such a gentleman to me and gave me a very fair interview.

We talked about the job the *News of the World* had done on me with their set-up and he asked whether I wasn't thinking of suing them. I said I had tried but I would have needed a lot of money. I'd already spent £8,000 on lawyers' fees but I would have needed more than £100,000.

He asked whether I had given away the storyline. He asked about the Ripper and Jean Jordan's body. I'd hoped he wouldn't ask about the Ripper but I'd known that he would from our chat beforehand. This time it really hurt me to talk about it and filming had to be stopped several times because I was getting choked up.

Piers also asked 'Why an award winning actor like you, someone who had won a European Actor of the Year award, an Actor's Guild award and someone who had won a Silver Heart from the Variety Club of Great Britain for his charity work was out of work?' He reckoned it was because the press needs a bad boy and that's where they liked to label me.

When we had finished filming I told Sandra this was the last time I was going to appear on a chat show because everyone wanted to talk about the Ripper and Jean Jordan. Sandra told me the same as Tony. People always want to know information about the Ripper no matter how hurtful it might be.

I have appeared on chats shows in Canada. Over there *Coronation Street* is massive. When you get there you really are treated as a star. It's hard to believe that *Corrie* has fans thousands of miles away tuning in to see a drama based on a cobbled street in Manchester. I love the chat shows in Canada, because I have never been asked about the Ripper.

CHAPTER THIRTY SEVEN
ON THE STREETS

So how can you tell me you're lonely,
And say for you that the sun don't shine?
Let me take you by the hand and lead you through the streets of London,
I'll show you something to make you change your mind
Ralph McTell *Streets of London*

My next step into the world of reality TV was in 2009 and this time, for the first time, it was something that I really wanted to do. It also turned out to be one of the most remarkable shows I've ever been involved with too. I really got into the whole programme from the word go. It was called *Famous, Rich & Homeless*.

This time Tony told me the programme was going to be all about living off the streets; to experience what those who live off the streets experience. I thought it sounded more like my kind of programme than *Celebrity Wife Swap*, so Tony and I went down to see the production company Love Productions in London.

They told me who else was going to be in it but the names wouldn't have mattered. What interested me was to know why people live on the streets anyway. I started thinking about whether people who live on the streets really are 'down-and-outs'; how they lived, were they sad and lonely? I wondered whether they were people who didn't want to work. I was up for it and said I'd do it, although I hadn't reckoned on the filming lasting 10 days.

The others who were going to be taking part were tennis player and *Treasure Hunt* TV presenter Annabel Croft; *The One Show's* Hardeep Singh Kohli; journalist Rosie Boycott and the Marquis of Blandford, who was a bloody pain in the arse right from the start and didn't even last a night. I think he took one look at how the other half lived and decided he didn't want to know.

We didn't meet until just before filming started, by then we'd all been checked over by doctors and given various injections in the lead up to the filming.

Our meeting place was a warehouse. There was coffee and sandwiches available as we arrived and we all met up. None of us knew exactly what we were going to do other than live on the streets of London.

We were introduced to John Bird, editor-in-chief and co-founder of *The Big Issue* and Craig Last, a former youth worker for a charity called Centrepoint. We also met our camera teams and security guards. We were each to have two camera teams – a morning team and night-time team. There would also be a roving bus with guards on it.

They stood us all in a line and John Bird stepped up to tell us what it was going to be like living on the streets. Craig then told us what not to do and how to keep ourselves safe. Even though we had camera crews and security he told us we still had to be very aware of keeping safe. I think at this point we all must have started looking at each other. He'd mentioned keeping safe a few times by then. How safe were we going to be?

We all still had our own clothes on at this time, as well as watches, money, credit cards, everything, but that was all about to change. That's when they told us where we were going.

'Bruce you're going to spend 3 days on the streets of Westminster. You'll be brought back in on the 3rd day in the afternoon, back to this warehouse. Now we want you all to strip off.'

They emptied black bags of clothes all over the floor and we were told to dive in and get our clothes. Even though the programme was shown in the Summer of 2009 we were filming this in November 2008. It was freezing, so I got two pairs of trousers, a shirt, jumpers, a denim jacket, an outer jacket and a big jacket. That's when the first row broke out because the Earl of whatever he was wanted the jacket I'd claimed. I told him he wasn't having it and that he should have dived in like we'd been told, but he was adamant he was having that jacket. I still wouldn't give him it and I walked away from him. I told the producers I'd smack him right on the nose. I didn't care who he was.

I think the producer realised that it was a stand-off which he hadn't wanted, so he said: 'Bruce we'll get you a brand new jacket, we've sent out for one, will that be okay?' I asked whether it was as good as the one I still had hold of and when he said yes I threw the jacket at the marquis. He was still a pain because when I got the new one he said 'I'd rather have that one'. Like a kid. He didn't get it – either the programme or the jacket.

Once the clothing had been sorted out we were all dropped off in a van to different parts of London. We really hadn't been told very much at all apart from keeping safe. I was dropped off at Westminster on some alley below Westminster Bridge. It was 11 o'clock at night. I said to the camera crew: 'What do I do?' They said: 'You're on your own, you can't ask us questions'.

I had two camera crew, a sound man, two security guards and there was a roving bus somewhere, but they were way off from me. Now I had to live on my own, on my wits, and survive these three nights. It was minus five degrees, it was freezing. My first thought was I wanted to go home there and then. I was in a part of London that most people know a little due to the landmarks, but I still didn't know too much about where I was at that time of night. The others taking part all knew London much better than me.

I could see the London Eye from where I was. I knew about that because Sandra and I have stayed in London. So I was at least able to get some kind of bearing. I'd got my sleeping bag, but I had no money and no cigarettes. Well I was meant to have no cigarettes but I had managed to smuggle some out with me by pushing them down the front of my trousers.

Where the hell was I going to sleep? No-one was going to tell me, it was just up to me. Unbeknown to me I wasn't far from Cardboard City but I found out later that would have done me no good, apparently it's dangerous and you can't just walk in.

If you sleep somewhere you're not supposed to, if it's someone else's spot, there's an unwritten code that says you can get picked up by both ends of your sleeping bag and the person whose spot you've nicked can kick the living daylights out of you. That was one of the keeping safe notes they had told us could happen.

I went and sat under Westminster Bridge. I didn't get inside my sleeping bag, I just sat on it that night for fear of what might have happened if I'd been caught inside it by someone who could have just thrown me or kicked me about without me being able to get arms and legs free. I must have dozed off because my head hit a wall and I remember waking up about four o'clock. It was still pitch black, I had a cigarette and just sat there.

The tunnel close to where I had been sleeping was lit up, but outside it was pitch black. I sat there for another hour or so, then stood up and set off walking. The crew had just got to follow me. They couldn't ask, couldn't direct me or tell me what I should be doing. That suited me. I was looking forward to making the most of my first day on the streets.

First thing I wanted to do was to see where all these people sleep. I got to Victoria Road, past Big Ben, and that's where I saw them. It was Sunday morning and I was walking down Victoria towards the station and every doorway had someone in it. They were all fast asleep in sleeping bags. I walked into Victoria Station at half past six so that I could get a bit warmer and had my first experience of being treated as someone living off the streets. I was kicked out.

It was getting a bit lighter by now and I started walking back towards Westminster Bridge. I was already making plans for my next night. I was going to sleep under the bridge again. It had a light.

I was taking in my new home for the next few days. I had the Houses of Parliament close by and I reckoned I'd stay in the area. I felt I would be quite safe if I didn't wander out of it. The one thing I hadn't given much thought to so far was how I was going to get money to buy a coffee or a tea and some food.

That's when my first stroke of luck came my way. I was stood at Westminster Bridge and it was somewhere between 10 and 11 o'clock when a couple came near to me. The bloke was trying to get a picture of his girlfriend with Big Ben behind her. They then swapped over and vice versa. I've always liked taking pictures so I said 'Do you want me to take both of you in that picture?' They were made up. And that's when I realised there was an opportunity here.

They were a lovely Italian couple and I explained I was homeless. I didn't ask them to give me anything for taking the picture and I didn't beg them to give me money for a cuppa or anything like that, but they gave me £4 - they obviously knew more about London coffee prices than me!

I had a radio microphone on all the time so the camera crew could hear everything, but they couldn't see how much I'd made. When they asked me I just told them to stand there and film, go away, get out of my face. If I wasn't to get any advice off them about what to do, I wasn't going to tell them what I was up to.

I was now Bruce Jones, freelance cameraman, without camera, but with a franchise for tourist snaps of Westminster Bridge and Big Ben.

That's when my next idea kicked in. Manchester City had been due to be playing Manchester United that Sunday afternoon and it was on television. I had given up hope on seeing the match when I knew I was going to be away filming *Famous, Rich & Homeless*, but now I had a chance of getting to see it and having a pint, something to eat and enough to live off for the next few days. So I took pictures of happy tourists from all over the world until 2 o'clock. By that time I'd made £40. I thought I've got a right money spinner here. That will keep me going for the next few days. And I headed off in the direction of a pub. I didn't know which one would have football on but I knew there would be one somewhere. The camera crew didn't know where I was heading.

I said: 'I can't ask you questions, so from now on you can't ask me them of me.' I got to Liverpool Road, walked down a few back streets and came down by New Scotland Yard police station. There was a copper stood in the doorway at the front.

By now I was starting to make sure that I didn't miss the kick-off, but everything's shut in Westminster on a Sunday. I couldn't even find a pub that was open, let alone one that showed football. So I thought if anyone would know it would be a copper.

He looked at me, saw what I was wearing and how I looked. I told him I was homeless and then he asked me. 'Don't I know you?' I said, going straight into an act because I wasn't allowed to say who I was: 'No, you've never arrested me.'

I told him I wanted to watch the Man City v Man Utd game. He gave me directions where he knew there was a pub open. So off we went -

and the camera crew are now getting happier because they've heard what I've said, so they're thinking right, we're okay here, we're going to be able to get warm, because if he goes into this pub we will go with him. It was freezing for them as well.

When we got to the pub I told the camera crew to put their cameras away and have something to eat, but they couldn't because the programme was all about everything we got up to. It wasn't a social experiment to find out about homeless people. The programme was about us and what we made of life on the streets. I was doing okay, and as it turned out I was taking to it more than the others.

I sat down and there were six blokes behind me. Almost immediately one of them come up to me and said: 'You're Les Battersby aren't you?' There is never any escape you know. All I said was: 'Not today mate'. He said 'Yes you are. What are you doing here?' I managed to tell him something of what was going on.

What followed next was as funny as it was unbelievable. This bloke bought me a pint of Guinness, but he and his mates weren't staying for the match. Instead they gave me £3 each, enough for 6 more pints is what they'd said. Then the landlord recognised me. I was just about to part with the first few quid I'd earned during the morning when he gave me a pint on the house!

So I'd got this £40 in my pocket that I'd made in the morning. Then I'd got £18 from the 6 blokes who'd left, and I still hadn't had to use any of it because my beers had been bought for me. I was starting to think this living off the streets game wasn't so bad after all. I had more cash in my pocket than I normally have when I'm at home!

I thought about getting something to eat, but the match was about to start so I left it until half-time before asking. This time it was the landlady's turn to look after me. Now don't start getting any ideas, it wasn't like that. She pulled me another pint on the house and got me a piece of pie. It was just a normal day for me by now. In the pub, pints and a pie watching a football match with my beloved Man City. What was so different about this to being at home? The only downer was that City lost.

The crew were having some food as well. I think they were dying to know how much money I'd made so far. One of the crew was an Arsenal fan and their game was on next so we watched that as well. By now I had actually bought my first pint. Then Craig, our welfare man came in to make sure I didn't drink any more.

I told him I'd earned the right to go in there. He agreed and told me to do what I wanted with it but to make sure to eat. I told him I'd done just that and I wasn't going to have another drink because I was going to walk the streets until I was ready to go to sleep.

When I came out of the pub I met a lad who was living off the streets. I got talking to him on the way back towards Westminster Bridge and asked him why he was living off the streets. He said he'd had wife troubles and had walked out. He'd just had enough and didn't want to go back. He'd lived on the streets about three years and I asked how he'd coped. He told me he begged. That's one thing we had been told we couldn't do. We couldn't beg. He told me some of the homeless' unwritten rules.

This bloke was living in Cardboard City. He backed up what we had already been told: 'Don't walk in there whatever you do. You've got to be invited into these places'. Then he told me about the soup kitchens, where you can get breakfast. I learned a lot from him in a short time.

The crew filmed him but they never showed the conversations I had with him and others. He said he wouldn't go back to his old life. This was his life now. Here he had freedom, his own freedom with no stress, he wasn't going back to the rat race. He would stay in the welfare centre all day. He told me that if you go in the welfare centre long enough you can use it as an address for the dole to get more money, so he was getting that. It was also somewhere you could wash and change there.

I started thinking that if there were more people like him on the streets maybe this life wasn't so bad. It was my second night now and as we walked back towards my 'bed' I bought a sandwich to take back with me. This time I unrolled my sleeping bag. My friend had given me some useful lessons about sleeping on the streets. He said that if you take your boots off sleep with them under your head, otherwise someone will pinch them.

He was quite a teacher for living rough and I learned quite a lot off him very quickly in an hour or so. I never saw him again after that. He didn't know who I was, or he didn't let on if he did. He didn't even see or notice the cameras. He just thought I was someone new who had arrived and was living off the streets for the first time, which I was. He was gearing me up for a lifetime of this.

One of the important lessons he told me was about the homeless population and how it has changed in recent times. When he told me it sent a shiver right through me. This is what John and Craig had meant by keeping safe: 'There's a lot of Russians out here now, sleeping on the streets, and some of them are very dangerous. They'll kill you for whatever you've got. They are very bad news.'

After he had gone I sat in my sleeping bag and had my sandwich. I fell asleep and woke up in a good mood. The funniest thing was that I could hear people running past me and I remember sitting up and going 'what the fuck are these people doing running through my bedroom at this time in a morning'. I heard the crew laughing at what I'd said.

That morning I went back up on the bridge again and Bruce Jones, cameraman, went back into business. I earned about another £16 quid before quitting for the day. I'd do it again tomorrow. I didn't need much money. You don't when you're living off the streets, just enough to get by. I'd now made quite a bit of money already and knew I could live on the streets and not beg. I got the impression that if you're willing to give a service there are enough people willing to pay for it.

My next experience was living off the streets when it rains. By now I'd walked to Victoria Bridge. The rain started so I went back to Westminster and tried to get into Westminster tube station. I had no chance. They won't let homeless in, so I sat about for the rest of the day under a cover near the station. I went to get hamburger and chips and couldn't get a bag of chips anywhere, in Manchester there's a chippie on every corner.

Once the rain stopped I walked around again. This time I went right around the Houses of Parliament and back to Westminster Bridge ready for my third night's sleep in my temporary 'home'. But first I tried the places that homeless people go to regularly.

I went to this welfare centre and they wouldn't let me in, and later I went to the chuck wagon to see if I could get a sandwich and soup. I got the shock of my life. The queue was full of Russians and lots of foreigners, and every time I was nearly close enough to get served they pushed me out, so I started to argue with them. That's when one just went like that with his hand. He had a gun under his coat. I think one of the security guards saw it and he started to walk away. I knew then that my sandwich wasn't worth the effort. I never went near them after that.

We had been told by the production company that we would be on three-day stints but we didn't know what that meant other than we would be picked up at some time. So this was my third day of Westminster Bridge and Big Ben. My photography business was still doing well, but as for fitting in with other homeless people I now knew what the bloke had told me on my first full day was right. You weren't just accepted because you were homeless.

The morning of the third day saw the end of the first stint. I was told I would have to walk back to the factory – the warehouse where we had started. I thought it would be miles away and wondered why we were walking back rather than getting picked up, because the van had dropped us off. I thought it would take ages to walk back but the crew said we weren't far away and that the others were fairly close by.

As we were walking back I realised just how close I had been to some of the others, or at least one of them! Annabel Croft came walking over the bridge. She told me it was a nightmare and asked how I'd been doing. She said she'd had hardly anything to eat. I'd just had toast and tea for my breakfast, I'd eaten well each day – and I still had a load of money in my pockets. She said: 'How the hell are you doing it?' Anyway I was hustled on by the crew saying: 'Move on Bruce, you can't talk.'

We all met back up again at the warehouse and were asked about our three days. We were asked what we felt, how we had done, what we had experienced and the producers told me I'd done well for surviving so far.

They asked what I'd done with all the money I'd earned and I just said that they'd said whatever money we made it was ours to do whatever we want, so I did what I wanted with my money. Was that okay? And they said, fine.

We were back stood in a line once again. We'd had coffee and sandwiches, something to eat before we went back out again. This time it was going to be more difficult. We were all going to partner up, not with each other, but with someone who had been on the streets for a few years. I didn't know then just how unpleasant this was going to be, but I was soon to find out.

'Bruce you're going to be with an active cocaine smoking addict and he's living in a squat, you're going to spend three days with him. Just be with him, talk to him'. It sounded like they were asking me to help him in some way, but just what good they thought I could do God only knows. That seemed to be what they wanted for the programme, or at least that's the way I understood it - but it turned out I was wrong to think that way. And my God was I in for a hard time from John Bird when I was to come back after this second stint.

They told Annabel that she was going to be with an alcoholic; Rosie was going to pair up with some alcoholic drug addict. That was our debriefing and briefing. Out we went again. This time I wasn't somewhere I knew at all. I had to go to the East End of London where I was going to meet up with this crackhead.

What an experience this was. I can honestly say I have never experienced anything like it in my life and I'd never want to again. I was all set to leave the programme as soon as I saw where they had brought me. If you want to see squalor and the worst possible state some people live in then this was it.

You should have seen it. I was shocked and horrified by what I saw. Even the rats had moved out! We had to climb in to his squat through a hole in the wall. There were 2 damp beds there and it was a cold, horrible place. You could smell urine everywhere. I walked out and went to this pub around the corner. The crew came in. They contacted the welfare officer. I told them straight: 'That's it I'm quitting. I'm not going to go and live in that, no way, why would I subject myself to that? Why would anyone?' I told them I'd had rheumatic fever once in my life and I wasn't to put myself at risk of anything like that again.

Craig, the welfare officer, told me that this young man had lived in there for seven months. I went for a smoke and I looked at this addict who was now sat with the crew. He was only a young kid and I thought he should have plenty to look forward to in life, yet here he was - a crack/cocaine addict – crawling in and out of a hole in the wall to sleep in a disgusting place every night. Maybe I was meant to help.

I said ok I'll stay, I'll do it. I thought that if he could stay seven months I could do three nights for the sake of the programme and maybe for the sake of this young man.

It turned out to be another of the worst decisions of my life. I should have gone there and then. I hated it. This isn't a life at all. Don't let anyone ever try and dress it up for you in some way that opting out of a normal life is the right way if you end up like this. I remember getting into bed, into my sleeping bag and just feeling the damp all around. It was awful, it stunk of urine and God knows what else.

The building was an old block of flats, ready for demolishing and we were in one of the bottom flats that was boarded up. The security guards had to stay in the house as well. I'm sure they were hoping I was going to leave the show because they didn't want to do it. Nobody on earth would want to be here in the damp, horrible, disgusting place.

The crack addict started telling me about his life. He was from the East End of London originally but he didn't get on with his family and he'd moved out. He hadn't got on with his father and it turned out he was a father himself, he had a wife and a baby. He was stealing the money for drugs from his child support money or anyone else he could get it from. His wife had thrown him out on to the streets and he'd been in this squat for seven months as Craig had told me.

I never saw him actually take drugs. I don't know whether he injected with a needle, stuck powder up his nose or swallowed. He would just go through his own little hole and did what he did. I didn't want to see what he did.

When he got up the next morning he told me he was going to go and get a fix. The crew wanted to go with him, but I knew that wouldn't be a good idea. I told him we would wait for him in the café. That would be a safer place for us having been with him there the previous day. We couldn't be seen taking a camera crew near a drug dealer. That could have put him in real danger. An hour later he still hadn't got back. I remember saying 'I bet he's dead'. Anyway an hour later he turned up happy as Larry and said. 'Right we're going into town now. I've got my job to do now.'

That caught me out. I said: 'What job? You didn't tell me you had a job, what you do, where you work, what's all this about? I thought you just lived here and that was it.' He said: 'I give directions in theatre land, people pay me for telling them the way to each theatre then I sell them a copy of The Big Issue. That's how I make my money.'

One of the lessons this crack addict did teach me over the three days I spent with him was how to sneak on the buses in London for free. You get on the middle doors and sit on the back of the seats. I did it for the three days travelling there and back from West End to East End without paying a single fare.

Selling *The Big Issue* on the streets was something I reckoned I could do as well, and at least it might give me something to do that was more enjoyable than this had been so far, and add to my cash. I asked the crew to ring John Bird and tell him I would sell copies of *The Big Issue*. He agreed and said I'd get 16 copies. He said I could keep the money if I sold them all. I was starting to multi-skill on the streets. This was now my second career on the streets in a couple of days - freelance photographer and now a magazine seller. I sold every copy in an hour. Well, we were in 'theatreland' after all and people knew who I was. We sold out of his copies as well and we were doing something together.

That day I felt we had at least got somewhere. That's when I tried to help him get his life back on track and away from this smelly dump he was living in. I said we'd get up early in the morning, go to these toilets where you put your 20p in, and we'd get washed and cleaned up. Then we were going to go to this counselling place to start getting him off crack cocaine. He was up for doing it, or so he said, and he was on about getting his wife and kid back. We went to the counselling place. I couldn't go in with him, but I felt good. I actually felt we were making progress.

Whilst we waited for him I went and had a cup of tea back at the café he used, then he came back and said he was off to the Job Centre next. I said I'd go with him so we were going to go together, but then he said he needed his birth certificate. I asked him where it was and he said it was at his wife's house. He said he'd have to go on his own for it. He reckoned he'd be back for 4 o'clock.

That's when I said: 'You've got a chance here to clean yourself up, get yourself sorted out.'

But it didn't work out. He didn't get back at four o'clock and the café, where we had been waiting for him, shut at 6.30pm so myself and the crew had to come out of there. We ambled around for a while then went back to his nasty, horrible, infested squat.

He returned about nine o'clock and he was totally out of his head. I lost it with him. I grabbed him by the neck, got him against a wall and said: 'I've wasted a day with you. I tried to help you, get you back on the right track, but you don't want help. You need putting down.' I really felt he'd let us down, me and the crew, and the TV programme itself. I thought we were working with him, helping him.

He hadn't been to the house to see his wife. It must have been too much for him. Instead he'd been on the 'smack'. I had a right go at him and I walked off back to a pub for a drink and maybe some more pleasant conversation.

The camera crew followed me and when I got into the pub the barman asked if I was alright. That was when I really found out just how the class system still operates in this country, and how people are judged on their appearance not on who they really are.

There were three ladies together in the bar and I asked if they would mind if I took this particular stool. One of them said: 'How dare you? Who lets riff raff like you in this pub? You smell, you look a mess, you should not be allowed in these pubs you homeless people, you should stay where you belong, in the gutters.'

I stood there, looked at her and then walked away because I wasn't to tell people who I was, but the landlord had heard it and he had a word with the three women about who I was and what I was doing. I wasn't happy at what she had said, but I wasn't in a position to do anything about it. I felt like giving her a piece of my mind.

Once the landlord had a word the woman came up to me and said: 'I'm so sorry Mr Jones.' Her apology meant little to me. She was only apologising because she had now found out that I was not really someone who lived on the streets. I'd met some really friendly people who lived that way. They shouldn't all be banded together and be rubbished by idiots who have never probably been through what some of these people have had to cope with in their lives.

That woman, for all I know, may have been born into a family that was never stressed by money and relationships and where everything came easy. She probably came from a nice, respectable background; but she showed me no respect. I suppose we all make judgements on people by our first impressions. All I had asked was to borrow a stool in a bar. It wasn't as though I was committing some kind of heinous crime, yet she wanted rid of me because of the way I looked and smelt.

It's people like this particular woman that maybe should have an occasional taste of what the other side of life is really like; without the support of good parents, good family and a good upbringing.

Then I found out my crackhead partner for these few days was sat outside, so I gave him a piece of my mind as well. We had another row. I had tried to help him, but he had more or less kicked me in the teeth. I'd then had to suffer that awful, butter-wouldn't-melt, holier than thou, cow of a woman, someone who obviously just enjoys looking down on people. I was not in a good humour. At one end of the scale you've got ignorant, snotty-nosed types who would rather just forget about those who may be underprivileged; then at the other you have people who plainly and simply don't appear to want help. Some seem to be satisfied with floundering.

God knows there are probably thousands of others like this crackhead who don't want to be helped and don't help themselves, but surely everyone deserves to be treated better than this woman felt about me. There are too many people in this world with their heads shoved up their arses.

Not everyone is the same, but life has dealt some of the people who now live on the streets a bad card or two or three. As far as I can make out that's the reason why they are now on the streets. Many of those who sleep rough do so because they haven't been able to cope with what others call a normal life.

I've been pretty close to giving up on trying to live a normal life a few times myself, especially in the past two years, with all that has happened. Maybe that's why I took to a life living off the streets a bit more readily than the others in the show.

My own feeling is that I don't think homeless people, some of the ones I saw at any rate, want to be rescued and brought back into the routine of mortgages, paying for cars, televisions, mobile phone bills and building up debt. That's why they're here, largely, in the first place. For some of them it's because they prefer to be on their own, away from nagging partners and day-to-day family pressures that affect us all. Going back to that kind of 'normality' would probably be too much for them. The reason why they are on the streets is because that's where they want to be. I still can't imagine anyone ever wanting to be where this cocaine addict lived though.

It made me sad that night. The crew looked after me and bought me a pint. I still had my own money I'd earned and I was using some of that, but they took pity on me. They could see how upset I was over the cocaine guy and that idiot of a woman.

The next day, our final day together, we went into London and ambled around. We didn't talk much at first. I was still annoyed and I didn't think there was much more we really had to say. I had wanted to help him and it looked like he didn't want to be helped. That was the end of the story really.

When I did talk, because I couldn't let it go, I just said: 'You told me all this bullshit about your wife and kids and it's just that isn't it? It's bullshit. You went out and got more drugs. Why did you let me take you to those places, go with you and then not follow through? I supported you and then you kicked me in the teeth. You've stolen off your wife, your kid, your father. You're a cocaine addict, doing all this shite, living in this horrible squat – and you know you're going to die in there and no-one is going to know. All you do is count up your money for your next deal.'

He just said: 'That's my life, my next deal.'

I'd tried to help him. I kept thinking that maybe I could get through to him, but it was time for us to go back to the warehouse again. We said our goodbyes and he apologised. I told him not to be sorry to me. I just said: 'You're a crackhead and that's all there is to it.' I found it as difficult to accept his apology as I had the woman in the pub. As Sandra has said to me many times before, words are easy it's actions that speak louder. Their words meant nothing.

I was still all set to quit after that. I'd had more than enough. The first three days had been okay and I'd learned how to live on the streets in my own way, maybe not as a proper one of their community but I'd survived and made enough money to keep myself fed and watered. Then they'd thrown me in with this loser. It wasn't just soul destroying seeing someone like that, it had made me angry. I don't know why people can't see that someone is trying to help and then make something of it; and I just couldn't believe the squalor. The three days with the cocaine addict were awful, but it really did show me how some people live - if you can call it that.

On the plus side I'd developed two other careers in the six days just in case the acting and television jobs dried up.

When we returned to the warehouse we all had some horrendous stories. Annabel had a knife pulled on her in the soup kitchen she had gone to; Hardeep was ready to quit. I think he'd had an even worse time than me.

We were back stood in the line, six days in to the filming and totally knackered. John Bird and the care worker came out . They started off nicely enough telling us we had all done well. It proved to be the calm before the storm. We were in for quite a shock. They said Annabel had done a lot for the partner she was with, but then John Bird turned on her and said: 'But you're supposed to be homeless, you're not a nursemaid, you're nothing but a southern Jessie.'

He turned on me next. 'And you, you Northern twat, you took this guy and tried to clean him up!'

That's when all hell broke loose, the balloon went right up. I was livid. We thought we were meant to give some help, that's how it seemed when they sent us out there. I was under the impression we were supposed to help if we could, inject some of whatever we were into them. Now it looked as though that wasn't the way they wanted it to be, and they were turning on us. Hardeep went up to him nose-to-nose after what he'd said to me and Annabel and said 'What are you going to call me? A Paki bastard?'

Bird just said: 'You've got to live their life.' A massive row broke out. I told him that if he thought I was going to take cocaine just to be like the addict then he was stupid. Annabel, Hardeep and I all quit there and then. Since the marquis had quit early on – no surprise there – that only left Rosie Boycott. She stuck with Bird and said he was right that we were not there to help them. I felt Bird's comments were totally out of order and I felt for Annabel. Bird had no reason to subject her to the kind of verbal volleys he was blasting her way.

Hardeep had told me that he'd heard that he and I were going to spend the next three days up in Glasgow. Nobody had mentioned anything to me about Glasgow. The only city mentioned when the programme idea had been moted to me was London.

I told the producer I wanted to be off, to get on a train and go home. The producer then started giving me a load of flannel about me being the one who was giving them the programme. I knew he was trying to win me over, to get me back. He told me that he felt my street mentality, because of my working class background, had seen me through. He felt the strength of my character and my opinions were making the show interesting, but I still wanted to go home. I thought both Hardeep and I were on our way; and not to Glasgow. All I wanted at that time was to talk with Sandra and be back home.

I thought the producers could have gone a lot further with the show. We could have had some great interviews. They could have used some of the footage from when I was talking with these people, but it turned out that wasn't the point. The programme was about how we survived living in their world, how we reacted to it, and how we coped with being down there in the very pit of existence. That was what the programme makers wanted. They didn't want a Panorama programme. This was a celebrity reality format, not a 'let's make a difference' show. I misread it all, and I don't think I was the only one who felt that way.

What we had also not understood was that the reason you can't do certain things, such as showing those who live on the streets on screen, is that a lot of homeless people do not like TV cameras. Many of them don't want the people that they have left behind, and in many cases escaped from, to know where they are. Being on-screen will blow their cover. I didn't see that at first, but I see it now. We don't know what goes on in everyone's lives and the individual's privacy is precious. The lesson I learned from it is that sometimes, in trying to help, we can actually make things far worse.

The producers talked me around into staying on the show and going to Glasgow, as I guess you'd worked out by now. We went back out that night after our second debrief. I spent my last night with the cocaine addict in his grubby little pit. We said our final goodbyes the next morning. I didn't try to help him in any way. All I now wanted to do was get through the night and get away. A car came to take us back to the warehouse the next morning.

Hardeep and I had both agreed to complete the final three days. I remember saying to Hardeep that we'd gone this far, so we might as well finish it. That morning the production team gave us each an envelope. Inside was £40 - a week's dole money – and a one-way train ticket to Glasgow.

No-one would sit next to us on the train. I couldn't blame them because we stunk. It was at this point that I started to think about the woman in the pub again. Maybe if I'd been in her position I would have said something as well, but I just don't think I would have been as callous as she had been to me.

The production company filmed us on the train. We got to Glasgow Central at half past four. It was winter, pitch black and freezing cold. I went across the road; straight over to Greggs, the bakers, and bought four sausage rolls.

I had two of the rolls straight away and I was going to leave two for my supper. I didn't know what this place I was being sent to was going to be like; and I just hoped it wasn't going to be as bad as the crackhead's smelly den. Unbeknown to me where I was going was to have a meal laid on. After six days of what I'd been through that was a luxury to come.

I'd got quite a bit of money with me by now – photography money,

Big Issue cash, plus the £40 they had given me. I'd got more money than I have now!

This is when I realised that the programme makers finally had developed a sense of humour. Either that or I had struck incredibly lucky. Given my affection for going into a pub and having a pint, or two, or three, or more of Guinness, they had only put me into a 24-hour wet hostel; somewhere you can drink all day.

I arrived at the hostel about 5 o'clock. Hardeep had gone into a young drug offenders unit. My room was like a hotel room and it immediately relaxed me. It was as though all the pressure was being taken off after the past three days of hell. There were new clothes on the bed - jeans, shirts, new socks, new underwear, the lot - and everything I had on was to be binned and skipped. Hallelujah. Please God, I thought, let this continue. After the three days with the crackhead I wasn't sure whether this was some kind of cruel joke and that in an hour's time I would be flung out on to the street again.

I had a shower. I know this isn't big news in someone's story normally but it was absolutely gorgeous. I must have been in that shower for an hour or more and I could have stayed there a lot longer. All the grubbiness and smelliness was washed away. When I eventually stepped out of the shower; and put clean clothes on for the first time in nearly a week it felt so good. I made my way back downstairs and there was a meal waiting for me. It was mince and mash and to me it was like heaven. I'd still got the two sausage rolls, plus a bar of chocolate upstairs but this was just brilliant. I was inside, I was warm and I was eating a lovely meal. It might not have been Britain's Greatest Dish but it was very welcome.

The meal might well have been good but the people were a bit strange. At first no-one would talk to me. It was now about 7 o'clock and I went into the smoke room.

There was a guy there and he greeted me with: 'We don't like you...'

I was feeling good by now, so I wasn't irritated beyond compare about this, but I was still in no mood for idiots. I replied quick as a shot: 'I'm not that keen on you either mate, so don't give me any fucking hard luck stories. I've had enough of them in the last few days, so why don't you just sit and watch the television if you haven't got anything better to say than that. I can quite easily do without you in my life.'

It turned out to be the best thing I could have said as an ice breaker. The guy started laughing and he said: 'You tell it like it is don't you lad?'

He had enjoyed me standing up to him and he told me that at 9 o'clock he and his mates would take me somewhere. Then he started telling me his life story and how he'd ended up in this place. He was an alcoholic and he'd come here to die. It was sad but very true as it turned out.

When it was nearly 9pm he went away and two other guys came back with him, one was a little guy who was dead strange at first but turned out to be a cracking bloke and the other was an artist, a painter who was really well spoken.

No prizes for guessing where they were taking me. We went into a pub. I said that I'd thought they weren't allowed into a pub. I don't know quite how I'd worked that out. I suppose I'd just thought that since they were in a 24 hour wet hostel that they were meant to drink there rather than go anywhere else.

They told me there was no problem and that they went to the pub at 9 o'clock every night until half past 11. Once they were back at the hostel they would have a bottle of whisky or vodka in their room and keep drinking.

We left the pub at spot on 11.30pm as they had said. We were soon back at the hostel and at last I was in a proper bed, not some horrible place but a warm bed. And I had the room to myself. This was to be my first proper night's sleep in seven days, well almost. As part of the show I had to be up at six o'clock and do the rounds with the warden. What we were doing was basically making sure all the hostel inhabitants were still alive. I'm serious. The producers had sent me here to see what alcohol can do to you if you carry on a certain way and let the drink get you.

At breakfast I talked with the guys who I'd been out with the night before. I asked one of them how he'd ended up here. His story was amazing as much as it was sad.

'I murdered a man,' he said. I immediately thought here I go again, another murderer, what is it with me and murderers?

'He was my best mate and he raped and killed my daughter. He threw her off the bridge in Glasgow and she was found dead in the River Clyde. They caught him and when I found out I went and threw a brick through this window. Then I went and battered the bloke. We ended up in the same prison and I killed him there. I've not been out long. Now I drink. That's all I do and I've ended up here.'

All he wanted was revenge for his daughter – who wouldn't – and he got that. I know it sounds strange saying this about someone who has killed but he really was a great bloke. Who knows what's around the corner for any of us – and how we would react if the same thing happened to our children. If someone did anything to any member of my family I'd want revenge as well.

That same day when I'd been told his story the warden took me to the graveyard where the people from the hostel are interred when they die. It's a field with little wooden crosses in it. It was heartbreaking as you would expect. We went back to the hostel and I spent a lot of time talking with each of the regulars. From not liking me at the start we all became friends.

Every night when 9 o'clock came everything stopped at the hostel and everyone was back off to the pub again. The second night at the pub was a real party night. The landlady had arranged it and had told us there would be a surprise for myself and the crew, yes they were still there. I think they were enjoying this part of the show. We were all certainly enjoying it more than we had earlier. Our surprise was a bagpipe player who came in and played. I had a go but couldn't play it. The owner of the hostel was there too and she had brought her friends, so it was a really good atmosphere, a long way away from sleeping under Westminster Bridge and in a hole in a wall in London's East End.

My final full day was yet another interesting experience. The management at the hostel had arranged a trip to Loch Lomond for seven of the guys. There were a couple of carers or whatever their official title was, me and the crew.

I was to see another side to their personalities, and it seemed they had none for a while. It was as though someone had turned a switch off in all these guys' heads. They didn't say a word on the way to the loch; and when we went on a boat they were still silent. It was one of the weirdest things, a bit like those times when you've had an argument with your partner and no-one says a thing for a while. I wondered what was up with them, but you've probably worked it out already. We got to the hotel on an island in the middle of the lake and walked in. A few people in the hotel recognised me and did the usual thing of asking for a photograph with me or an autograph. I turned to look at the guys from the hostel. They still hadn't exchanged a single word since we'd left Glasgow.

Then the carers said 'watch this'. They put a pint in front of each of them and immediately they all started chatting away, laughing and talking. It was comical, like something out of an Ealing Studios film from the 50s.

When it was time to get back on the boat they all stopped talking again, no talk, no chat, not a word. It was one of the most surreal things that I've ever experienced. It was like these guys just couldn't breathe properly without having a pint in front of them. I asked them whether they had enjoyed their day but I didn't get an answer.

Of course we had to get them back to the hostel before 9 o'clock. I think that's what they were worried about. Where do they go at 9 o'clock? You know the routine by now. We got back around 7pm and they all disappeared off to their rooms. There was still not a word said coming out of the hostel. This was strange because they were now back in their home area, but still they were quiet. At 9 o'clock we went back across to the pub, the pints were in front of them and conversation and laughter started again. One of the strangest things I have ever seen.

I spent four days at the hostel, one more than I was supposed to, it was the way the programme makers wanted it. Later I was told that everyone else had finished before me. Hardeep had not managed to make it through the last part.

I couldn't say I enjoyed being a part of *Famous, Rich & Homeless*. You probably wouldn't expect me to either, but it was an experience that will remain with me. I saw sides of life that I would never want to see again, but I'd never be in a hurry to go back to any of them.

On my final morning I was told I had some interviews to give before I left and that I would have to do them outside. When I went back in one of the production team told me they were sending me home by plane. They were flying me home. That was a nice surprise. The three guys I had been closest to at the hostel also came to see me off.

I'd got on with everyone in my short time there. I'd made friends with the staff and the guys who were preparing to spend the last days of their lives in that hostel. I've been labelled an alcoholic so many times in the press and media but they should see what it really is like living with real alcoholics.

If I'd said no to going for a drink at 9 each night it could have been a different matter. They probably wouldn't have taken to me, but I talked to them. I didn't say things like 'you look a right mess'. I treated them as human beings, the way I think everyone deserves to be treated.

For all of the 10 days I was with human beings, no matter what situation they were in. I wanted to know why they were homeless and I found out. For me it wasn't because they didn't want to work, it was because something had happened in their lives where they had been either sexually abused, badly beaten by their parents, had their daughter killed by a best mate, or just weren't able to cope with all sorts of pressures. These are all things that can knock your life off balance and send you to another place.

The producers said they could see I wanted to know why people were on the streets. Whatever these people I saw had been through could happen to any of us. I found out there are reasons why everybody is where they are.

Images stay with you and even now if I'm in a car I sometimes look and think that's not a bad place to sleep if you're homeless.

Coming home though is a great feeling. When I got home Sandra had prepared a massive pot of chilli and there were loads of our friends around. I had a tear or two before really enjoying the night. I'd seen things that you hear about and read in the news and in 10 days I'd experienced an amazing take on life, but never again, never!

CHAPTER THIRTY EIGHT
FISH, FISH, FISH!

You couldn't get a TV programme much more different than *Famous, Rich & Homeless* for my next 'reality' show. I had a lot of fun with this and all four of us on the show had a great time.

I have liked watching *Come Dine With Me* since it started and so does Sandra, so when I was given the chance to go on the *Celebrity Come Dine With Me* version of the programme I didn't need to think about my decision. I also couldn't have wished for a nicer group of people to share the evenings for a week.

Yvette Fielding, who presents *Most Haunted* was so bubbly and friendly all the time; Natasha Hamilton, of the girl-band Atomic Kitten was so down-to-earth, as well as being stunningly beautiful; and Roy 'The Legend' Walker proved how funny he still is. I seem to recall he was appearing in his own show on the North Pier when I was filming *Bob's Weekend* years previously. All three of them were great company and the production company must have been pleased with us because some time later we were asked to attend a TV awards evening. Our programme was nominated.

Roy kept calling me Les, but when I mentioned that he'd done it each night he simply said that I should really take it as a compliment. He said: 'How dare you. You've invented this character and you've accomplished what you started out to do. You created a national institution with Les and you should be proud of what you did.' National institution, I can't say I disliked what he'd said. He's got a way with catchphrases you know.

I like cooking and what I do best is cottage pie, but the production people thought that was a bit boring so I cooked a chicken roulade with black pudding. I've this mate who's a top chef and I got him to write the recipe for me, but when I came to slice it the chicken just crumbled. I'd had it boiling for an hour.

My sauce was a triumph, though I say it myself. If you see our show one time you'll see just how much I worked on the sauce. The one thing they didn't show was when I'd invited my chef mate around to check on it. I was caught with him in the house but it doesn't get mentioned in the show. Naughty Bruce! But it was all my own work. I just wasn't confident about it and needed a bit of reassurance. The cheeky bloke who does the voice-overs takes the piss out of my lack of confidence unmercilessly.

My starter was a prawn cocktail. I didn't think I could go wrong with that and I didn't. Sandra has always made a great prawn cocktail and I did my best to get it her way using salad, nuts, apple as well as the prawns and Marie Rose sauce. Natasha said it was the best starter she'd had all week; and my dessert was a summer pudding. It was the first dessert I have ever made properly and although they all laughed at it when I brought it to the table, because it looked like a turkey, Yvette said it tasted 'fab'. She's a good girl that Yvette and so happy.

All of the others cooked fish. It didn't matter whose house we went to, it was fish on the menu everywhere. I don't usually like fish apart from fish and chips or salmon out of a tin. It became a running joke every day with the voice-over man when I looked at the menu. 'Fish!?' you would hear me say. We had salmon at Yvette's; blackened cod at Natasha's; and smoked haddock at Roy's. I thought they were all ganging up on me. Yvette said she should have done me egg and chips. Roy said if I didn't eat what he was cooking he would just give me a bag of crisps – Walker's of course!

When they all came to Alderley Edge I got a band in. They were a folk band, a jug band, but they didn't make it to the final edit. They were great, but the producers only have so much time and I think they were enjoying the banter between the four of us. I still came in last with 22 points. Roy won with 26 points. I gave both Roy and Natasha nine points and Yvette eight.

I found *Celebrity Come Dine With Me* a complete change for the better after *Famous, Rich & Homeless*. All four of us laughed, smiled and enjoyed ourselves throughout the week. I was more than a little stressed when it was my turn to cook, I don't mind admitting, but it was a lovely show to do.

What I also liked about our version of the show was that there was none of this business where you go through the drawers in people's houses. We didn't do any of that. Why do they do that?

Celebrity Come Dine With Me was shown in November 2009. When you see me on screen I am happy, enjoying life and having a good time. But just four months before I had done probably the most stupid thing I have done in my life. And I have done some stupid things in my time. Are you ready for this?

CHAPTER THIRTY NINE
ROAD TO HELL

'Former *Coronation Street* star Bruce Jones tried to kill himself and his wife in their Mercedes in a drunken argument at 70mph, a court heard yesterday.' *The Daily Mail.*

'Les Battersby actor admits grabbing wheel while wife drove' *The News.*

Here are the basic facts of what happened. I'm going to make this first part short and straight to the point.

On Friday 28 August 2009 Sandra picked me up from a pub. I had been drinking all afternoon. We were heading off for a weekend away in North Wales. I was being argumentative. I then grabbed the steering wheel, causing Sandra to zigzag on the A55 and be a danger to other motorists, whilst I was vowing to end it all for both of us.

They're the basics. I put her through hell that day. I had put her through hell several times before by carrying on drinking when I didn't really need to, and I continued putting her through hell by not admitting I was guilty in court until I could see the damage I was doing to her.

The rest of this chapter is not about justifying what I did that day, although it might sound as though it is. It's about lots of things that contributed to making me feel the way I did – and it's not all about too much drink.

I had been finding life increasingly tough being out of work. I was depressed and I had been drinking heavily for a while. Depression and drinking is not a very healthy mix. That's the way it was. I had been seeing a psychiatrist for about six weeks and he had helped but I was still suffering.

Each time I have ever suffered from boredom or depression, whether it was when I was not at work for a year when the cowling slashed my wrist or when I wasn't getting regular TV work after *Coronation Street* there were arguments at home. Things would calm down for months and then something would cause me to blow again. The arguments were my fault.

Sandra talks of a lot of our fall-outs being down to my drinking more than I should. She believes that is what makes a big difference. I agree with her, but it's not all down to drink, although I admit sometimes that hasn't helped.

I knew we were meant to be going to Abersoch that weekend with our friends Mark and Lesley Wheetman and I had gone to the Bird in Hand pub in Mobberley for a few drinks. I hadn't gone there to drink all day. I'd meant to go for a couple of pints and then go home but, as was becoming the trend for me, I didn't. I'd had more than just a few by the time Sandra picked me up. She'd rung me beforehand, telling me my tea was ready, but I had something else playing on my mind at the time.

A while before what happened that night I'd lost the ring my mum had given me. My mum was close to dying. I was upset that I'd lost it and Sandra and I had looked everywhere for it. Unbeknown to me Sandra had found it but was looking for the right time to give it back to me. She'd never found the right time because I was either drinking or coming home and being argumentative. I'd found it one day when I'd gone in Sandra's bag to find something else, car keys or something like that.

During the time I thought I'd lost the ring I'd told my mum a little white lie saying I'd left it in the bathroom. That's because my mum had seen me without it one day and had asked where it was.

When I'd found it in Sandra's bag I was angry with her. All of these thoughts were running around in my head, along with copious amounts of alcohol, that day when she picked me up from the pub. The ring, and it being in Sandra's bag was messing with my brain and I became obsessed with it. I was thinking more about my mum than I was about Sandra. I know I should have just been glad that I'd got the ring back and thanked her for finding it but I really wasn't thinking straight.

Once we were together in the car I was telling Sandra about this old school friend I'd met in the pub who had become a bit of a bad lad. Sandra wasn't really interested. After a while I started on about my mum's ring. It turned into a rant and before long I was having a go at her.

The two of us really had looked for it everywhere in the house and hadn't been able to find it. Sandra had found it on our drive. We had a pebbled driveway, she'd been doing some weeding and that's when she found it.

I think I still had the *Coronation Street* job on my mind as well. I was feeling very sorry for myself. I'd lost a job I should never have lost. I'd never done any of what the *News of the World* said I'd done.

I'd been on good money in *Coronation Street* and we were able to afford nice things, but now I had been out of the show for two years we still had a huge mortgage but with little coming in.

The more Sandra moaned at me for drinking, and I know she was right to, the more I thought she was moaning at me for not bringing in the money I was earning before. I thought she was mad that I was not giving her the lifestyle that we'd had for the past 10-15 years whilst I was in films and on television. She had her own job as a hair stylist, but I thought she hated me for what I had lost and what I had become. I felt guilty that I wasn't bringing in the money I had before.

I thought she wanted to be with her friends more than with me, so I started to hate her mates. I was jealous. I know her mates are fantastic and just how much they've stood by her when she has needed them. I felt kicked about. This was the way my head was, spinning around, the same thoughts churning around and around in my head.

Sandra's dad was ill too; so between us we were going to hospitals all over the place from Bakewell to Bury. I went through it all again as Sandra was driving. My mind was full of my mum's ring, losing my job on *Coronation Street*, not bringing in the money I had done before and thinking my wife hated me; but I concentrated on my mum and her ring that day. I said: 'Why didn't you give me the ring back?' And that's when the drink and my emotional state took over in the most dramatic way.

Sandra was driving along about 60-70mph and my mind was getting so twisted up. I just found it all too much. I was depressed about everything and had now wound myself up so much. That's when I said: 'I'm going to kill us' and 'we're going to drive this car in front of a truck'. That's when I started trying to get hold of the wheel.

I grabbed the steering wheel, jerking it up and down. We were in the outside lane of the A55 dual carriageway. There were cars at the side of us and in front and behind. It was the Friday of the bank holiday weekend so the road was very busy. It was getting dark and the road was damp.

We swerved and zig-zagged across the road. The driver of the car behind us was flashing his lights. Sandra managed to rescue us and pull off the road and in to the car park of a pub called The Traveller's Rest in Rhualtt, Denbighshire. Sandra was so frightened, as you might expect, but she hadn't wanted to pull up on the hard shoulder of the A55 just in case I did something else so stupid. She felt it was best to get somewhere that when she got out of the car there were others around.

I was jailed. The police arrested me, took me to St Asaph police station where they interviewed me; and banged me up for the night.

I was in overnight and released the next day on bail. I contacted my mate Paul Lord in Rhyl. He's a family friend and a bouncer at a club in the town. He said to get a taxi to the club and he would take me to his house. When Paul turned up, and saw that I was in the club rather than being stood outside, he told me that I'd better get to his house quick.

I still wasn't thinking straight, and was feeling mad with Sandra, because she hadn't given me my mum's ring. It was so stupid really. I should have just been able to let it go, but I couldn't. I don't know why, I just couldn't. The thing is I know that Sandra would have given it to me at some time. I know that, but then I get paranoid about things, especially when I'm depressed.

My head was an absolute mess. I hadn't got it sorted at all. It was a good job I went to Paul's and that he took me in. After three days of being at Paul's house I went to live in a caravan, a really nice luxury caravan that Paul and Louise Massey let me stay in. I was on my own there. Paul and Louise are also good friends and both of the Pauls talked with me and tried to help me get my head around where I was at.

Nearly three weeks after grabbing the steering wheel I rang Sandra for the first time since that night on the A55. I remember that I couldn't stop shaking whilst I was talking with her. I knew I'd done wrong and I was remorseful.

I thought that Sandra sounded okay, but no sooner had we started talking then it seemed it was time to finish the call. I knew that Sandra didn't really want to talk to me and I couldn't blame her for that, but between us we also had to agree to another bail address for me to go to.

I had been in the caravan for three weeks over in Wales, but it was time for me to return nearer to home. We agreed on me staying at Mark and Lesley Wheetman's house which was not far from where we lived in Alderley Edge.

One of the conditions of my bail was that I didn't go near Sandra but I wanted to be back home with her. I went to see her, breaking my bail twice, and got into trouble for doing it with Macclesfield Court.

Sandra and I had always spent a lot of time together, apart from the time when I was away for long periods of filming. I was finding these weeks of being apart very difficult, even though I knew the reason for us being so was all down to how I had behaved.

I still had it in my head that Sandra was blaming me for not providing the same lifestyle as we'd had in the past 15 years. We had bought a yacht, which we'd then exchanged for a cruiser. Sandra liked going on the cruiser with her friends. I felt guilty that she couldn't do that any longer and embarrassed about what I had put her through that night.

As guilt trips go I was really on one by now. When I was in *Coronation Street* we'd taken on a £650,000 house in Disley which it had turned out we hadn't been able to afford. It was my fault too. I'd been talked into it and hadn't considered how much it was all going to cost. Later we had moved into a cheaper property in Alderley Edge and we were in the process of having to sell that. We were close to selling off everything apart from our bungalow in North Wales in order to pay off the bills.

Financially there had been nothing left until I landed my next big role, or until I landed any role. I'd had one or two approaches but there was nothing definite and certainly no long-term job on the horizon. The celebrity programmes were all very well, but they were one-offs and they weren't going to come around that quickly.

I didn't have a plan. To be fair I'd never had a plan and had never needed one, but I was now on a downward spiral. I'd found that in those moments it was easier to go out and have a few pints, but then those regularly started turning into more than a few.

People say I'm an alcoholic but I'm not. I can go days without a drink, it's not that I need it when I wake up in a morning and have to put it on my cornflakes or that I need it like the blokes in the hostel in

Glasgow. I can just as easily sit at home writing poetry, learning lines or researching for my children's book.

I will always admit I love being in a pub. You can talk in a pub, have a laugh. And when I'm in a pub I drink. It's just that the longer I'm in there the more I drink.

Sandra says that she thinks some days when I go down to the pub I do try not to drink heavily, but then there are some days when I go and get talking with people and can't leave, because I enjoy the social gathering and the conversation. She knows that I know I should leave, but that I just get too involved with everybody.

One thing I do know is that I love Sandra more than anything in the world. I know that you will be thinking that I've got a funny way of showing it by what happened in 2009, but there it is.

Sandra has saved my life so many times over the years – and it was Sandra who listened to me all those years ago and helped me start on my acting career. It was Sandra who again saved me that night.

I'm not proud of this by the way and I would rather have not written either this chapter or the next one, but they are both part of my life and as I said at the start of this book I didn't want to miss anything out. This next part hurts too and it would have been far easier to leave it, but here we go.

CHAPTER FORTY

COURT

Before I go any further I just want to thank Sandra for helping me with the last chapter and also this one. I know you might think it's a bit odd thanking your spouse for taking you to court but this was different. This was my wife trying to help me.

My case was held at Mold Crown Court on 19 March 2010 and I was fighting against the charges of dangerous driving, drink-driving and assaulting Sandra. Crazy I know, and I had one of Manchester's top barristers Mr Dominic D'Souza defend me and boy was he going to do just that. He really did put Sandra through it, and I know that means I did too. When I saw what Sandra was put through in the witness box I finally came to my senses and pleaded guilty.

No-one ever wants to go to court if they can avoid it but Sandra had felt that she had to try something to get me back on track. I can totally understand why she felt that way. After all, trying to end it all is a pretty desperate act.

She says this was her attempt to make me realise how far I had gone and that I needed to get my act together. She had hoped this might make me think more about my actions and stop drinking as heavily as I was at the time. Sandra has always tried to make things work and although this was an extreme way of helping I think she felt that desperate times called for desperate measures.

Sandra says that nothing could have prepared her for that day in court. She felt that rather than me being on trial it felt like she was the one who was to blame. The questioning of her was very hard and I felt so bad about the way it was all going. When I finally changed my plea to guilty I know that all she wondered was why hadn't I done that in the first place?

It really was all down to my head being in a mess. I'm not blaming anyone else at all. Mr D'Souza was simply going about his job and trying to get me the right result, the one I'd said I wanted, but I hadn't realised what this would mean in the way Sandra was treated in the witness box. I know I was not in the right frame of mind at all during this time but even in my state I could see the hurt and pain I was causing.

Just before the court case my mum passed away. There was only one person I wanted with me at the time and that was Sandra. She took me to the hospital where my mum had died during the night. I was so grateful that she'd come with me. She let me stay back at our family home for a while after that even though we weren't supposed to be together. But I was upset about my mum dying and Sandra took pity on me.

I returned to court in April 2010 for sentencing.

CHAPTER FORTY ONE
REHAB

I was ensconced in a rehabilitation centre before my sentence was passed. This wasn't my first time in rehab of course, but this time it was for a far different reason than when I had checked in to The Priory nearly a decade prior. This time I was going a long way from home because I'd been an idiot. That's the way I saw it; I'd done something really stupid; and it wasn't simply to give me a few days off from the outside world, as it had been previously, because I'd been working hard.

Basically, this time rehab wasn't down to my employer looking after my welfare either. I no longer had an employer. This was no 'holiday' from a TV filming schedule. This was a serious case of trying to straighten my life out so that nothing like the incident on the A55 ever happened again.

I'd admitted during the trial at Mold Crown Court that I had an alcohol problem. This didn't mean that I felt I was an alcoholic. I'm not trying to split hairs here; but I feel there is a distinction to be drawn between the two.

I had been booked into East Coast Recovery (ECR) in Lowestoft on the Suffolk coast, which specialises in drug and alcoholism rehabilitation. The *Daily Mirror* paid for my stay, in return for a story from me about my drinking problem. Whilst I've had quite a few stories about me in the press over the years, they've not all been bad and the *Daily Mirror* and *Sunday Mirror* have been two of the newspapers that I feel have always given me a reasonably fair go.

There is absolutely no way I could ever have afforded to go to ECR without the support of the newspaper as money was now very tight. It was my old mate Kev Kennedy who had told me a little about ECR, the way in which they worked and he had felt it might do me some good.

Lowestoft is a very pleasant seaside town. It's the most easterly point of the UK and it also seems to have quite a proliferation of older people. As if to bear this out, during the six weeks I spent in the town I found myself dodging mobility scooters. I'm not kidding you; some of these people must have been watching too many Grand Prix races. Jensen Button and Lewis Hamilton could learn a thing or two from these people. It wouldn't surprise me if, back home, they hadn't turbo-charged their machines.

Whilst I was in Lowestoft I recorded my feelings and emotions in the form of a diary. I don't think I have ever been more honest with myself than when I put pen to paper each day and much of what I put in my notes is here.

No offence to those who were the course leaders, but I probably received more therapy in writing my notes than through the people who were supposed to be helping me. But then the idea of the course is for you to help yourself understand the actions you need to take. That's what they try to instil, so in that regard my time wasn't wasted.

I had no problem with not being able to have any alcohol during my time there. I've always been able to go quite a while without a pint if I've wanted to and I knew that this was one of those times. That's the reason why I never saw myself as an alcoholic, but rather someone who has an alcohol problem.

When I had admitted to having a drink problem I had done so for two reasons. Firstly, because everyone else seemed to think I had, so it was easier to go along with it; and secondly, because my drinking, although not alcoholism, had now landed me in serious trouble.

The day I was supposed to travel down to Lowestoft, Thursday 25 March 2010, was fraught with problems. We knew where we were going, but it was a case of two steps forward and one step back. We had set off from Mark and Lesley Wheatman's house, where I'd been staying in Alderley Edge. Obviously I couldn't drive so Mark was doing the honours and we had travelled quite a distance when I received a phone call telling me that since the judge had not yet passed sentence that also meant he hadn't given his permission to allow me to travel either. I was already nervous as hell about going and this was just piling on the agony. Should we turn back?

We made several calls to no avail and, although some of the advice had been to keep travelling and the clearance would come, we turned around and headed back towards Cheshire. What should have been a five hour journey ended up taking nearly eight hours after my agent's partner Susie rang with clearance for me to go. Mark was a star. This was to be a very long day for him because he still had to drive back home afterwards, but he just got on with it and finally deposited me in Lowestoft.

I knew I was there to try and put my life back together and do whatever I could about my 'drink problem' but I really didn't want to be there. I know this sounds daft because I'd been a long way from home many times before through filming, but this was far different to those days. I felt alone. This wasn't some great adventure; as though I was going to take part in some exciting new show where I would meet up with other actors and have a great time. I just felt this was all going to be very hard. But I also knew I had to try to embrace it and hopefully it might bring me one step closer to being back with Sandra.

When we had arrived in mid-afternoon I was told that I would be sharing a house with others who were in various stages of their rehabilitation. I don't mind admitting that my first thought was this wasn't the kind of rehab I had anticipated. In rehab I think I had expected to have a room of my own and that I would talk with people who were going to help me, probably on a one-to-one basis. Kev Kennedy had mentioned a little about what happened at ECR, but I couldn't remember him telling me that you had to share with others.

You have certain mental images of what you expect, no matter where you go, but this had been nothing like the mental picture I'd conjured up in my head. I would be living in a house which was away from the centre with others who were either alcoholics or drug addicts. It didn't exactly fill me with the joys of spring, but I suppose the idea was to keep us living in the real world rather than thinking rehab was some kind of hotel where everyone waited on you hand and foot.

This certainly wasn't to be some kind of cushy number at all. Anyone who had heard that I was going into rehab probably had the same picture as me, something like a hospital-cum-hotel with lots of people in white coats. This was as far from that as you could imagine. We made our own meals on a rota basis, so that everyone did their share; and we washed and ironed for ourselves too. This was as far away from what you imagine as a pop star's rehab as you could get.

My belongings were taken from me. Cash, mobile phone, laptop – I wasn't allowed any of those. After just a few minutes I already wanted to go home; or to the nearest pub. I would have gladly taken the offer of going to a pub, even without having any alcohol.

On my first evening I saw the centre's doctor who put me on a course of tablets, which I was told was my medication detox; later I met up with my fellow 'inmates' at the house which was to become my home for the duration of my stay.

My first full day was an embarrassment. It was frustrating because I had been trying hard to get off to a good start. I was prepared to give this my best shot, although I didn't exactly know what that would entail. But I knew I had messed up and by agreeing to come here I was hopeful that Sandra would see I was making the effort. But just a short while into our first group session the national press turned up in their droves, which meant the paparazzi were crawling all over the centre causing a bit of fuss, trying to get their pictures of me. I ended up apologising to my new colleagues and course leaders for the intrusion. Fortunately everyone was very good about it, but the photographers' intervention didn't help, as you might expect, particularly as some of my colleagues had come here without telling loved ones.

I broke down on the second day of sessions. I had started thinking about the normal, everyday things that Sandra and I had done together over the years. Nights out; going on holiday and perhaps crazily, even supermarket shopping. I desperately longed for going back to those days when we were happy and having fun together with our kids. We were a happy family back when they were all just growing up playing on their bikes and going together for picnics. Yes, like any other family, we all had our moments but there had been plenty of good times too. I talked openly about Sandra that second day, about the kids, our family life in our early years of marriage. I also shared with the group the horrific discovery of Jean Jordan's body. It didn't take long for my tears to come.

All I could see now, especially after what I had done that evening on the A55, was that Sandra was going to leave me for good. That was my recurring theme throughout my time in ECR. She'd left me before, following other arguments, but now my biggest fear was that it was over, she wouldn't want to be with me again.

There were a couple of newspaper stories about me whilst I was in East Coast Recovery and one of them was published in the *News of the World* on the first Sunday of my stay. I knew that I had pretty much offered myself up on a plate to all of the tabloid press as an easy target with what I had done, and so I had felt nothing would surprise me.

However, I felt very disappointed by some of the material that was published in some of the tabloid press in the coming weeks as what they had reported was patently untrue. I won't name them here, or the people who gave them the stories, because the media concerned don't deserve the individual publicity, and also because I haven't got the money to be able to afford to go to court in actions against them.

What I would like to say though is that regardless of what was printed, and whether it came out even worse than had been intended by those giving the interviews, I can understand some of their reasons. All I found that I really wanted was to move on, to put any bad things behind me and start afresh. Getting back together with my family was a priority.

Throughout my time in rehab I found that I suffered tremendous mood swings. If I woke up in good spirits it would have turned around to depression at least by lunchtime and it seemed as though the slightest thing would knock me back. The group sessions seemed to help at times, but invariably I found that these became more of a negative influence than positive.

My medication detox course of tablets was finished after five days. I have to say that I wondered why I had been on them at all, because I didn't feel I had anything to detox from. I hadn't been drinking regularly for quite some time before I went into rehab; and I hadn't craved alcohol. Mark and Lesley had looked after me and whilst I'd had the occasional Guinness that was my lot.

I'll admit that in the five days I'd been there I'd had the urge once or twice to go off to a pub, but I had resisted doing so. I might have struggled to get served with having had my money taken away from me.

During my stay at ECR we would often go somewhere together as a group and inevitably this would bring back those thoughts of when

Sandra and I were bringing up our family. Go-kart racing did it to me on one occasion but there were a number of other times that brought about similar feelings of nostalgia and a longing for normality once again.

One week into my stay I endured the first full-scale cross-examination of my personality. I was told that I had an anger management problem, that I was a control freak, manipulative and extremely selfish. I'd say that was quite a bag of problems. I'd never thought of myself in any of those ways and I'd managed up to now without ever finding this out. But when I took the time to take in what they had said I started thinking about each area.

Both my counsellor, and the group members, had told me that who I was and how I reacted stemmed from fear. They told me that losing my temper showed a lack of control, and that what I really wanted was to control others around me. That way I would always feel that I could get what I wanted. They felt that if I wasn't successful in getting what I wanted I would become very angry. The following day, Easter Saturday 3 April, anger management became the main topic of conversation in our group discussion.

The biggest problems I had throughout my time in Lowestoft were depression, loneliness and the recurring fear of losing Sandra. Each evening, when I would write my diary, I would finish every date with 'I love you Sandra'. I knew that when I went back I would probably have to live on my own for a good long while and that kept bringing me down.

Losing my mum had been another major body blow. All of a sudden, in the space of a few months, my mum had died and Sandra was no longer with me. The pair of them had been the cornerstones of my life, and now one of those had gone for good; and the other, understandably because of what I had tried to do, didn't want me. I was stuck out here, five hours away from home, with no job, no money, away from all my friends. I knew this was meant to be rehabilitation and that talking about life was useful but it didn't stop me feeling all of those other emotions. I wondered whether the feeling of depression, lonely and fearful was really supposed to be the cocktail towards setting me on the right track?

Two weeks in to my time at ECR and phone calls were now allowed.

We were given our mobile phones for a short while each day. Hallelujah! I had contact with the outside world again. My son Jon said he was coming to see me, with his son Jake. It was like a light had been switched on in my life again. This was what I needed, people who I cared about talking with me. Unfortunately none of the calls that followed were from Sandra, but I did keep in touch with what she was up to through Mark and Lesley. It's amazing the difference a few phone calls from friends can make. Those calls started to make me feel good about myself again. My sister Glynis called, and my Uncle John and Auntie Marjorie. Dene Michael from the pop group Black Lace also rang. He'd been a friend for quite a while and had some ideas he fancied chatting over with me. And to top it all off Tony (Nyland) came up with some very positive news on the jobs front. For all my fretting in ECR it seemed as though things were working out for me back home, without me being there.

Tony told me there had been quite a bit of interest in me appearing in pantomime again; and that I was on the shortlist for a few reality programmes, plus he'd had an interest from a couple of producers about TV dramas that were in the pipeline. He felt really positive about me picking up good, regular work once I was back out in the real world. For all the two weeks I'd had in rehab, this had been my best rehabilitation of the lot. All I ever needed was to feel wanted, and in the space of one evening I felt that way again.

One of the most interesting times I had at ECR was when we had a talk and watched a DVD all about quantum physics. I can't begin to explain it properly here and, probably like you're thinking right now, I thought it would be just a bore; but it turned out to be one of the best things I have seen about the human brain and addiction. But then again maybe I was in such a good humour at the time because I was looking forward to Jon and Jake coming in the next couple of hours of that morning. It's amazing how much more bearable things can be when you have other things to look forward to.

There really is nothing like having family around for making you feel better about life, and when I walked out of the centre there they were, my son and grandson, complete with football in hand ready to blast a few shots past me. No chance! I became 'competitive granddad' for an hour or so. The rest of the day was just how I'd wanted things to be when I had been thinking back to family days, when I had first come to Lowestoft. We played football together on the beach and I spoke with Jake about how well he was doing. He's a good player. You wouldn't expect me to say anything other than that would you? Now this was the rehabilitation I needed. The only problem was that it all seemed to fly by; you know how it does when you're enjoying yourself. Jon visited me again a few weeks later. Steven would have come too but he works on the railways and his shifts wouldn't allow.

Dene Michael and his family turned up next. Dene had some great ideas for things we could do together when I was back. We talked about show ideas and going to play in Benidorm. He reckoned I'd go down a storm over there, and he was proved right. Within the space of a couple of days I had gone from wondering whether things would ever come good for me again to feeling decent about myself – and that had all been down to my family and friends.

Of course the one phone call I really wanted was from Sandra. Two and a half weeks into my stay in rehab we talked for the first time. It was about signing papers to sell our home in Alderley Edge; so it had some sadness about it, but I didn't care, at least I had the opportunity to talk with my wife again. It wasn't the longest conversation we would ever have but we both asked how each other was coping. We were at least talking and I felt better that we had talked; regardless of what it had been about. Just to hear her voice at the other end was a major step forward. That night I slept well for the first time since I had been at ECR. I'd talked with Sandra, I'd seen Jon and Jake. And people still seemed to want me and know me.

Right from when I was with Eddie in Clarke & Jones, I had always written. I had written sketches for us, gags and short stories. I had also written hundreds of poems. They're not written for anyone else but me, and what they do is allow me to put my feelings down on paper. It's my own kind of therapy. Buoyed from the previous day's visits and calls I spent three hours concentrating on my poetry. We had been taken for an afternoon's boating on the Broads but I'd opted out because it was so windy. I was more than happy just to write in a nearby hotel whilst drinking coffee.

Around three weeks into rehab the course leaders turned the attention of all of us to how our behaviour changed whilst drinking heavily. In the group we talked about the ways in which we became different people and how that affected those around us. I knew, from past experience, how Sandra would dread me coming home after I'd been drinking for a long time. I knew where we were heading here and that I needed to control my drinking better. The group discussions we had made me think back over the years about how my drinking had caused pain and suffering to my wife and family. It made me amazed that Sandra had stayed with me as long as she had over the years.

At this point I hadn't had a drink of any form of alcohol since arriving, and hadn't craved one either. Sure, I might have thought about going for a pint a few times, but it wasn't because I particularly needed alcohol. So much for being an alcoholic, even though I had by then got used to saying things in the group like: 'Hi, I'm Bruce and I'm an alcoholic.' I still didn't believe I was, even though I was saying it.

The longer I stayed in rehab it seemed the more good news I received. It did cross my mind that I might be better off staying here whilst all of the positive things happened at home. That way there was little chance of me cocking them up! I jest, of course all I really wanted was to be back home. There was more good news to come. Tony (Nyland) was working hard with additional work for me and two of my promoter friends, George Wilkinson from Huddersfield and Mikey Ellis from Devon also rang with further offers. I was more in demand in here than I was when I was at home.

Even more of my friends started picking up the phone to me. It really was a great feeling. Reg Glass, who ran a B&B in Blackpool, put in a call telling me I was welcome anytime. Both my sisters, Carol and Glynis, called and my brother John wrote me a letter to make sure I was okay. He also sent me some money to buy cigarettes.

Maybe the stuff that had been printed about me in the national press hadn't turned out so bad. It had put me back into the minds of booking agents and TV executives. There is a saying that goes 'all publicity is good publicity' and maybe I'd benefited this time around. I hoped so.

Sandra had done something else for me too. She had changed the phone number on my mobile phone. At first I wasn't sure that this was a good move but then Tony told me it was to avoid some of the national press, who had managed to get hold of the number. Bearing in mind what happened in 2011, over the phone-hacking scandal that led to the end of the *News of the World*, Sandra had done exactly the right thing. She was thinking of me, as she always had. She was still protecting me, even if she didn't like me very much over the A55 and the court case. Now that gave me another reason to be cheerful. I wasn't getting carried away with feeling that everything was back right, but it did give me a warm glow.

I was amazed at the variety of people I met who were in rehab. The only ones we all ever normally get to hear about are the likes of poor Amy Winehouse who sadly died whilst I was writing this book; Robbie Williams and Michael Barrymore. We generally only think of pop stars and television personalities when we think of rehab.

But with me were people from all walks of life, from every type of job. There were social workers, teachers, white collar management, housewives, chefs and top business men. Hearing their life stories certainly made me sit up and listen. When I heard what some of them had gone through in getting to the top, then sliding down that greasy pole, and losing it all through drugs or alcohol, I could see how easy it was for us all to lose our way.

There were times when I couldn't quite believe what I was being told about me by the course leaders. Most of the time things involved a great deal of common sense and I understood them; but the biggest laugh I had was when I was told that my humour was just a mask for my fears; and that it could also be a sort of addiction. It all sounded totally crazy to me but I listened to what they had to say. I still couldn't work it out. It's funny really, because Sandra always says I have no sense of humour! Humour as an addiction? Hmm.

My second main grilling came from a combination of the counsellor and the group, which centred on me resisting change. I couldn't help but feel that they hadn't thought much to my take on 'humour as an addiction' the previous day and wanted to get me thinking differently, but I let it go after arguing against it for a while.

What actually happened had been that I was forced to admit they were right in what they were saying – that I resisted change; but because I hadn't gone along with their opinion straight away I had then been accused of being controlling. This again provoked much debate and arguing from me.

I wasn't trying to play games with them, but I wasn't just going to lie down and accept what they said. We ended up going around in circles and finally I found it easier to admit that I did resist change and I was controlling; or we would never have been able to move on.

It was around now, about four weeks in to rehab, that I was beginning to lose a little faith in what was happening here. I had enjoyed many of the sessions, talking with the others, sharing experiences. I had also enjoyed our meditations, reading excerpts from the bible and the Dalai Lama of Tibet. I had thought deeply about what I had done back home and how I wanted to make things right again. It looked like work was coming back through for me too. I was feeling ready to go back.

But they hadn't finished with me just yet. My key worker, one of the course leaders, wanted to know where all my anger came from. He told me that I had this pent-up anger that manifested itself from time to time, but that he wanted to know from me how it came about, what triggered it. I told him that I hadn't a clue, and that I was able to get angry very quickly when I needed to, as I had to playing Les in *Corrie* or Geoff in *Twentyfour Seven*. There wasn't some dark secret lurking in my past that made me like this so far as I knew.

He must have gone away to think about it because the following day I was put through what must have been a process they hoped would get me to give them some clues. They told the group that everyone was to ask me any question they wanted to about me, my life and my career. I felt this was all turning into a bit of a game.

I tried to answer every question the best that I could; and then the key worker jumped in asking questions himself. I cannot remember what he asked, but he then started what he called 'pushing my buttons'. So far as I was concerned he was simply trying to upset me; and for no apparent reason. How was this all going to help? I thought that the people at the centre, as leaders and key workers, were meant to lead us the right way; not back into anger and frustration.

Perhaps he was trying to find out which questions would get me angry, and perhaps he thought that might help unlock some of the things he felt were lurking under the surface. Either way, I felt it was a strange of going about it and it didn't unlock anything.

East Coast Recovery uses two houses in Lowestoft for those who attend the courses. The house I stayed in was very orderly and we were a good group who behaved ourselves. As time went on some left and others came new to the centre, but there was never a problem where I lived. However, over in the other house there had been one or two issues and myself and my roommate were in hysterics one day when it all blew up. Once again this landed me in trouble. My humour getting in the way again!

It was something and nothing, but when you've been cooped up for a while with the same people you will probably laugh at the daftest thing.

This particular morning there was a big argument over the other house's cooking of dinner the night before. We were all listening to this in the group and the argument was raging over who was to blame. As my roommate and I did not live in the house we both sat back finding it very funny. It reminded me of that old proverb, 'too many cooks spoil the broth' and I think I might even have said so. Naughty Bruce!

Me and my roommate were then reprimanded for laughing. But we found the argument was getting funnier and more stupid by the minute. We couldn't stop ourselves from doing that kind of silent laugh, where you put your hand in front of your mouth as though you're trying to make sure you don't make too much of a sound. Needless to say we were frowned upon by the leaders.

One date which had been etched on my brain since I had been incarcerated in Lowestoft (I know it wasn't prison by the way; just that humour of mine again. I use it as a mask you know) was now imminent.

My sentencing was due on Tuesday 27 April, somewhat ironically as it was also Sandra's birthday. Given what I had done in 2009 I could not blame her if it had ever crossed her mind that this would be a good birthday present. I travelled from Lowestoft to Wrexham; and then on to Mold in Wales. Daniel from ECR came with me and we stopped off overnight in another rehab centre in Wrexham on the Monday evening after picking up my suit from Mark and Lesley's house and meeting up with Tony and his partner Susie.

Nervous couldn't adequately describe my feelings the night prior to my sentencing. On edge; restless; fidgety; unrelaxed; and all of the other words that would have required too many asterisks here. Take your pick from those. I'll go with the asterisks. I honestly now felt that I was going to be sent to prison.

I'd been trying to put a brave face on things for ages, but now that the time had come I felt absolutely bereft of confidence. Fortunately I had Tony and Susie there, along with Mark and Lesley. We arrived at court for 9.45am. We met the barrister who took a look at my probation report. We were called in at 10.15am. I was in the dock as the barrister went through my case. I saw Sandra and so much wanted to talk with her and be with her, but I wasn't allowed to. But at least she had come.

As you might expect there were plenty of media people around. I was fortunate to come out with the sentence the judged passed. If I had been banged up I'm sure the press would have had a field day with me.

On 27 April 2010 I was sentenced to eight months imprisonment, suspended for 18 months. I was ordered to undertake 100 hours of unpaid work and to complete a 12 month supervision order. I was disqualified from driving for 12 months and was ordered to pay a £1000 fine.

At least it was over. The wait had been the worst thing, constantly worrying about whether I would be locked up. And now that I knew I wasn't going to be I could start rebuilding my life. Tony and the other guys had all been working on my behalf to get me back in work. It was now time for me to get back under way, but first I still had another two weeks to go through in rehab.

Later that day I was back in the land of mobility scooters in Lowestoft. You take your life into your own hands running the gauntlet with them as you travel around town. But at least I was able to walk freely and have the opportunity of being run down. My humour again, what would they say at ECR?

In a strange way I was pleased to go back to Lowestoft after the sentencing. It gave me a time to take stock again, without any outside pressures. And I was soon getting involved in the community service hours that were part of my sentence.

The Seagull Theatre in Pakefield, Lowestoft is a community theatre that puts on a very diverse mix of drama, musicals, stand-up comedy and dance. My probation officer had arranged for me to go there and I was looking forward to getting involved in running drama workshops and basically anything else I could do to help. It felt good to be back in a theatre again. As soon as I entered the auditorium it was as though I was back home. Television and film acting is great to do, and I had earned very good money from it, but as most actors will tell you there's nothing like being on stage. I only had a brief time at The Seagull, but I will definitely go back to put on a charity show in the future. It's a lovely small theatre.

There are two theatres in Lowestoft, the other being the Marina Theatre and it turned out that a mate of mine, who had also been a long-running character in a TV soap, Peter Amory (Chris Tate in *Emmerdale*) was appearing as Prof. Jeffrey Fairbrother in the stage version of *Hi De Hi*. I'd called in to the theatre to see whether he was around one day. He hadn't been there, but he rang me back and we talked about the Street, *Emmerdale* and what he was up to. I mentioned that I had several offers of work in the pipeline, but wouldn't know how they would all turn out until I was back home. He mentioned something about a TV show he had been approached about that might be good for me as well.

I now felt that something good was happening. By being in the theatre I was back somewhere that I felt I belonged; I had not had a drink or even thought about having a drink for quite a while; jobs were on the horizon; the only remaining piece of the jigsaw was hopefully to be able to get back together with Sandra. I wasn't kidding myself. That would be the trickiest of the lot.

Because ECR specialises in helping drug addicts as well alcoholics I attended a number of Cocaine Anonymous meetings. I've never taken drugs in my life and yet here I was sitting in a group as though I was a drug addict. I suppose what they were trying to do at the centre was to show that whether you are a drug addict or an alcoholic it is a similar problem.

I attended my first Alcoholics Anonymous meeting in my fifth week at ECR. I received my '60 day sober' badge; my 30 day badge, and my first AA meeting badge. It was a bit like going back all those years when I used to be in the cubs and scouts. I wondered whether anyone would sew them on to my sleeves for me!

Seriously though, Alcoholics Anonymous is a fellowship of men and women who share their experiences, their strengths and their hopes to try and solve their problems. The only requirement is that there is a desire to stop drinking and to remain sober. There was a recognition, early-on when the movement started, that one recovering alcoholic needed another who has recovered to help them as a sponsor. I now needed a sponsor.

Fortunately, one of the calls I received when at ECR during this final week was from Lee Otway, who played 'Bombhead' in *Hollyoaks*. We had met before and he had called to talk with me about a TV pilot he had written and was due to shoot shortly; and to offer me a role in it. Perhaps Peter (Amory) mentioned my name to him. Whichever way it came about it was more good news, but what was also very useful was what I found out next.

I hadn't known that Lee was an alcoholic and when we talked he offered to take on the role of sponsor for me. I think the people at ECR would have preferred one of their own choices but once Lee had offered that was good enough for me.

Going to a centre such as East Coast Recovery doesn't guarantee that you will come out of it as clean as a whistle, or that you won't relapse when you've finished your course. We heard of several of those who had completed their time at ECR whilst I was there, who had then gone home and backtracked to where they had been previously. And there were those who relapsed whilst they were there too. It didn't exactly fill me with confidence.

The Alcoholics Anonymous meetings were a different matter completely. Within those meetings I found out a great deal about other people; and the consequence of doing so meant that I thought back about my own life far more. A lady who had been married 30 years talked about how she had lived with an alcoholic. This really brought home to me the state of my own marriage and how I had so very nearly killed us both.

I left the meeting upset, but it gave me a purpose. I got back to the house and immediately phoned Sandra. Thankfully she was available. I hadn't had contact with her except for that earlier brief conversation when things were very strained. I was trembling as I waited for her to pick up my call and tried not to worry about what she might say to me; or worse still that she wouldn't talk with me at all apart from one word answers. I needn't have worried as it turned out. Sandra was great on the phone, asking if I was okay and being very supportive. Once we had finished our call I cried. Part of it was in remorse, but another part was a feeling of release. My wife and I were talking again.

In my final days at ECR it seemed as though the course leaders and counsellors were ramping up the pressure. I would imagine that's what they have to do in your final days with them, in order to prepare you as best they can for returning home. They put me through the mill, constantly questioning me about my anger, my control over others and ability to accept change. I was finding it all a little too much, probably because my mind was now set on getting back home, wherever home was to be.

I was set on working on the ideas everyone had come up with and seeing Sandra and all my friends and family. Many of my family and friends had called with their best wishes during my six weeks in Lowestoft. All of the calls I received meant a great deal to me, particularly those from my granddaughters Sophie and Frankie; and my daughter Lisa. I knew I'd hurt everyone by what I had done that day on the A55 with Sandra and that I was paying a price for it.

This had been at times a gruelling period and at other a little bit like Groundhog Day, but it was over. And it wasn't because my funding had run out. ECR offered me another two weeks there free of charge, but I declined.

I was ready to go home.

Home turned out to be Reg and Christine Glass's hotel in Blackpool for the first couple of weeks as Lesley and Mark Wheatman were on holiday when I returned. There had been no suggestion that Sandra and I would be back together straight away, if at all, although of course I hoped it would happen.

On Friday 7 May 2000 I boarded a train for Manchester to pick up a few things before heading for Blackpool. Forget about *Bob's Weekend*, this was Bruce's Return. I left behind the land of mobility scooters!

CHAPTER FORTY TWO
REHAB WORKED

Rehab worked for me because I was so far away from everybody, from my friends, relatives and the life I had been leading. It allowed me time to gather my thoughts, to get my head sorted; and to write my diary documenting all my frustrations and my emotions.

Overall, I enjoyed my time at ECR. The people who try to help are considerate, but they don't give you some kind of easy ride. You are in there to take a look at yourself and get your act together. The course leaders and key workers are watching and listening all the time, doing their level best to guide you. There are times when I didn't like what they were saying to me, but I could also see why they were doing so.

I went there because everyone was worried about me, and because of what I had done on the way to North Wales in 2009. I didn't drink for the whole time I was in there, apart from once when I had a pint one afternoon nearer the end of my time in Lowestoft. It was still frowned upon by the course leaders and I was severely reprimanded for doing so, but I was back in a pub watching a football match and it seemed the most natural thing to do. I didn't need a drink, but since I was there I had one. It wasn't as though I had craved a drink during any of that time.

I've always been a guy, like most working class men, who when he finishes his working day likes to go for a drink before going home for tea, then maybe going out for a drink later, but not every night. The drink problem I sometimes have is not alcoholism, it is more a case of 'pubism'. I like being in pubs; and when I'm there I drink, usually Guinness.

I hate being lonely and a pub is where I have always found I can talk to people, have a laugh and a joke. Loneliness is a funny thing. You can be lonely and have nothing, or lonely and have everything in the world. I can still be lonely when I'm with a load of mates. They'll ask what's wrong with me. I have these moods where I don't want to be with anyone, but I don't like being on my own. Being in a pub gets rid of that feeling of loneliness. It's just that sometimes I end up staying a long time and during that time I can end up drinking up to seven or eight pints. I don't believe that is alcoholism because if it was I would be dependent upon alcohol all the time.

I can be at home for four or five days working on my poems or my story I'm writing and not need or want a drink. When I'm not in a pub I don't actively go looking for my next beer wherever I can. I'm quite happy at home drinking a cup of tea.

Stories get around about drinking, particularly when you are someone who is in the public eye, but I wasn't an Oliver Reed type of drinker. The only problem is that when stories appear in whatever media after a while they tend to stick. You then struggle to shake off the persona that others feel about you.

I'm not hiding from the fact that I drink, or that I like drinking. I've always liked a pint. I'm also not hiding from the fact that if I have too many pints I become argumentative and aggressive in the way I speak. That has caused me problems over the years and is one of the reasons that Sandra and I are currently not together.

Sandra knows there are things in my head that she can't get to. I don't think anyone can get there. I haven't been able to explain them myself and even the professionals at ECR could not unlock them when they 'pushed my buttons'. However, they at least pointed out several areas that I have thought about since – anger, control, resistance to change. I cannot say that I have mastered these but what rehab did was to make me more aware of some of my failings.

I've learned, not just from rehab but also through the time since rehab during 2010 and 2011, that whatever has happened has been my own fault. I cannot and should not blame anyone else for what I have done in the past. I know that some will chart my demise back to when I was drinking heavily. I cannot deny that I did drink heavily either. No excuses.

Thankfully what rehab also showed me was that I have lots of people in my life who think of me and who care about my well-being. I cannot thank all of them enough for the kindness they all showed by ringing me or sending messages when I was in rehab.

Whilst Sandra and I might not be together at present we are still in contact nearly every day. She comes to see me and still cares for me even if she isn't here with me day to day. Even after all that has happened between us she is there and I am so grateful for her support.

CHAPTER FORTY THREE
CHARITY

One of the great things about being known, and there are lots of things that I have found are not so great by the way, is being able to use your name and face for charity. I've been involved with charity concerts and helped organise shows to raise money for those who need it most for many years and I'm always happy to help.

I won't go through all the concerts and events here but I must tell you the heartwarming story of little Charlotte Speddy from Bethesda in North Wales; and also the time when I visited the armed forces bases in Cyprus.

Charlotte was three years old at the time, back in 2001. I was in The Mulberry pub on the marina at Conwy. The pub is run by Brett and Annie. Brett is brother of the lovely Sherri Hewson who played Maureen Naylor in *Coronation Street* and is now in *Loose Women*.

Charlotte's mum and dad asked whether I could help, because they knew I was involved in charity work. They were desperate. Charlotte's rib cage was twisted and her lungs were not being allowed to grow, they were getting crushed by the rib cage. When she had been born she had only weighed 1lb 4ozs, less than a bag of sugar. Angela, Charlotte's mum, and her husband brought her in. My heart went out to Charlotte and her parents instantly. She was in plaster from her chest to her waist. I had never seen anything like it. Her legs were plastered up and she had a bar separating her legs. But there was one other thing about her that I will never forget until the day I die, regardless of her condition.

She had a smile on her face that could have lit up the world. There she was this poor girl, plastered up and yet she could still smile – and boy did that make a difference to anyone who saw her. If she could smile whilst like this, with what she was having to cope with, well I was touched. I was hooked. I held her in my hands and thought of my children and grandchildren. I told Angela I would do whatever I could to get the money for them to get her to the American hospital where they fitted titanium ribs. Charlotte's parents had raised £10,000 themselves and they'd done well, but they needed a lot more. And they needed it quickly. We needed publicity.

I got a team together of my friends in Wales. There was John Dutton, Mark Evans, Paul Lord and others. Everyone had specific jobs. We raised £25,000 in one charity auction evening at the Mulberry. A jeweller friend of mine made a unique, gold and diamond Charlotte Speddy broach. That raised £15,000. Many of the *Coronation Street* cast came along to lend their support, as well as stand up comic Stan Boardman and other stars of sport and television.

The evening was interrupted twice by the fire service, because the pub was overcrowded. There was a traffic jam trying to get into the pub car park, which stretched right into town. It was mayhem, but a good mayhem. But the evening carried on nonetheless.

That was just the start of our activity. We contacted the government asking for their support too, and the Welsh Assembly agreed to make up any shortfall of up to £100,000. Now we were getting somewhere. I appeared on the *Esther Rantzen* show and on *Granada Reports* to talk about Charlotte and what we were aiming to do. Esther was fantastic. She has always worked on behalf of children and the response to our appeal grew considerably thanks to her show.

We ended up raising £80,000 towards the appeal in just six months, as well as having the Welsh Assembly's promise in our back pocket. Charlotte's parents had been told they would need £150,000 so that meant that, with the assembly's underwriting, we had achieved what was needed and she was able to go to Texas where her operation was a success. That was the main thing we were all concerned about. Raising money is one thing, actually getting through the operation was another. This was one brave little girl – and with such a radiant smile.

Charlotte will be 15 now (in 2011). The last I heard she was enjoying dancing and her mum described her as having the body of a mouse but the heart of a lion. She is also extremely lively and bossy; probably 15 going on 25 like most girls of her age. She still has to have an operation every six months because as she grows the rib cage moves, but these days the operations she requires take place in Cardiff. I am so pleased we were all able to play a small part in helping Charlotte.

The other main charity work I'm going to mention wasn't a case of raising funds, it was purely a visit. But it was an important one and one that brought home to me just what our troops do and how their families are affected.

Sandra and I were on holiday in Cyprus. We were stopping at a fabulous hotel renting our own bungalow with a private swimming pool. George Wilkinson, who organises personal appearances for me from time to time, rang me to say that whilst we were over there would I be able to spend a day meeting the armed forces' families who were stationed on the island. He said that a lot of the women's husbands were in Iraq.

I made sure it was okay with Sandra and off I went to meet up with each of the armed forces in turn – army, navy and RAF. The day I was going was one of the days when some of the soldiers who'd lost their lives were being sent back to the UK. I went to the army barracks first and spent a couple of hours with the wives and their children. I didn't know what to expect, or how they would react to seeing me, but I just felt proud to be able to do something.

I knew it could very easily have been a heartbreaking day for any one of them at any time. Their husbands were out overseas doing their duty, and yet they, their wives, could receive a call at any minute giving them bad news. It brought home to me just how on edge they must feel all the time whilst their partners are away on active duty.

There were one-year-old babies at the base and I just prayed that all of these children would see their fathers. I'd never done stuff for the armed forces before. This felt very special.

I moved on from the army base to the naval base. This time I went on ship and met the wives; and from there I met our RAF families. One of the pilots took me up in a helicopter. He left the door open, so I asked him to close it. I might well have been there to meet them, and hopefully they were enjoying my visit, but I certainly wasn't up for falling out. I met wives of the squadron and some of the top fighter pilots. They wear a scorpion on their t-shirts. It's their motif, like a badge of honour, and they presented me with one for my visit.

It was a great day and in my own small way I hope they all got enjoyment from my being there. I was sad when I was leaving. The day ended so quickly. I felt very humble to have spent time in the company of these brave families. Our armed forces deserve the most fulsome praise as they serve us wherever they are.

I'll try not to go on too much about my charity work, but it is important to me. One of my proudest moments in showbusiness came in 2005, when the Variety Club of Great Britain held a special evening for me at The Palace Hotel in Manchester. I was presented with the Silver Heart award for the work I had done.

There were some extremely nice things said about me that night. Sam Aston (Chesney) said that I was a really funny man and that I always called him a 38 year old midget. Sam said that I'd been very kind to him and that I have a heart of gold when it comes to charity shows. Wendi Peters (Cilla) said: 'It's a brave man who can spend two days looking at me in a grass skirt and coconut bra.' We're back to the Jacuzzi sketch again! You did look good Wendi!

In more recent times I have been raising funds for sufferers of asbestosis and the MacMillan nurses. Two couples who have had a big influence on my life in over the past few years have been John and Wendy; and John and Liz. John suffers from asbestosis and Liz has gone through heartbreak with him. They live in Cheadle Hulme. John and Wendy have always been there for John and Liz. All four of them are an example of how friends should be.

And I'm back in a camper van for charity this year as well. Myself, Dene Michael and Ian Robinson of Black Lace, and my great script-writing friend Ryan Dior are taking to the road with the camper van – not bought off Charlie West – to raise funds for St. Ann's Hospice which is celebrating 40 years. Ryan's mum died of Non Hodgkin's Lymphoma in 2009 and was treated at Heald Green Hospice. Ryan has always been one of my favourite scriptwriters on *Coronation Street*. We have shared some great moments, not least when we raced Rolls Royces around a hotel car park. Yes we got in trouble for that. Firstly for racing; secondly because we were in a hotel car park; and thirdly, and perhaps most importantly, the cars weren't even ours! We won't be doing anything like that with the camper van.

I'll go anywhere to help, it doesn't matter how far and it doesn't have to be in a camper van. I love working on behalf of children. I know it sounds corny but children really are our future, and I firmly believe that no child should have to suffer, especially the way Charlotte Speddy has, without a fight from others to help. I might have well and truly cocked up many things in my life but this is one area that I know I haven't.

CHAPTER FORTY FOUR
AGADOO'S

When I came out of rehab it's fair to say that, despite the possibilities that I'd heard about whilst being away for six weeks, the jobs weren't stacked up in front of me. Our house at Alderley Edge had been sold and the bungalow at Conwy was being rented out so neither I nor Sandra could live there until it was out of contract with the tenants.

I'd been working with comedian Ronnie Oliver in the North East and was good friends with Dene Michael of Black Lace who had come to see me in rehab. I'd appeared with Dene when I'd been working in Benidorm. I'd also met another great comedian, Lance Edwards whilst I was in Spain. He and Olly (Ronnie Oliver) are two of the funniest men you will ever see on stage and the great thing about what they do is that neither of them needs to resort to gutter language to get their laughs. Promoter Stephen Lloyd had organised some gigs for me back in Benidorm; I shot a TV pilot and landed roles in a couple of films; and there were more charity shows and my own shows. There was plenty more in the pipeline.

All of the work that was coming was gladly received, but I needed more. That's when Dene (Michael) contacted me with something I had never even thought about. How would I like to be involved in running a themed bar?

John Kerr ran a nightclub in Sunderland and he had contacted Dene, who then contacted me about this idea of opening up a chain of nightclubs named after the famous Black Lace party anthem *Agadoo*.

The first one would be in Sunderland, the next in West Yorkshire. I know what you're thinking. I'd just come out of rehab for drinking problems and now I was going to be involved in themed bars. Not the wisest move in the world.

I just thought it was something to do. All I had to do was shake hands with everybody and be there as Les Battersby. Sunderland is a great place. I had a great time in the three to four months I was up there. I didn't have any money in it, because I didn't have any money anyway.

We had some great plans. The idea was to create each of the nightspots as really fun places to showcase up and coming talented comics. We were also setting up a TV production company with a reality show format for comics. We had a lot of acts in and good crowds but it just didn't work as a seven-night-a-week venue.

What killed me during that time in 2010 were the four o'clock in the morning stints. At my age I was finding it all too much. The one in Batley opened up and then closed within a few months. I hear the Sunderland one is now a lap dancing club. That's not exactly what we had in mind. Dene is now involved at a place called Long Can Hall, near Halifax.

CHAPTER FORTY FIVE
BACK ON SCREEN & ON STAGE

In a way playing Les Battersby has been both a blessing and a curse. I will still always see it as more of a blessing; but it was not just the thing that built me up, it also saw me lose nearly everything and mess things up big style. I say nearly because thanks to people like Sandra, my family, my friends Mark and Lesley, Tony, Stephen, Ronnie, George, John and Liz, John and Wendy, Kev Kennedy, Lee Otway and probably so many more, I'm getting things back on track in 2011. I might not be completely there yet, but it's a lot better than I have been.

My first feature film role since *The Full Monty* and *TwentyFour Seven* was released in the cinemas early in 2011. I filmed it during 2010 and it's called *Soulboy*. I play the manager of Wigan Casino, which was the hub of the Northern Soul music scene that was very big in the seventies. Funnily enough it wasn't filmed in Wigan at all because the Casino is no longer there. The film was all shot in Stoke-on-Trent. It received some nice reviews. My character is the guy who does the throwing out. He's okay if you're okay, but if you fight you're out.

In 2010 I also shot another feature film which has the title *Down Our Way* and is being produced by Gritish Films. It's not out yet. There has been a trailer or two. I play such a violent role and it is such a violent film. In the film my character has lost his brother and his brother's wife in a car crash. My character ends up with their two kids. He is meant to be their guardian, but beats them. The girl leaves but the boy stays. It turns out my character only wanted the kids for the family allowance. This guy is a complete and utter bastard. There is little to like about him. He goes to a karaoke night and if he can't sing then he makes sure no-one can. It is a great cast of largely new actors.

There is one scene where it is just all guns and blood. It's quite topical in one sense, particularly as the riots in London and other British cities have been taking place in the Summer of 2011. The film in some ways mirrors what's happening in some places now, so maybe the producers can make an awareness of that and it may do some good. My character in this film is completely different from the way I normally look. I had to grow a beard, dye my hair black and wear glasses.

This year (2011) I am currently working on a film with Darren Wharton, keyboard player with Thin Lizzy and lives in Conwy. In this film I play a detective. And my name? It's Detective Jones. No prizes for guessing the type of criminal I'm after. A serial killer. Well it just had to be didn't it!

I've also filmed a half-hour pilot episode of a sitcom about a boy band called *That Band*, which has already had 14,000 hits on YouTube for the trailer. In the impending series the band has just won the vote on a TV talent contest. I'm their manager, Pete. I'm a bit rough and ready, but I'm going to get the lads straight. My rival in the series is Max, played by Peter Amory from *Emmerdale*. We made this trailer in 2009 which is why I knew Peter and why we made contact when I was in rehab in Lowestoft after I'd found out he was working there.

We filmed it all over a long weekend in Leeds. I had such a great time making this. The band is called Overdrive, which relates to how they run their lives. They're useless but they're young lads with a massive sex drive and that leads to some great scenes and great one-liners for me. It has been promoted to TV bosses as a send-up of *X Factor*. It involves groupies, sexy stuff and general bad behaviour from the boys and I'm supposed to keep them all in check. Do they know what they've done putting me in charge? I loved filming it and I'm sure it will work as a format.

Lee Otway is excellent and there are stars from *Coronation Street* and *Emmerdale* also involved.

Benidorm is one of my current favourite programmes and I would love to play a role in the show. I think I'd make a good idiot on holiday. You know the type, the guy who wants all the women but who's never going to get them no matter what he does. I'd be the sort of man who thinks he's Don Juan, but he's really Don None. Some actresses could have a real field day with him. They could really put him down. They could play him all the way but it would never get through to him. It would be like water off a duck's back. I met Crissy Rock (Janey York) and Tim Healy (Les Marshall) and spent some time on set with them in

Benidorm when I played a couple of gigs out there recently.

And just before this book was going to press I found out that I was being shortlisted to appear on the reality show *Celebrity Coach Trip* and that I have been offered another pantomime role for Christmas. Oh yes I have! I've had offers from three productions. So the work is not looking bad at all.

But it wouldn't be me if there hadn't been a calamity or two as well would it? That came in the shape of last year's pantomime. And what a shame that was.

I was scheduled to appear as Doc Hard Up in *Cinderella* at Hyde Town Hall in Cheshire, but the production company must have been even more hard up than my character, because they didn't pay the cast. What really upset me though was that they tried to make a story out of it, by saying I stunk of booze when I turned up for a performance. The whole cast backed me against the production company on that one. The real fact was that ticket sales were low and they were looking for a scapegoat. I offered to complete the run for free rather than disappoint the youngsters but I was told Tameside Council couldn't cover the running costs.

That's the only blip I've had over the past year, which has seen me back acting again in a feature film; a yet-to-be released feature film; and a pilot for a TV series. I'm performing regularly with my own variety show; have another pantomime in the diary; and the possibility of another TV series. So life's certainly not all bad. I'm also working on a children's fairy story.

When we lived in Disley we had some woods on our land and I used to tell the kids that there were fairies in there. I'm researching mythology to make sure I get the book right. I'm nowhere near getting back on a proper even keel with my finances but I am working. And I'm still doing the job I always wanted to do. And there are not many who can say that.

So am I Les Battersby to you; or am I Bruce Jones? I hope that you have seen the real me, with all my flaws and my dreams here.

AFTERWORD

BY

The Variety Club of Great Britain

Bruce Jones has been a wonderful supporter of the Variety Club North West region since 2002. He has raised many thousands of pounds through his commitment and dedication to disadvantaged and disabled children throughout the North West.

Bruce has always been on hand to present our famous Sunshine Coaches to schools and organisations and has always found time to have photographs with the children and parents.

The Variety Club has been extremely grateful for Bruce's support. He is a major television character, not only in *Coronation Street* but in many wonderful films, which has helped raise the profile of the charity in the North West.

We have always been able to rely on Bruce to attend our high profile fundraising events, our children's parties and indeed we were delighted when Bruce donated his winnings from a major television programme to our charity.

Bruce also kindly persuaded some of the cast members of *Coronation Street* to perform at a spectacular Soap Star Evening at the Opera House Theatre in Manchester, which raised thousands of pounds for our children.

The Variety Club will always be grateful to Bruce for his amazing dedication in supporting the Variety Club North West region.

Kindest regards
Lyn Staunton
Development Director

APPENDIX 1:

Films on DVD

RAINING STONES (1993)
Directed by Ken Loach
Bruce Jones plays Bob Williams
Also in Cast:
Ricky Tomlinson & Julie Brown
(Available on FILM 4 DVD)

BOB'S WEEKEND (1996)
Directed by Jevon O'Neill
Bruce Jones plays Robert Askew
Also in Cast:
Brian Glover, Ricky Tomlinson & Charlotte Jones
(Available on GUERILLA FILMS DVD)

TWENTYFOUR SEVEN (1997)
Directed by Shane Meadows
Bruce Jones plays Geoff
Also in cast:
Bob Hoskins
(Available on PATHE FILMS DVD)

THE FULL MONTY (1997)
Directed by Peter Cattaneo
Bruce Jones plays Reg
Also in cast:
Robert Carlyle, Tom Wilkinson & Mark Addy
(Available on 20th CENTURY FOX)

SOULBOY (2010)
Directed by Shimmy Marcus
Bruce Jones plays Wigan Casino Manager
Also in cast:
Martin Compston & Felicity Jones
(Available on SODA PICTURES DVD)

Major Films & TV Series Chronology

This list includes the order in which Bruce Jones has appeared in his main TV and Film roles to date:

RAINING STONES (FILM)   1993
ROUGHNECKS (BBC TV) 1994 & 1995
BOB'S WEEKEND (FILM) 1996
TWENTYFOUR SEVEN (FILM) 1997
THE FULL MONTY (FILM) 1997
CORONATION STREET (ITV) 1997 – 2007
SOULBOY (FILM) 2010

Bruce Jones has also appeared in HEARTBEAT; A TOUCH OF FROST; CREWE STORIES; HILLSBOROUGH; and JOHNNY WATKINS WALKS ON WATER

Bruce Jones has also appeared in a number of celebrity-based TV shows including:

CELEBRITY STARS IN THEIR EYES (as Dean Martin)
CELEBRITY WIFE SWAP
FAMOUS, RICH & HOMELESS
CELEBRITY COME DINE WITH ME
Bruce Jones' current projects include:
DOWN OUR WAY (FILM)
DETECTIVE JONES (FILM)
THAT BAND (TV PILOT)
CELEBRITY COACH TRIP (TV REALITY)

Also available from Great Northern Books:

JOE LONGTHORNE
the official autobiography
with Chris Berry

At last, the book all Joe Longthorne fans have been waiting for - his life story, in his own words, in a fully illustrated, high quality hardback book. The ups and downs, the triumphs and tragedies, Joe doesn't hold anything back. From his childhood in the travelling community and singing on the streets for money, to early successes in talent competitions followed by national success and a TV series that attracted over 12 million viewers. His rock 'n' roll lifestyle was dramatically curtailed when he was struck down with leukaemia. But he's a fighter and his voice – and his true fans – have never deserted him.

"The highs and lows are extraordinary. It's the real truth." "A fascinating autobiography."
Lorraine Kelly, GMTV and The Sun

www.greatnorthernbooks.co.uk